"Many companies have fallen victim to the trap of pursuing growth at all costs. Driving shareholder returns requires a different mind-set, which the authors have succinctly captured."

—**ANDREW CLYDE,** President and CEO, Murphy USA Inc.

"In an increasingly complex world, Paul Leinwand and Cesare Mainardi make a compelling case for sustained business success via simplification and focus. Linking strategy and execution through a set of differentiating and coherent capabilities is a winning idea, making *Strategy That Works* a fresh and inspiring read to help answer today's leadership challenges."

—**BENNO DORER,** CEO, The Clorox Company

"In a refreshingly pragmatic guide, Leinwand and Mainardi describe how senior leaders can bridge the gap between strategy development, execution, and delivery of results."

—**NEIL C. MCARTHUR,** CEO and Chairman of the Executive Board, Arcadis NV

"Leinwand and Mainardi have laid out a playbook for executives to close the 'strategy-to-execution' gap, lighting a path for businesses that want to become more profitable and more influential, and delivering invaluable insight for CEOs who aspire to be 'supercompetitors.'"

—**ERIC A. SPIEGEL,** President and CEO, Siemens Corporation

"*Strategy That Works* provides a clear and compelling framework for executives to use in developing a cohesive and effective strategic vision. It provides a behind-the-scenes look at the characteristics of unconventional leadership and the importance of culture and identity as foundational components of a strong corporate strategy. Using tangible examples, this book presents the transformational journey that companies across all industries have undergone to remain successful and relevant in the twenty-first century."

—**MARK T. BERTOLINI,** Chairman and CEO, Aetna

"Any successful large enterprise must remain entrepreneurial, changing as needed to continue to do pioneering work. It must strike the right balance between openness to change and having a powerful, long-lasting core identity. *Strategy That Works* shows how to bring these two contrasting ideas together."

 —ZHANG RUIMIN, Chairman and CEO, Haier Group

"Leinwand and Mainardi show you how to transform your value proposition into real results."

 —MARSHALL GOLDSMITH, author, *New York Times* #1 bestselling *Triggers*
  and global bestsellers *MOJO* and *What Got You Here Won't Get You There*

"Strategy is all about making clear plans and sticking to them. Yet organizations get easily distracted. This great new book explains how to gain coherence across an organization in strategy setting and execution."

 —SALLY BLOUNT, Dean, Kellogg School of Management, Northwestern
  University

"*Strategy That Works* is simple and astonishing at the same time. Coherence is a critical ingredient for success, but it is so difficult to find such coherence in organizations. This book will help you think about whether your organization is really aligned with your strategy: from the company's value proposition to its distinctive capabilities to the products and services it provides."

 —ALESSANDRO CARLUCCI, former CEO, Natura

"A great book! *Strategy That Works* demonstrates how capabilities shape successful markets, enable winning companies, and sustain on-target execution. The case for capabilities-driven strategy strengthens with every turn of the page."

 —KARIM MICHEL SABBAGH, President and CEO, SES

STRATEGY THAT WORKS

STRATEGY THAT WORKS

HOW WINNING COMPANIES CLOSE THE **STRATEGY-TO-EXECUTION** GAP

Paul Leinwand
Cesare Mainardi

with Art Kleiner

HARVARD BUSINESS REVIEW PRESS

Boston, Massachusetts

PwC refers to the PwC network and/or one or more of its member firms, each of which is a separate legal entity. Please see www.pwc.com/structure for further details. Mentions of Strategy& refer to the global team of practical strategists that is integrated within the PwC network of firms. For more about Strategy&, see www.strategyand.pwc.com.

10 9 8 7 6 5 4 3

The web addresses referenced in this book were live and correct at the time of the book's publication but may be subject to change.

Library of Congress Cataloging-in-Publication Data

Leinwand, Paul, author.
  Strategy that works : how winning companies close the strategy-to-execution gap / Paul Leinwand and Cesare Mainardi; with Art Kleiner.
    pages cm
  ISBN 978-1-62527-520-2 (hardback)
1. Strategic planning. 2. Management. 3. Organizational effectiveness. I. Mainardi, Cesare, author. II. Title.
HD30.28.L44933 2016
658.4'012—dc23

                                                                          2015026915

The paper used in this publication meets the requirements of the American National Standard for Permanence of Paper for Publications and Documents in Libraries and Archives Z39.48-1992.

ISBN: 9781625275202
eISBN: 9781625275219

To those we love.

CONTENTS

STRATEGY
THAT WORKS

Overcoming the Strategy-to-Execution Gap

Almost every business today faces major strategic challenges. The path to creating value is not clear.

In one ongoing global survey of senior executives conducted by Strategy&, PwC's strategy consulting business, in recent years, more than half of the forty-four hundred respondents said they didn't think they had a winning strategy.[1] About two-thirds said that their company's capabilities didn't support the way they create value in the market.[2] In another survey of more than five hundred senior executives around the world, nine out of ten conceded that they were missing major opportunities in the market.[3] In that same survey, about 80 percent of respondents said that their overall strategy was not well understood—even within their own company.[4]

These problems are not caused simply by external forces. They are the outcome of the way most companies are managed. There is a significant and unnecessary gap between strategy and execution: a lack of connection between where the enterprise aims to go and what it can accomplish. We have met many leaders who understand this problem, but very few who know how to overcome it. In another global study, this time of more than 700 senior executives, only 8 percent said the top leaders of their enterprises excelled at both strategy and execution.[5] Some business leaders try to close the gap on the strategy side, looking for a better market position. Others double down on execution, improving their methods and practices. Despite their efforts, both groups struggle to achieve consistent success.

Yet a few companies seem to have this problem solved. They naturally combine strategy and execution in everything they do. Their products and services have an enviable position in the markets they care about, and they reliably deliver on their promises. At every level of the hierarchy, from the top to the front lines, they seem to have an uncanny ability to make the right choices—even when those choices run contrary to the conventional wisdom of their industry. Each of these firms has its own unique way of competing, but they all have one thing in common. Their success is clearly related to the distinctive way they do things: their capabilities.

Consider these three examples:

In the early 1950s, a young European entrepreneur decides to sell elegant, functional, inexpensive furniture so that people without much money can have better lives. To draw customers to his relatively remote retail store, he designs it so shoppers can comfortably spend all day, eating in the store's restaurant and leaving their children in its play area. His business rapidly grows, opening new stores and attracting employees who share a blunt, frugal, and empathetic perspective. Together, they build a remarkable group of capabilities, including an innovative manufacturing and supply chain; a proficiency in designing elegant furniture that ships flat in a box; and a keen ability to understand the way customers live at home and translate that insight into new products. Gradually this business expands to many other countries, becoming the world's largest home furnishing enterprise. Its name, of course, is IKEA.

is IKEA. In its fiscal year 2014, there were 361 IKEA retail stores in forty-six countries, with total annual revenues of €30.1 billion (about US$40 billion).[6]

A small cosmetics company opens in Brazil in 1969 to sell high-quality, natural personal care products—the kind of products generally unavailable then because of import restrictions. The founders soon expand their ambition, adopting the slogan *bem estar bem* ("well-being, being well") to celebrate women's health and quality of life at every age, rather than the forever-young ideal of beauty many competitors promote. They foster a network of direct sales consultants, who eventually number 1.5 million and who have close relationships with seemingly every woman in Brazil. To give the consultants a reason to visit their customers every few weeks, the company becomes proficient in rapid-fire innovation, releasing more than a hundred new products every year. It builds on its heritage of respect for nature and local communities by sourcing many raw materials from remote villages in the Amazon rain forest. You may not have heard of Natura Cosméticos S.A., unless you live in Latin America, but its distinctive capabilities have made it the largest beauty products company in that region. It had revenues of 7.4 billion reais (about US$2.6 billion) in 2014.[7]

Two brothers with a commercial real estate business based in the United States acquire an ailing motor vehicle components supplier in the early 1980s. When they discover that its leaders are successfully reviving it using lean production methods adapted from Japanese automakers, the brothers encourage other businesses in their portfolio to do the same. They soon realize they have a knack for buying underperforming companies, improving the way they operate, and bringing them back to profitability. They assemble a distinctive portfolio of enterprises, first in tools and industrial components, and then in the more specialized and profitable arenas of medical, life sciences, and diagnostic devices. These businesses respond well to operational improvements, and most of them have science-oriented professional customers who comprise a welcoming market for innovative new products—so the company raises its game in innovation. The Danaher Corporation, named after the brothers' favorite fishing creek, gradually becomes recognized among management experts for its remarkable performance across multiple businesses and its phenomenal M&A success rate. It had revenues of about US$19.9 billion in 2014, and its proposed split into two companies, planned for 2016—a focused science and technology company and a diversified industrial growth company—is generally seen as one more step in its profitable evolution.[8]

Several other well-known enterprises, including Apple, Frito-Lay, Haier, Industria de Diseño Textil (Inditex), Lego, Qualcomm, and Starbucks, have also transcended the strategy-to-execution gap. These companies are all idiosyncratic; at first glance, they seem to have little in common, and they are rarely thought of together. And yet, they have all built the kind of differentiating capabilities that give them a major strategic advantage.

Capabilities are the link between strategy and execution. They are the place where a company truly differentiates itself, and where the work takes place. But it's not enough to simply have good capabilities; all companies have them, or they couldn't compete. A truly winning company is one that manages itself around a few differentiating capabilities—and deliberately integrates them. When companies accomplish this, we say they are *coherent*.

The word coherence means something specific to us. It refers to the alignment among three strategic elements:

- A value proposition that distinguishes a company from other companies (we sometimes call this a "way to play" in the market)

- A system of distinctive capabilities that reinforce each other and enable the company to deliver on this value proposition

- A chosen portfolio of products and services that all make use of those capabilities

As we'll see later in this book, these elements shape your company's identity, its practices, its culture, its approach to managing resources, its role in the world at large—and its ability to close the gap between strategy and execution. Coherence among these elements is a big deal; in our view, it's the most important factor in building sustained success.

When your company is coherent, you don't have to struggle to overcome the strategy-to-execution gap. There is no gap. All your products and services are supported by the same group of distinctive capabilities, serving the same value proposition. Your strategy is thus inherently executable. Your growth is supported by the capabilities you already have, augmented by those you know you can build. The close fit between strategy (which is typically seen as "what business to pursue") and execution ("how to pursue and sustain it") is ingrained in every decision that people in your company make. Your strategy is no longer just about where to go or where to grow. Now, it's primarily about who you are and what you're great at. This defines how you win.

Incoherence, by contrast, dissipates a company's vitality. Incoherence is the state of following many roads to value creation. The products and services in an incoherent company require different capabilities to succeed; they don't take advantage of the same common strengths. Incoherent companies tend to operate without a distinctive identity, and it is hard for them to differentiate themselves. When you perceive that there's a gap between strategy and execution in your company, that's usually a signal that your company is incoherent. (Appendix A describes how the natural state of management is incoherence and how, historically, business theory has failed to address the issue of the strategy-to-execution gap.)

Many leaders of incoherent companies try to solve the problem by putting their attention on what they perceive as an execution issue. "Why can't my functional leaders get things done? If only we could hold people more accountable!" But no individual function has caused this gap, and no narrow solution can solve it. The solution is to dynamically connect strategy and execution together, through the distinctive capabilities you build. By focusing your attention there, you bring these two seemingly disparate activities into one.

The Unanswered Question

In our previous book, *The Essential Advantage: How to Win with a Capabilities-Driven Strategy* (Harvard Business Review Press, 2011), we described the differentiation that coherent companies enjoy—how they stand apart from other companies—and the competitive advantage they consistently maintain. And we articulated some of the tangible reasons why coherence yields these benefits: it leads to greater effectiveness, greater efficiency, more focused investment, and an atmosphere where every employee understands what the company does well, how their own efforts fit in, and how all of this creates value.

As part of our research for *The Essential Advantage* and in our subsequent studies, we tracked the coherence premium: the financial benefit that companies gain from focusing their activity through a small group of distinctive capabilities. This premium is prevalent in every industry we've looked at, including aerospace and defense, automobiles, chemicals, consumer packaged goods, health care, and financial services. Repeated studies have found that coherent companies were twice as likely as other companies to report greater-than-average profitability levels compared to competitors.[9] Analysis of our survey of more than 700 senior executives reinforced this conclusion. We asked about the sources of success for companies they know. Companies perceived to compete on distinctive capabilities—instead of assets, scale, or diversification—consistently scored higher in terms of average annual total shareholder return (TSR) between 2010 and 2013.[10]

The coherence premium reflects the reality that distinctive capabilities are not easy to build; they are complex and expensive, with high fixed costs in human capital, tools, and systems. But they are critical for sustained success; even a company with genius ideas needs powerful, distinctive capabilities to bring them to life time and time again. No matter how large and well-managed a company may be, it can only compete at a world-class level with a few distinctive capabilities—say, three to six. Therefore, enterprises that organize those capabilities in a mutually reinforcing system and apply that system to everything they do have an economic advantage: a new kind of economy of scale. That is why companies have felt tremendous pressure in recent years to realign themselves around the things they do exceptionally well.

We have also found evidence of the coherence premium in studies of mergers and acquisitions (M&A). One study looked at 540 major global deals in nine industries announced between 2001 and 2012. Deals with a coherence rationale—those that brought in new businesses that fit the acquirer's capabilities system or brought in strengths that improved it—led to compound annual shareholder returns on average 14 percentage points higher than other M&A transactions.[11] Another study of deals done between 2001 and 2009 found that capabilities-oriented deals led to a 12 percentage point premium in TSR.[12] All our work and research, in short, has reinforced the idea that coherence is a sustainable, accessible, and reliable path to success for major businesses.

There was still, however, a major unanswered question: How do businesses like IKEA, Natura, and Danaher build the distinctive capabilities that give them their edge? How do they stay true to their value proposition over time—especially amid the melee of pressure and potential disruption in today's business environment—and translate it into results? How do they consistently close the gap between strategy and execution?

To answer these questions, we conducted a study between 2012 and 2014 of a carefully selected group of enterprises that were known for using their distinctive capabilities for competitive advantage. We sought businesses that had reputations for being extraordinarily proficient—the kinds of companies that could do things, regularly and seemingly easily, that other companies found difficult, with success attributed to their capabilities systems. From the dozens of companies suggested to us by industry experts, we used several criteria to select a few companies to study. We looked at their coherence, of course, and also their representative diversity. We ensured that they came from a range of industries and regions. Relative performance was another consideration; there had to be a correlation between the company's management approach and consistent business success. Finally, we chose companies that we could learn about in depth—either from published materials or interviews with current and former executives. We set out to study how these firms had evolved, the decisions they had made, and how they had shifted course when things went awry. (Appendix B summarizes our research methodology and company selection process.)

We looked at fourteen enterprises closely. These were Amazon, Apple, CEMEX, Danaher, Frito-Lay (the snacks enterprise within PepsiCo), Haier, IKEA, Inditex, the JCI Automotive Systems Group (the seat-making division of Johnson Controls Inc.), Lego, Natura, Pfizer (specifically its consumer health care business, sold to Johnson & Johnson in 2006), Qualcomm, and Starbucks. For each of them, we developed a profile of the company's identity. This profile combines the value proposition that carries the company forward, the capabilities system that supports that value proposition, and the products and services that it offers. We have placed these profiles throughout the book, each next to a story about that company.

We also looked more generally at a few other companies—Adidas, Campbell's Soup, McDonald's, Tesla Motors, and Under Armour among them—that seem to have deliberately sought to build capabilities for success. Using these examples and other examples from our experience and that of our colleagues, this book describes the path of differentiation through capabilities. It explains how to build and maintain a coherent enterprise, no matter what kind of company you are in today, and how to avoid the painful strategy-to-execution gap.

This book might seem similar to the genre of management books that seek to learn from the example of high-powered, successful companies—works such as Tom Peters's *In Search of Excellence* and Jim Collins's *Good to Great*. The authors of those books, many of whom we know and respect, have researched successful companies and discerned a set of factors that successful companies have in common. They have articulated some very insightful principles and practices, from "management by walking around" to "level-five leadership."[13] But when companies try to replicate these practices in their own businesses, they don't always get the results they want.

We have taken a different approach. This book does not attempt to represent every winning formula for success; it focuses on the only approach that we've found that generates consistent results. We started with a working hypothesis, supported by our research and our experience: There is a path to value creation that comparatively few companies have followed in the past, but that would lead many companies to success if they followed it. It is consistent, practical, and sustainable—albeit counterintuitive to many business people. We identified companies that had demonstrated success through that approach. We set out to learn how they made decisions and how they operated on a day-to-day basis, to see what they had in common. (Of course, these are not the only companies following this path that are worthy of study. You might have assembled a different list, and we would probably agree with many of your choices. But these companies represent a broad enough cross-section that it is reasonable to draw conclusions from them.)

The five acts of unconventional leadership at the core of this book are the practices that enable all of these companies to win, time and again. These five acts should not be seen as a list of management elements from which to pick and choose, but rather as five facets of a single approach. If they lead you to business success, that's because they all help you do the same thing: close the gap between strategy and execution through the everyday work your company does and the capabilities that distinguish you.

Five Acts of Unconventional Leadership

As we got to know companies through our research, we discovered that coherence had not always come naturally to them. The companies had all moved deliberately to develop capabilities that were special for their business. To accomplish this, they had to run their companies in ways that differed, sometimes dramatically, from the conventional wisdom of mainstream business practice.

Conventional wisdom, for example, might lead you to focus on growth, looking for revenue wherever it seems most available. But these companies focus their growth efforts on arenas where they are well-equipped to win, taking advantage of the things they already do exceptionally well. You might assume that the best way to build capabilities is to adopt the best practices of your industry or develop functional excellence, but these companies design and build their own bespoke capabilities that set them apart from other companies. You might seek to solve performance problems by rethinking incentives and restructuring the org chart, but these companies do it differently. They recognize the power of their culture and foster performance by tapping their cultural strengths. Nor do they try to reduce costs across the board by going lean everywhere, spreading their investments across a wide range of promising opportunities, as many companies do. Instead, they marshal their resources carefully, doubling down on the few capabilities that matter most for long-term value. Finally, instead of trying to become agile, to respond to external change as rapidly as possible, they focus on creating the change they want to see. They use their distinctive edge to reshape their business environment on their own terms.

The problem with conventional management practices is that they have mostly developed through trial and error, without a fundamental theory for value creation. Since they developed independently, often without any direct link to a company's strategy, following them can often lead to incoherence. Table 1-1 provides an overview of conventional management practices and their unintended consequences. They foster incoherence by focusing attention on narrow, fragmented, expedient measures, aimed at getting things done rapidly and in line with the rest of the industry. This naturally divides global decision from local action, and strategy from execution.

The five acts of unconventional leadership are shown in table 1-2. They take different forms in different companies, but there is a family resemblance across all of them. They are all critical to engendering

TABLE 1-1

How conventional business practice creates a strategy-to-execution gap

Conventional wisdom	Unintended consequences
Focus on growth	Getting trapped on a growth treadmill: chasing multiple market opportunities where you have no right to win
Pursue functional excellence	Striving to be world-class at everything but mastering nothing: treating external benchmarking as the path to success
Reorganize to drive change	Falling into a habit of organizing and reorganizing: trying in vain to change behaviors and create success by restructuring alone
Go lean	Cutting costs across the board: starving key capabilities while overinvesting in noncritical businesses and functions
Become agile and resilient	Constantly reacting to market changes: shifting direction in the misguided conviction that if you listen hard and act fast, you will survive

TABLE 1-2

Closing the strategy-to-execution gap: five acts of unconventional leadership

Conventional wisdom	The five acts
Focus on growth	*Commit to an identity:* differentiate and grow by being clear-minded about what you can do best
Pursue functional excellence	*Translate the strategic into the everyday:* build and connect the cross-functional capabilities that deliver your strategic intent
Reorganize to drive change	*Put your culture to work:* celebrate and leverage your cultural strengths
Go lean	*Cut costs to grow stronger:* prune what doesn't matter to invest more in what does
Become agile and resilient	*Shape your future:* reimagine your capabilities, create demand, and realign your industry on your own terms

management habits that keep strategy and execution closely integrated, so that there is no gap between them. Together, they comprise a playbook for creating sustainable value.

Here is a description of each act in more detail, and a bit about how coherent companies put them into practice:

1. Commit to an Identity

Companies become coherent by making choices about who they are. They define and develop a value proposition that distinguishes them from other companies, and identify the few capabilities that will enable them to deliver on this way to play more effectively than anyone else. They build and expand their portfolio of products and services, always in line with their distinctive capabilities. In short, these companies deliberately commit themselves to an identity based not on what they sell, but on what they do. Having made this commitment, they only enter competitive markets where they believe they have a "right to win": where their identity and their capabilities give them an edge.

Thus Apple has applied the same design, consumer insight, and technological integration capabilities to its computers, mobile devices, retail stores, online services, and wearables (the Apple Watch). Its identity is clearly evident in everything it offers. Haier has expanded from appliances to air conditioners to water and air quality monitoring services, always customizing products to consumers' needs in the same distinctive way. Qualcomm has moved into new telecommunications domains, continually relying on its ability to develop breakthrough technology and to enable other companies to license it. IKEA, Starbucks, Lego, and Zara (an Inditex brand) are all recognizable brands not because of any particular product, but because they have built a strong identity for the enterprise as a whole and for the unique way they do business.

Staying true to your identity doesn't mean becoming complacent or losing your ability to change. It means using your strengths as a guide as you move through a rapidly changing world. With the entire company aligned around your specific way of creating value, you are not easily distracted. You can concentrate on differentiating your enterprise in ways that naturally outpace your competitors. If a business segment slows down, you don't chase every opportunity that appears; instead, you look for areas of growth where you will have the right to win, based on the capabilities you have now or those you can develop. As you grow more coherent, you shed the products, services, or entire businesses that don't fit and expand only to markets and businesses where your most distinctive capabilities apply.

2. Translate the Strategic into the Everyday

With this act, you create a blueprint that defines your most distinctive capabilities. You build and refine them, and then bring them to scale across your enterprise. These capabilities are complex and highly cross-functional combinations of processes, tools, knowledge, skills, and organization—all put in place to reliably and consistently deliver a particular outcome. You will need a great deal of focus and expertise to blueprint, build, and scale these capabilities. The effort will involve the commitment of leaders and employees throughout your company. Though these capabilities tend to pay off their investment even in their early stages of development, it can take some time to bring them to full fruition. If they could be created overnight, they wouldn't be worth very much, because anyone could copy them.

Highly coherent companies are particular about their capabilities. They don't aim for functional excellence or external benchmarks. They make their processes and practices their own. They know that if every company is capable in the same way, they'll all end up in the same place—fighting for an ever-smaller share of the same market. This awareness typically extends throughout the company. Employees are keenly aware of why the capability matters and how their contribution adds value.

If you ask people at Starbucks what they know about the customer experience, people at Danaher how they manage postmerger integration with consistent success, or people at Natura how they organize their supply chain throughout Brazil, they respond with both precision and artistry about what they do and why it matters. They are like virtuoso chefs, operating with a high level of mastery at a large scale. It's not just their skills and talents that matter; it's the way they weave those individual skills and talents together with larger-scale infrastructure, operations, and technology, to produce something that no other enterprise can match.

To translate strategic priorities into everyday execution across a large and incoherent enterprise might seem daunting, but it doesn't have to be. You can draw on multiple practices, some of which are familiar and some of which involve thinking and talking in new ways. As you turn distinctive cross-functional capabilities into habitual behavior across a global enterprise, you develop the kind of culture that fosters coherence and collective mastery. This leads you naturally to the next unconventional act.

3. Put Your Culture to Work

Business leaders know that the culture of a company—the way people collectively think and behave—can either reinforce or undermine their strategy. Since culture is difficult to manipulate or control, many executives tend to regard it as an enemy of change. Indeed, at companies stuck in the strategy-to-execution gap, executives tend to complain about cultural resistance and disharmony. This complaint is itself a symptom of incoherence.

But highly coherent companies view their culture as their greatest asset. The details of their culture may vary dramatically from one company to the next, but they all have cultures that reinforce their distinctive strengths. In all of these companies, people bring emotional commitment to work; they feel mutually accountable for results and develop a kind of collective mastery that is hard to duplicate. To boost performance, these companies don't have to change their culture; they have to recognize its value and use it to reinforce the way they coalesce across their strategy and execution. These cultures make it easier, not harder, for people to work together across internal boundaries (like those of functions and business units). They have a climate of grand aspiration, drawing people to contribute and excel, and to bring more of themselves to work. The interplay between capabilities and culture becomes a defining feature of the enterprise.

The relatively high level of trust and enthusiasm you feel when you enter the building of a company like Starbucks, Danaher, IKEA, or Natura is testament to the power of this type of energetic, strategically-oriented culture. You can also detect it in the way people talk about their companies. Natura's people refer continually to the importance of relationships to everything they do, and Starbucks employees speak to their genuine love for coffee and the ambiance of a barista-style establishment. At Qualcomm, you hear about their persistence in solving complex technological problems and fostering them throughout the industry, "even when others doubt us." At Danaher, people refer to their willingness to learn from each other at a moment's notice, taking every opportunity to raise their management game. When truly taken to heart, these attributes reinforce their capabilities and coherence.[14]

How do you develop a culture that helps you close the strategy-to-execution gap? In part, it's a natural outcome of the first two acts: committing to an identity and translating the strategic into everyday behavior in your company. Making a commitment to a collective identity and devoting everyone's efforts to building distinctive capabilities help create conditions for a healthy, thriving culture.

If you don't have this kind of culture to start with, you may be tempted to try to change your existing culture wholesale, with a massive change initiative that legislates new behavior from the top. ("From now on, everyone must act decisively," or, "We will all be customer-focused.") That approach inevitably backfires. Instead of fighting your culture, pursue a form of cultural intervention called the "critical few." Find a critical few cultural behaviors that relate to the value proposition you support. Empower a critical few managers and employees who understand them and can help you bring them to the forefront. Articulate a critical few attributes of your enterprise that people genuinely care about and that can help you move your strategy forward.[15] This relatively subtle approach has far more power, in the end, because it lets people bring their own emotional energy to an enterprise where they feel they have a stake.

4. Cut Costs to Grow Stronger

Companies that bridge the strategy-to-execution gap spend more than their competitors do on what matters most to them and as little as possible on everything else. Rather than managing to a preconceived bottom line, they treat every cost as an investment. They know that the same sum of cash could either be used to fund either amazingly powerful distinctive capabilities or incoherent activities that hold a company back. They base their decisions about where to cut and where to invest on the need to support their value proposition and differentiate themselves through their capabilities.

These companies don't treat costs as something separate from strategy. Cost management itself is a way to make critical choices about identity and direction.

Managing costs in this way moves you to a new level of financial discipline, redirecting your resources from the projects that distract you to the core capabilities that drive your profits. It brings new life to financial practices (for example, to your annual budgets). When times are good, you don't dilute your investment dollars by making bets on dozens of new projects. Instead, you figure out the areas where you are most likely to succeed, and focus your investments there. When times are tough, you don't completely stop spending money or cut costs across the board. Instead, you find ways to double down on your strategic priorities and cut everything else.

CEMEX, a global building materials company, cut most expenses to the bone when it, like its entire industry, suffered during the 2008 housing crisis and the recession that followed. But even in the midst of a company-threatening debt crisis, CEMEX continued to develop its internal knowledge-sharing platform, an investment in technology and training that other companies might have considered superfluous. But the leaders of the company knew that its return to growth depended on maintaining a distinctive edge as a solutions provider, which required knowledge management.

When you're first on your way to closing the gap between strategy and execution, you may be in dire financial straits. You will probably need to eviscerate anything that isn't a strategic priority and pare back most expenses to bare necessities. Then, rather than banking the money you save, reinvest it to further your capabilities system.

(At PwC and Strategy& we sometimes call this the *Fit for Growth* approach.)[16] As you continue to grow, don't lose that willingness to reinvest. Develop the kinds of financial practices and rewards that make it easy to say no to projects that don't fit and yes to projects that do. This financial rigor allows you to cut costs and grow stronger at the same time, throughout the long life of your enterprise.

5. Shape Your Future

Over time, focusing on what they do best allows highly coherent companies to develop capabilities that go beyond their original goals. They stop talking about the constraints in their environment and dare to take control of their fate. They seek out higher aspirations—applying their capabilities toward a broader range of challenges and loftier goals, serving the most fundamental needs and wants of their customers, and ultimately leading their own industries. In other words, they build on their early success to enhance and extend what they do best.

Some successful companies fall into the trap of coasting on their past success. But the companies we've studied generally work hard to avoid complacency. They explicitly try to anticipate how their capabilities will need to evolve. They make the necessary investments early enough that they will be out in front of changes in the world around them. They build privileged relationships with their key customers, creating demand instead of just following it, launching products and services that define and fill unarticulated customer needs. Finally, in the same way that species like beavers and earthworms (known as ecosystem engineers) transform their environment to better meet their needs, these companies stake out a dominant role in the markets where they are clear leaders—adding superior value in a way that attracts suppliers, distributors, complementary producers and other companies to join or emulate them.[17]

Frito-Lay, facing the threat of disruptive competition, equipped its sales force with the first handheld computer, took charge of the snack food retail shelf, and changed the way the industry thought about the distribution of fast-turning impulse purchases. Inditex, with its direct links between the shopping floor and the factory, created a form of fashion-forward retail that made the conventional discounting practices of the apparel industry seem archaic. Apple became the leader of the digital technology industry in the late 1990s and early 2000s by foreseeing that consumers would want to connect devices for computing, writing, music storage, video streaming, downloading documents, taking photographs, telephoning, texting, and every other type of media activity. Its success is sometimes attributed to the genius of Steve Jobs and a few other individuals, but it was not just a matter of genius; it took decades of capability development and deployment to shape the relevant industries and bring that concept to reality. Moves like these are pragmatic and achievable, but only when your leadership is intensively aligned, with the same people working on both strategy and execution.

Our name for the companies that operate at this level is *supercompetitor*. These companies are so capable and influential that they realign the relationships among other companies in their industry. Coherence is a necessary prerequisite for achieving the status of a supercompetitor, but it is not sufficient in itself. You need to be able not just to play the game of your business well, but also to change the rules. All the companies we have studied have, to some significant extent, become supercompetitors as they practiced these five acts of unconventional leadership. You can do the same.

How the Five Acts Fit Together

We have been presenting these findings in business and academic settings for the past few years. At one business school, an MBA student raised his hand. "I get that the conventional wisdom is problematic," he said. "But most of our professors are telling us to do those things."

Executives tell us something similar. The five acts of unconventional leadership contradict what many believe is the right way to run a business. Companies that focus on growth are universally applauded, even if the new offerings don't fit well together. Functional excellence, organizing for success, going lean across the board, and agility are all regarded favorably in business circles. But those are precisely the approaches that often lead to a gap between strategy and execution. The companies we studied manage to stay resilient and adaptive, often beating their competitors to the punch, while also maintaining a solid, coherent, cohesive identity.

Another telling comment came from a high-ranking official of a branch of the US military. The conventional wisdom on table 1-1, he said, accurately captured the management style of his overall organization. "But there are small groups that do [the unconventional acts shown in table 1-2] very, very well." These groups he said, were typically special forces: Green Berets, Navy Seals, and other elite groups that are used for highly sensitive jobs. Most companies also have similar elite groups, which are insulated from the rest of the enterprise. They assume that the larger enterprise can handle run-of-the-mill operations, and they delegate the elite activities to their special forces. But if you truly want to have strategy linked seamlessly with execution, throughout your company, then you can't rely on elite groups. You have to give up the idea of special forces, and instead create distinctive capabilities that will scale across your enterprise, involving everyone in applying them to all of the company's products and services. That takes a level of attention, and a way of thinking and acting, that may seem difficult to achieve at scale. But these five acts embody practices that help companies reach that state.

The five acts themselves are so interconnected that it would be very difficult to pick just two or three to focus on. Consider what happens if you overlook any one of them.

- When you don't commit to an identity, you risk becoming scattered among a variety of objectives. It is all too easy to continually shift your focus—to deal with exigencies and never quite build the capabilities you need. You gain a right to play in many markets, but a right to win in none.

- When you can't find a way to translate the strategic into the everyday, you have to rely on your existing functions to achieve your strategic goals. These functions naturally operate according to their own self-contained perspectives. However good your capabilities may be, they will be too narrow to fully deliver your strategy. You risk becoming a company that perennially promises great things but never seems able to deliver.

- When your company doesn't put its culture to work, your people feel trapped and disengaged. They lack commitment and enthusiasm. Yours might be one of those passive-aggressive companies where new strategies fail because people pay lip service to them while waiting for the next shake-up in the org chart.

- When you fail to cut costs to grow stronger, you become, in effect, malnourished. You starve the parts of your company that matter the most and overindulge those you don't need. Your critical capabilities will be diminished and will blend and blur into the rest of the enterprise.

- If you can't shape your future, then you run the risk of falling behind competitors that do, or worse, being disrupted by them. In many industries, supercompetitors are emerging. They are continually improving their capabilities, anticipating customer needs, and staking out a clear part of the market to control. You might lose the opportunity to become one of them and thereafter be dependent on larger, coherent players in your industry.

The IKEA Story

For a good example of how the five acts of coherent leadership can lead to success, consider the story of IKEA, the world's largest furniture manufacturer and retailer. The identity of this company is embodied in two simple statements. The first lays out its value proposition, which founder Ingvar Kamprad articulated this way in the mid-1950s: "to create a better everyday life for the many people." The second is a succinct reference to the way IKEA involves customers in its operating model: "You do your part. We do our part. Together we save money." Each store thus invites people to pick up their furniture from the warehouse and assemble it on their own.[18]

From its earliest years, IKEA has devoted itself to building and managing a capabilities system that enables this value proposition and applies it to everything the enterprise sells.

Ingvar Kamprad started the company as a college-age entrepreneur in 1943, selling seeds, postcards, and stationery. It was always a personal business for him; the word IKEA includes his initials and the first letters of the farm (Elmtaryd) and village (Agunnaryd) where he grew up. But it wasn't until the 1950s that the IKEA we know today got started. Kamprad realized that furniture in Sweden was so expensive that many people, especially those moving into their first homes, could not afford it. Part of the expense came from an elaborate system of middle merchants who bought and distributed furniture. IKEA would be the enterprise that figured out how to give people low-cost elegance at home.

IKEA's Identity Profile

Founded in Sweden, IKEA is the world's leading home furnishing brand.

Value Proposition: IKEA delivers value as a low-price player and experience provider. It creates a better everyday life at home for many people around the world—providing functional and stylish home furnishings at very low prices with a high level of customer engagement, quality, and sustainability.

Capabilities System

- *Deep understanding of how customers live at home:* IKEA applies this capability to a variety of design, production, and retail practices.
- *Price-conscious and stylish product design:* IKEA integrates customer engagement, supply-chain efficiency, and price considerations into the design process itself.
- *Efficient, scalable, and sustainable operations:* IKEA has developed its own distinctive operational capability integrating supply chain, manufacturing, and retail practices.
- *Customer-focused retail design:* The company knows how to create a distinctive combination of immersive and open-warehouse environments that provide engagement, inspiration and a distinctive "day out" shopping experience where people can comfortably spend time choosing the things they live with every day.

Portfolio of Products and Services: Known for its flat-packed furniture and its self-pick, self-carry, and self-assembly model, IKEA sells affordable furniture and other home-oriented products.

Kamprad demonstrated his commitment to this identity when he began buying furniture direct from manufacturers, bypassing distributors to reduce the price to customers. When Swedish industry leaders saw the threat he posed to the them, they tried to prevent their suppliers from selling to him. So he moved on to producers in low-cost Eastern Europe, where manufacturers could customize the product to his needs and give him a still better price.

The first IKEA retail store opened in Älmhult, a relatively remote Swedish village, in 1958. To attract people to make the full-day trek out into the forests, the company lowered its prices further and began developing its distinctive retail design, including distinctive room settings, a self-serve restaurant, and a supervised children's playroom—all to support the full-day shopping experience it became famous for.

Kamprad and his staff put a great deal of time and thought into translating the strategic into the everyday, by building capabilities that set IKEA apart. For example, they sought not just to learn what furniture people came to buy, but to gain a broad-based understanding of their customers: how they lived, how they aspired to live, and what frustrated them about their current living situation. Kamprad became known for habitually walking up to shoppers in IKEA stores and asking, "How did we disappoint you today?" That framing of the question helped draw out insights that customers wouldn't otherwise offer. Today's companywide requirement that managers visit customers in their own homes is a direct extension of this original practice.

Starting in the mid-1960s IKEA locations spread throughout Scandinavia and then the rest of the world. Becoming a global organization required IKEA to scale its capabilities in a way that was completely new. It established a franchise system in 1983, codifying and standardizing many practices around the world. At the same time, IKEA deliberately fostered an entrepreneurial and participative culture, in which managers routinely let their coworkers figure out "how we do things" to facilitate the innovation of their capabilities over time.

As Torbjörn Lööf, CEO of Inter IKEA Systems B.V. (owner of the IKEA concept and worldwide IKEA franchisor), puts it: "Of course there are areas where we're very strict and structured. But people don't resist it. They know it's been extensively tested, [and] they know we're constantly trying out new things, and if they prove out to work, they'll become part of the concept."[19]

IKEA is known for its ability to cut costs to grow stronger. Its people look for cost-saving opportunities relentlessly in every way that doesn't affect the quality of the merchandise, the customer experience in the stores, or the efficiency of operations. For example, designers continually work on packaging to shave the materials and space, so they can fit more pieces into a container. This type of congruence between strategy and execution is rare in product design. In many companies, products are designed by designers who are not responsible for managing expenses. The designs are often costed out by a separate group, generally part of finance or the supply-chain function, and the retail price is set by a third group in marketing. Each group is accustomed to managing trade-offs against the priorities of the others. Design, cost, and price are all considered together in product innovation; there are relatively few trade-offs, because everyone is seeking the same goals. This integration gives IKEA's highly advanced design capability its distinctive edge.

IKEA managers typically insist that corporate guests, no matter how important, have lunch in the store's own cafeterias. "If we took our visitors to fancy restaurants, that cost would eventually land in the customer's price," notes Montserrat Maresch, global marketing director of the INGKA Group, the largest of the thirteen IKEA franchisees. These franchisees generally plow their savings back into the business, often in the form of price cuts, expansion to new locations, or building the company's capabilities even further.

That frugality is reinforced by an annual moment of discipline that drives IKEA's businesses to improve their practices every day. Since 2000, prices have been reduced 1.5 percent to 2 percent on average at the start of every fiscal year. "This means we always start with a minus," says INGKA Group CEO Peter Agnefjäll. "If our group turns over €27 billion, we start with a minus of €500 million. We don't start on zero. If we don't do more, we're going to lose."

IKEA's culture reinforces all of the other practices and is interwoven with them. "The glue, or the inner strength, of IKEA is the cultural part," says former INGKA Group CEO Mikael Ohlsson. People at every level immediately recognize when someone is behaving counter to the company's values. If you visibly waste resources or reprimand a subordinate for suggesting an idea, you'll hear about it immediately, not just from your boss, but from everyone around you. People know that their continued attention to each other's behavior makes the entire system work.

IKEA built up its capabilities system and prospered accordingly. It is now the world's largest home furnishing brand. It uses its global scale within its chosen market as any supercompetitor does: to shape its future. For example, it purchases furniture in enough volume that suppliers go to great lengths to meet IKEA's specifications. As for direct competitors, they pose such a small threat that IKEA's leaders don't even track them consistently. Despite the fact that a few have tried to compete directly with IKEA in local markets, they are so far behind in developing their capabilities system and amassing the right kind of scale that they haven't been able to catch up. Although the IKEA leaders are conscious of this enviable market position, that doesn't make them complacent. In our interviews with them, they regularly express the concern that their success can always be emulated and they must stay on point to stay ahead.

As IKEA of Sweden's range and supply manager, Jesper Brodin, puts it: "Our number one threat is not the markets or the European economy or the recession or anything like that. It is ourselves and our own capacity to transform and deliver."

Meanwhile, IKEA continues to define itself in broader terms, capturing new domains without losing its distinctive identity. For example, as of this writing, the enterprise is rolling out a worldwide online shopping venture after carefully testing and refining it in the United Kingdom. It has ramped up its sustainability efforts through an innovative product-recovery initiative (so that returned furniture is repaired instead of discarded) and major energy-saving moves (converting its entire lighting product line to LED bulbs), among other things. These efforts are all carefully considered in light of IKEA's capabilities; like all coherent enterprises, IKEA only has time, energy, and investment capital for activities that fit.

IKEA's power stems from the way it has mastered the five acts of coherent leadership to close the gap between its strategy and the execution of the strategy. It stays true to its identity. Its capabilities all fit together, support a single value proposition, and are applied to every product it makes and sells and to every service it offers. IKEA routinely improves its practices, calls upon its culture to reinforce those practices, watches every dollar in the service of its strategic purpose, and pursues its customers in a way that gives the company great control over its destiny. Finally, its management habits, and the discipline inherent in everything it does, keep the company from losing its edge.

Every company we looked at has its own story involving these five acts. Natura, for example, built a powerful and successful identity around *bem estar bem*, carving out a role as a purveyor of natural products that build relationships, rather than promoting glamour. It developed a capabilities system to match, including a remarkable set of relationships with small Amazonian villages and with their many consultants. Natura has a powerful culture, grounded in mutual respect, accountability, and creativity; the culture is credited with enabling the constant innovation that gives the company an edge over competitors. The company carefully parses its resources, spending little (for example) on packaging and advertising but a great deal on its foray into online enterprise (where it needs to find a distinctive way of keeping relationships front and center). And Natura is now transcending the limits of the Brazilian national boundaries, seeking to become a supercompetitor in the world at large.

There is a similar narrative around Danaher. Its identity as a high-performance-oriented manufacturer of scientific and technologically oriented tools and instruments is based historically on its legendary ability to turn around ailing enterprises through its "Danaher Business System," a singular adaptation of lean and other management principles. The company's relentless competence in training and developing its own executive teams has given Danaher an almost unequaled track record in post-M&A success. Its employees and executives are proud of their culture, which despite its no-nonsense, austere ambiance, makes people feel welcome within an elite group. Danaher also works diligently to decrease or eliminate unnecessary costs, while focusing on the investments that matter (generally in R&D and operational improvement). Danaher is also shaping its industry—most recently with the announcement in mid-2015 that it would split into two companies, one focused on science and technology and the other in diversified industrial businesses. Building on its original prowess in operations improvement, the company had advanced and scaled up its capabilities systems enough that they were evolving in different directions, adapted to two increasingly different types of enterprises.

The Path to Coherence

We do not hold up the five acts as the only path to success. But it is the only path we know that closes the strategy-to-execution gap. And no other path seems to provide the same kind of long-term, sustainable success.

It is also an appealing path that feels intrinsically rewarding. Even taking a few steps down the path toward coherence can boost your company's performance and morale.

Becoming coherent doesn't depend on luck or individual genius. You do have to be discriminating and decisive: willing to say no to opportunities that don't fit your strategy and persistent enough to bring your entire organization along for the ride.

Each of the next five chapters describes one of the acts of unconventional leadership in greater detail and shows how the companies we studied put them into practice:

- *Chapter 2 ("Commit to an Identity")* covers strategic intent: how you can discover who you are as a company and stay true to your value proposition and capabilities system over the long term.

- *Chapter 3 ("Translate the Strategic into the Everyday")* looks at the way a company can blueprint and build a distinctive capabilities system and then bring it to scale across a global enterprise.

- *Chapter 4 ("Put Your Culture to Work")* considers how you can leverage and enhance the culture you have to develop and maintain coherence.

- *Chapter 5 ("Cut Costs to Grow Stronger")* explores how you can marshal your resources for the greatest impact.

- *Chapter 6 ("Shape Your Future")* describes how companies that close the strategy-execution gap can then move on to become the supercompetitors of our time.

It's a lifetime journey, so let's start now.

2

Commit to an Identity

If you asked your employees, "How do we create value for our customers?" would you get a clear answer? And would different people within your company hold the same view?

This question—how do you create value?—is the most fundamental inquiry about strategy that anyone could ask. Instead, many people think strategy has to do with choosing a direction: where are we going to grow next?

That's why so many executives focus their attention on creating purpose and mission statements. They are trying to define where the company should go, in a way that everyone can support and that will lead to profitability and growth. But these statements tend to ring hollow because they reflect the incoherence of the company that makes them. To encompass all of its disparate activity, the statements have to be generic and vague. A statement like "We want to be the company of choice for our customers," or "We are committed to delivering the highest quality and widest selection" affirms a goal, but it doesn't explain why this company is special or why it should have any hope of achieving that goal with distinction.

A true identity, by contrast, expresses what your enterprise does exceptionally well and why it matters. When the company is coherent, the people who work there can typically talk about its identity with certainty and clarity. Just as an individual identity is grounded in the things that make a person special—what the person does, how he or she does it, and what the person cares about—the identity of a company expresses what distinguishes this company from all others.

It takes time, dedication, and persistence to construct a truly differentiating identity—an identity that sets a company apart, grounded in the complex, difficult-to-build capabilities that no one else can copy, and that shape its attitudes and collective behavior. That's why we titled this chapter "Commit to an Identity." Commitment implies staying true to that identity over the long term. You develop the ability to change when necessary, but you recognize that the source of your greatest strength involves a commitment that may last for years. In this chapter, we'll explain how companies forge that identity, make the commitment to stay with it, and use it as a vehicle for sustainable growth.

Choosing and developing an identity requires a great deal of reflection, for the same reason that choosing a career does for an individual. Your choice is limited by the capabilities you have, or can reasonably build or buy. Where your company can go in the market—what products and services you can offer and to whom—is a function of who you are and what you do exceptionally well. Only when you understand your company's capabilities can you understand where you can expect to win, why you would win there, and what else you must do to enhance your capability system to capture a winning position.

A good example of a strong identity is Apple, which iterated and refined its identity over three decades. In his biography *Steve Jobs*, Walter Isaacson describes the early years of the company, when Apple's cofounder and ultimate CEO foresaw a compelling future in which computers would become powerful tools that would deeply improve everyday life. Jobs's unwavering conviction was echoed in his original description of the Macintosh, in the early 1980s, as a "computer for the rest of us." Most computer users were programmers; even consumer programs were as complex to learn as programming languages. Apple would be different; it would produce elegant, engaging computers that met people more than halfway. This powerful value proposition was possible because Apple already had the necessary capabilities: breakthrough innovation, customer insight, a well-evolved prowess in technological integration, and a facility for intuitively accessible design. Together, these capabilities overcame all the obstacles that Apple faced during its early years, including those that stemmed from Jobs's own temperament. They were instilled deeply enough in the company, even in those relatively early years, that they gave Apple an identity that lasted into the 1990s, long after Jobs was pushed out of the CEO position.[1]

Then in the late 1990s, when he returned as CEO, Jobs took the company's identity a step further. He began by reminding the attendees at a Macworld conference in 1997 that their job wasn't to compete with Microsoft. "We have to let go of this notion that for Apple to win Microsoft has to lose." He later explained his reasoning: Apple couldn't beat Microsoft at its own game. "Apple had to remember who Apple was."[2] Creating yet another Windows-like clone would not suffice; Apple had to find its own distinctive path.

But that didn't mean returning to the identity that it had ten years before. It was too late to base a computer's success just on being distinctively well-designed and user-friendly, like the original Mac. Jobs didn't unveil the next incarnation of the Apple identity until the annual Macworld conference in January 2001.[3] In his keynote address, he said that the first great era of the PC, the golden age of productivity, had passed around 1994 and had been replaced by the age of the internet. Now, however, the internet had matured and the PC was "on the verge of entering its third great age." Cell phones, camcorders, and other digital devices were exploding in popularity. Digital cameras represented 15 percent of all cameras sold in the United States. "Soon it will be fifty percent," Jobs said. Apple's computers, he added, would "become the digital hub of our emerging digital lifestyle . . . not just adding value to these devices but interconnecting them as well." Apple would be the company that brought that digital hub to life.

Apple's Identity Profile

With headquarters in Cupertino, California, Apple had the highest total shareholder value of any company in the world in 2015. Also, in surveys of business leaders, Apple is consistently ranked as the world's most innovative company.[4]

Value Proposition: Apple combines the roles of innovator, aggregator, and experience provider. Its computers, tablets, and smartphones form the hub of a single digital system enabling consumers to easily manage media production, consumption and communication.

Capabilities System

- *Consumer insight:* the ability to spot a burgeoning consumer need, based on a deep understanding of how people live, work, and play.
- *Intuitively accessible design:* of products, software, the retail store experience (including the Genius Bar), and online environments.
- *Technological integration:* combining superior technology (including that developed by other companies) in ways that work together as a seamless whole.
- *Breakthrough innovation of products, services, and software:* packaged and delivered with elegance and artistry.[5]

Portfolio of Products and Services: Apple designs, manufactures, and markets mobile communication and media devices, personal computers, and portable digital music players. It sells a variety of related software, online services (such as iTunes and iCloud), peripherals, networking solutions, and third-party digital content and applications.

Articulating this grand ambition led, over the next few years, to major investments of money and attention in Apple's capabilities system—for example, the development of the negotiating and packaging skill to procure and sell recorded music online. Apple would also revolutionize digital photography by including cameras in the iPhone, incidentally giving Jobs's prediction about digital cameras a whole new meaning.

"Some people argue," says Harvard Business School strategy professor Cynthia Montgomery, who uses the Apple story in executive education, "that a strategy is understood only in hindsight, retrospectively trying to make sense of a group of haphazard, reactive moves. But here's a case where, when the stock price was still very low [in 2001], Steve Jobs laid out his animating idea in public, in advance. When Apple came out with iTunes, the iPod, and the Apple Store, it all made sense in light of that idea."[6]

Starbucks is also known for the clarity of its identity. Its retail stores vary significantly from one location to the next, but they are all recognizably Starbucks. This strong presence didn't happen accidentally. It developed because CEO Howard Schultz and many others in the company have deliberately stayed true to a single identity. As with Apple, the company's identity is grounded not in one particular product, but in its value proposition and everything it does. Having a single powerful identity opens up diverse paths of growth, including product sales in supermarkets, its own distinctive food menus, snacks, and pioneering differentiation in mobile payments. Starbucks never stops being Starbucks, and it will probably never stop roasting and selling gourmet coffee. But it is resilient in the face of change; it moves easily into and out of a variety of changing markets.

In 2008, Schultz summed up the way the company manages its identity in a statement he called "seven bold moves." Two of the seven were directly linked to the company's value proposition: "Be the undisputed coffee authority," and "Ignite the emotional attachment with our customers." The other "bold moves" were related to the company's distinctive capabilities. Each move specifically had to do with how the company would be able to create value as a whole. Schultz didn't say, "Become the top performer in our global category." He said, "Expand our global presence while making each store the heart of the local neighborhood." High performance would naturally follow. He didn't say, "Employees will be our greatest asset." He said, "Engage and inspire our partners." (All Starbucks employees are called "partners," which reflects the fact that although they are paid retail-worker salaries, most of them hold stock in the company and receive health-care benefits.) He didn't even say, "Sell the best coffee," or anything else limited to product quality. He said, "Create innovative growth platforms worthy of our coffee." In one area he was vague, because this area required new levels of innovation: "Be the leader in ethical sourcing and environmental impact." And when it came to financial results, even there he focused on the necessary capability: "Deliver a sustainable economic model."[7]

As you think about your own company's identity, keep thinking about what you do and who you are. You may be tempted to define your identity in terms of what you sell—your sector, category, or industry: "We are a leader in Asia," or "We are at the top of the energy industry." But your people already know that you do something more specific than that. While you might have defined yourself through particular products or services in the past, don't limit your identity to that definition. Products and services may change. Your company may well evolve to transcend the current limits of your sector or category, enabling you to move into new enterprises without losing the qualities that set you apart.

How Haier Found Its Identity

For an example of a company that has achieved prodigious success from humble beginnings while always staying true to their identity,

TOOL

Assessing Your Company's Identity

This is a diagnostic assessment of the coherence that currently exists in the thinking and actions of your senior leadership—and thus in your company's identity. The exercise will challenge your perceptions and those of your colleagues. You may be surprised by how your existing perceptions of your supposedly best products and services, your highest-growth markets, or your most significant competitors differ among top leaders.

Use this diagnostic more than once—it's a valuable tool to measure and track your company's progress. For an online version, visit www.strategythatworks.com.

In a small group, talk through the answers to these questions as candidly as possible. This exercise benefits from more than one person's perspective. The more questions to which you can truthfully answer "yes," the more coherent your company.

	Strategy: Can we state it?	Execution: Do we live it?
Value proposition	• Are we clear about how we choose to create value in the marketplace?	• Are we investing in the capabilities that really matter to our value proposition?
Capabilities system	• Can we articulate the three to six capabilities that describe what we do better than anyone else? • Have we defined how they work together in a system? • Do our strategy statements reflect this?	• Do all our businesses draw on this superior capabilities system? • Do our organizational structure and operating model support and leverage it? • Does our performance management system reinforce it?
Product and service fit	• Have we specified our product and service "sweet spot"? • Do we understand how to leverage the capabilities system in new or unexpected arenas?	• Do most of the products and services we sell fit with our capabilities system? • Are new products and acquisitions evaluated on the basis of that fit?
Coherence	• Can everyone in the organization articulate our differentiating capabilities? • Is our company's leadership reinforcing these capabilities?	• Can we compete effectively and consistently well in our chosen market? (Do we have the "right to win"?) • Do all of our decisions add to our coherence, or do some of them push us toward incoherence?

consider the Haier Group. Founded in Qingdao, a coastal city of three million people midway between Beijing and Shanghai, this company is the world's fastest-growing appliance maker and enjoys the largest market share in white goods worldwide. It holds about 14 percent of the global market, facing at least seven other major competitors, including Whirlpool, Electrolux, and GE Appliances. Haier is also a world leader in technological innovation. That's not bad for a company with its roots in Chinese Communism. Moreover, only three decades ago the company was in such desperate straits that the CEO had to borrow money to pay workers' salaries, and many of the products it was selling needed to be repaired before they could be used for the first time.

Haier's value proposition is that of a solutions provider: a company that not only understands, but also does something about, problems people have with daily life. This unique identity began in 1984, when current CEO Zhang Ruimin took the helm, only a few years after Premier Deng Xiaoping came to power and began to open up the Chinese economy. For millions of Chinese people moving out of a subsistence existence, the "big three" aspirations were to own a television, a refrigerator, and a washing machine. ("Just a decade before," wrote Bill Fischer, Umberto Lago, and Fang Liu in *Reinventing Giants*, a history of Haier, it "had been a bicycle, a watch, and a sewing machine.")[8] Qingdao was one of China's first enterprise zones, and the Qingdao Refrigerator Factory, a city-owned company that had been founded in the 1930s, sold all the refrigerators it could produce. That was only eighty per month; would-be customers crowded around delivery trucks to buy the scarce devices before the machines were unloaded.

After three managing directors resigned in rapid succession, a thirty-five-year-old deputy manager in the company named Zhang Ruimin was asked to find a replacement. He found no acceptable candidates, and he reluctantly took on the challenge himself. His reservations were understandable. Despite its captive market, the company was a mess. It was in debt for RMB1.47 million (about US$11 million), and its eight hundred workers were owed several months of back pay. The doors of the factory had been broken up for firewood the previous winter, and so many employees were using the floor as a toilet that Zhang had to institute a rule forbidding it. He also had his hands full solving urgent operational problems, like refinancing the debt and installing new production lines.

Then, an almost unprecedented event happened. A customer sent a letter to Zhang complaining about a refrigerator that wouldn't stay cool. Zhang sent a few staff members into the warehouse to find a replacement, and they reported back that seventy-six of the almost four hundred refrigerators in inventory were unusable. Zhang was frustrated, but he saw an opportunity. China's middle class was poised for growth. People would not tolerate faulty products in the future. By solving the problem of poor quality, ahead of other companies, this little old refrigerator manufacturer from Qingdao could set itself apart.

From now on, Zhang announced to his staff, "everything that leaves our plant should be a grade 1 product."[9] He told the employees to line up all seventy-six defective units in the street outside the factory. He brought a sledgehammer, and one by one, they smashed the refrigerators to bits in full sight of the rest of the plant workers and the community. (The sledgehammer is now on display in a national museum in Beijing.) Everybody knew that Zhang could have easily sold those refrigerators; even the defective ones could have been repaired, and then they would have been worth more than two years of a worker's salary.[10] But instead, he literally hammered home the company's new identity. It would not be like most other Chinese companies, assuming that its customers' low incomes and nonconsumer backgrounds would lead them to accept anything they could afford. This company would provide solutions to Chinese customers' real problems—starting with the problem of poor reliability.

To deliver, Zhang knew, the company had to rapidly ramp up its capabilities. He was one of the first Chinese manufacturing executives to adopt Western quality approaches. He set up a joint venture with the German industrial company Liebherr and brought Six Sigma and other innovative lean production methods to Qingdao. Within two years, the company was winning local awards for quality and reliability. Even then, Zhang and the other company leaders understood that quality was just the means to their true goal: to be the company that met the real needs of consumers by solving their problems. In China, that meant delivery problems, so Zhang explicitly sought out mastery of China's notoriously complex supply chain. By 1989, when he reorganized the company and renamed it Haier (derived from the second half of Liebherr's name), it was the largest Chinese appliance manufacturer, holding its own in China against rivals from the West and branching out to washing machines, dishwashers, and stoves.

During the 1990s, Haier expanded its value proposition and leveraged its capabilities system by providing solutions in a different way: to niche markets. The company set up cross-functional product launch teams where marketers and engineers worked together on products that other companies didn't even consider producing. For example, on discovering that Chinese farmers were using its washing machines to clean their sweet potatoes, Haier produced new machines designed specifically for washing vegetables. This innovation capability enabled it to expand rapidly overseas. For example, Haier makes large washing machines for Pakistani robes, small ones for Chinese undergarments (which are often washed separately in China), and wine coolers and small dormitory-style refrigerators for the United States.

In the 2000s, it further expanded its role as a solutions provider by developing a capability for on-demand production and delivery: setting up a multichannel system that allowed customers to specify the color and features of appliances over the internet. Haier also expanded its customer support capability, with staff in China who often form ongoing relationships with customers, visiting them on a monthly basis. This customer support capability has allowed the company to launch a new line of water purifiers that are tailored to remove specific pollutants for each purchaser's neighborhood, with 220,000 variations in China. This remarkable site-specific system emerged from a collaboration with the Strauss Group (an Israeli food and beverage company) and Dow Chemical (which jointly holds more than 20 water purification patents with Haier). Other solutions-oriented innovations include a design service helping thousands of Chinese country-to-city migrants get used to apartment life and buy the furniture as well as appliances that they need, and an air conditioner and purifier with a miniature wind tunnel that excels at cooling the air a bit but not making it too cold. This feature was originally suggested by consumers on a Haier social media forum. The model, dubbed "Tianzun" (Mandarin for "heaven"), also has a circle of light in its center that shifts from red to blue when the air quality improves, and software that connects it to smartphones for control. It has proven extraordinarily popular in China.

Through all these changes, Haier's employees are always conscious of one company aspect that stays the same: its core identity as a solutions provider. Though it is sometimes associated with low prices in the West, Haier has never identified itself as a value player. It doesn't offer every appliance in every market, but only enters markets when its leaders believe Haier has an advantage in solving a particular problem. The company has also remained coherent; all the capabilities reinforce each other's value to the strategy. For example, the degree of customization Haier can create is possible partly because of the on-demand production and delivery capability. On-demand production and delivery, in turn, builds on Haier's operational excellence. All of it can be traced back to that moment when Zhang Ruimin realized that he could create a company that solved problems for potentially millions of loyal customers, first in China and then everywhere else.

Haier's Identity Profile

With headquarters in Qingdao, Shandong, China, Haier is a Chinese multinational consumer electronics and home appliances company. Since 2011, the Haier brand has held the world's largest market share in white goods.

Value Proposition: Haier is a solutions provider and innovator, with a track record of meeting customer needs, either for niches and regions or for individual customer tastes.

Capabilities System

- *Consumer-responsive innovation:* Haier rapidly tailors products and (increasingly) services for local markets and specific customer needs (notably the needs of China's emerging middle class and niche markets elsewhere).

- *Operational excellence:* The company is geared to produce high-quality products at very low cost through continuous improvement and internal competition.

- *Local distribution networks:* This capability was honed in China's highly decentralized value chain and is used in emerging markets and other locales.

- *On-demand production and delivery:* Haier incorporates a "pull"-oriented distribution system and zero-inventory logistics, allowing immense variety at minimal cost.

Portfolio of Products and Services: Haier products include water and air purifiers and conditioners, heaters, computers, televisions, washing machines, and kitchen appliances. It also offers related services, including water quality monitoring, home design, and microcredit lending.[11]

Defining Who You Are

The profiles scattered throughout this book show the identities of companies we have studied. Your own identity can be as powerful as theirs. You may expand successfully to new lines of business with the same identity—as Haier did with home design and water purification services, Starbucks with its instant-coffee innovation, Apple with its smartphone and iTunes store, CEMEX (the Mexican cement company) with infrastructure design consultation, Lego with its Mindstorm computer-driven products and Bionicle characters, and Amazon with cloud computing. You might also discover, as Amazon did with its Fire Phone or Starbucks with its hot breakfast menu, that there are limits to what you can successfully develop. And you may sometimes need to push the boundaries of your identity: to expand who you are.

A good place to start closing your strategy-to-execution gap is by first defining two or three primary elements of your identity: a clear, recognizable value proposition and the capabilities system that supports it. You continue to iterate these; with each iteration, you match them more closely together. At some point you must consider how these fit your portfolio of products and services and how to drive coherence among all three elements.

Let's look at these three elements of your identity—value proposition, capabilities system, and lineup of products and services—in more detail.

Your Value Proposition

By assessing your mix of industry conditions and your current capabilities, you can find the value proposition that is most promising for you. You can generally start determining the right value proposition for your company (also known as its "way to play" in the market) by looking at common, generic ways of creating value. We call these *puretones*—basic, self-evident value propositions such as aggregator, innovator, value player, and experience provider. These basic value propositions alone may not fully capture the nuances of your business, but like primary colors they can be combined to reflect a more complex value proposition. (You can find an extensive list of puretones we've identified in appendix C and an interactive tool to help identify your own value proposition at www.strategythatworks.com.)

In every company profile that you'll find throughout this book, we've included the puretone "building blocks" that come together into the company's value proposition. We also link those ways to play to the capabilities systems that enable them.

Every company combines the puretones in its own way to create its own custom approach to providing value. For example, Qualcomm, IKEA, and CEMEX are all innovative enterprises, but each in a different way. Qualcomm is also a platform provider. Its innovations are all oriented toward industry leadership through franchising fundamental forms of technology that other players adopt. IKEA is a value player. Its innovations in packaging and logistics shave costs, while its design innovations enable it to provide stylish home furnishings at very low prices. CEMEX is a solutions provider; every innovation is oriented to addressing a particular customer problem or group of problems.

These value propositions define in detail what the capabilities system needs to do. For example, IKEA's capabilities in product and retail design clearly involve ongoing innovation, but this is always in service to being a value player and experience provider: finding ways to make products less expensive and the retail environment more engaging. CEMEX has a well-honed innovation capability, used to deliver solutions to homeowners and commercial and government customers. This reinforces its value proposition as a solution provider—differentiating itself in an industry, in this case cement and concrete, which is prone to commoditization.

At the same time, the capabilities system of your company—the capabilities you already have and those which you know you can build, buy, or borrow (through joint ventures)—should help determine your value proposition. Your value proposition is a promise. You'll need a distinctive capabilities system to keep it. You should only adopt a value proposition that you'll be able to deliver.

Don't assume you have to follow every opportunity that promises returns. Instead, look at your capabilities. Pick the places to compete where there will be no gap between strategy and execution, because you already have prowess that fits that challenge. The value proposition you are aiming for should fulfill the following criteria:

- It is supported by your strengths and is therefore feasible.

- It is differentiated from the value created by your competitors. No other company could offer it as well or as completely.

- The parts of it that you can't deliver on yet are within reach, at least in the long run. With the right investment and attention, you can build the necessary capabilities.

- There is a market that will appreciate and respond to this value proposition.

- You can offer it profitably.

- Your value proposition will continue to be relevant, given the changes that you think are likely to take place in your industry.

Your Capabilities System

In chapter 1, we defined a capability as a well-designed combination of processes, tools, knowledge, skills, and organizational design. Together, these generate the capacity to reliably and consistently deliver a specified outcome relevant to your business. A distinctive capability is more specific: it is what you do well, what customers value, and what your competitors can't beat.

Your capabilities system is the group of three to six distinctive capabilities that differentiate you from other companies and that allow you to deliver on your value proposition. These critically important capabilities do not stand alone; they are part of a mutually reinforcing system, which is the key to a company's differentiation. Apple, for instance, is not a superior company just because of its exquisite

Thinking Through Your Value Proposition

In developing the strategy of your enterprise, which comes first: the value proposition, or the capabilities system? The answer is both: You develop them together, because each should influence the other. This exercise can help you do just that. It is simultaneously outward-looking ("market-back") and inwardly driven ("capabilities-forward"). It will help you develop a value proposition that matches your own strengths and can differentiate your enterprise in your industry.

1. Start by going through the list of available puretones and identifying which are relevant in your industry. How do your competitors create value? Which competitors could be described by which puretones? What distinctive capabilities do they have that help them deliver that value?

2. Look at the rest of the market for your industry—the entire landscape. Are there value propositions that are not yet occupied—that could, in fact, be relevant in your industry, but that have not been taken so far? Which value propositions will be relevant in three to five years?

3. Now imagine your enterprise in each of those value propositions. How well could you deliver? How would you set your company apart from others? What would be your identity— your value proposition, the capabilities that would differentiate you, and your products and services?

4. Finally, look at your company today. For each value proposition that you might occupy: What relevant capabilities do you already have in place? What gaps would you need to fill?

5. Of all the possible value propositions you might occupy, which have the most potential? Why? Of these, which is the top contender? What makes it attractive to you, and how does it fit with the capabilities system that would best distinguish you?

This exercise could (but does not have to) occupy your senior team for an extended period of time. You can use it to explore the many options available to you and your competitors, and to settle on the one "way to play in the market" that will serve you best in the years to come.

design capability alone. Its "secret sauce" is its combination of capa-bilities. This includes the consumer insight needed to spot a latent need; the ability to integrate technology (often technology originated by others, but Apple always brings it to fruition and improves it); design prowess that makes its user interfaces intuitive, elegant, and easy to use, and its products packaged and marketed with cachet; and a breakthrough innovation track record that extends even to cus-tomer support (the Genius Bar in its retail store). All of this together has made Apple the default consumer standard, difficult to overtake even by much less expensive computers and mobile phones, earning high margins long after the offerings are launched. Whether Apple will succeed in extending this system into cars, televisions, or wear-ables isn't yet clear. But the full system of capabilities allows Apple to transcend any particular product or service. It gives Apple an identity to which employees, customers, and shareholders will continue to commit their time and money.

CEMEX gains a similarly strong identity from the several capabili-ties in its system. We've already mentioned one: its solutions-oriented innovation capability. Another is operational proficiency; the com-pany is known for its precision in timing deliveries in many loca-tions. A third is relationship-building through guidance. CEMEX's community-based salespeople are trained in providing local officials and homeowners with knowledge about building and design. The company also knows how to share knowledge about customer prob-lems (extending to financing and construction advice), and how to promote energy efficiency and other aspects of environmental sus-tainability related to the building industries. Its use of alternative fuels grew from 5 percent in 2005 to an industry-leading 28 percent in 2014.[12] Capabilities like these are not just functional activities. Each of them combines people, processes, technology, and organiza-tional measures like incentives across a range of functions.

Some readers may associate a capabilities system with the con-cept of a value network, as articulated by Clayton Christensen in

The Innovator's Dilemma. A value network is the group of common capabilities shared by every company in an industry: the common standards, efficiencies, and interoperability that allow many suppliers and customers to interact easily.[13] As we'll see in chapter 5, these value networks are like "table stakes" in a card game. Every company must ante up, developing some level of proficiency in each of them, just to survive in that industry. These industry-wide capabilities are important. (In appendix D, we name some prevailing table-stakes capabilities relevant to particular sectors.) But they do not lead to competitive advantage. Your systems of distinctive capabilities are the opposite of value networks. They include the few capabilities that aren't table stakes, that other companies don't share, that help you succeed because they are difficult to copy or emulate.

It takes some precision to describe the distinctive capabilities that differentiate you. A conventional functional label like logistics—or innovation, marketing, merchandising, or analytics—is generally too broad. It overlooks the precise elements that make this capability effective. C. K. Prahalad and Gary Hamel recognized this back in 1994 when they proposed the concept of core competencies (a forerunner to the idea of distinctive capabilities): "A substantial amount of effort is required," they wrote, "to cluster and aggregate the skills and technologies in some meaningful way, and to arrive at labels that are truly descriptive and promote shared understanding."[14]

That's why the best descriptions of capabilities are grounded in specific observation, reflecting their complexity and bespoke nature—their ties to this particular company. For example, at Starbucks, one distinctive capability is the company's consistent proficiency in developing and retaining skilled, committed staff in a storefront retail environment. This is not easy to do, and it would be too simplistic to describe it simply as a "human capital" capability. It involves skillful recruiting and the delivery of a far-sighted health care policy, to be sure, along with a carefully thought out approach to employee stock ownership. Most staff members (who are called "partners") also own shares in the company. Moreover, every "part-ner" in the company gets involved in training others. The company has developed processes and tools to help staff members succeed at this, and to ensure that training is closely aligned to Starbucks' desired customer experience. All of these facets, and more, combine together to establish a high level of loyalty and commitment among Starbucks employees, especially in that high-turnover industry.

Another example is the logistics capabilities of three very different companies: Frito-Lay, Amazon, and Inditex. Frito-Lay's supply chain, which we will describe in detail in chapter 3, is geared toward delivering snacks tailored to local tastes, using highly sophisticated and increasingly automated direct store delivery (DSD) systems. Amazon's supply chain makes use of other companies for trucking, but relies on its own robotics- and cloud-computing-facilitated warehouse system, delivering a broad variety of goods around the world, generally with next-day service at very low rates. (The company spent $775 million in 2012 to acquire Kiva, the company that makes the robots.[15]) Inditex uses its supply chain to link its factories with its Zara retail stores, with the intent of making its manufacturing responsive. It takes as little as two weeks for an idea to bubble up from a random conversation in the store, gain the attention of Zara management, go to a clothing designer, be translated into a manufactured garment, and appear on the retail racks.[16] All three of these capabilities could be called "logistics," and all three are IT-enabled, but you could not easily substitute one for another.

Despite all this precision and detail, however, a distinctive capability should not be seen as being "in the weeds." It is the core driver of strategy. While it is cross-functional and many-faceted, it is also intrinsically whole—it stands on its own, with all its related activities complementing each other. You cannot remove any part without compromising the entirety. Thus, any description of the capability should be simple and clear enough to convey a sense of its power. It should galvanize leaders, including the top leaders of the company, to make the necessary commitment to it to propel the company to success.

In chapter 3, we'll describe how companies design and build distinctive capabilities and bring them to scale. As you develop your capabilities system, keep in mind the needs, strengths, and culture of your company. It does not do you much good to emulate some other company's capabilities, not even if it's world-class. Just about every business leader these days would love to have Apple's capabilities system at his or her disposal. But unless you have the same value proposition and a similar lineup of products and services, it won't be economically or culturally feasible. You need to identify the capabilities system that fits your own enterprise.

Your Product and Service Mix

Becoming and remaining coherent also requires that the products and services you offer fit seamlessly with your value proposition and drive scale to your capabilities system. A portfolio review should give at least as much weight to strategic fit as it gives to financial performance. Ideally, every one of the company's individual businesses should link strategy to execution in this way.

When they look at their portfolio with an eye toward capabilities fit, many companies realize that some offerings don't fit their chosen identity, even if the offerings are individually successful. Other companies have the capabilities to do better with these offerings and are benefiting from the resulting advantage. That is why a growing number of companies are divesting businesses that don't quite match their capabilities system—so that they can release funds to acquire products and services that fit more closely.

Though products in the same industry are often assumed to fit together, a capabilities-driven view on portfolios forces business leaders to discard conventional views of their portfolios and growth opportunities. The Standard Industry Classification (SIC) definitions, most of which were last revised by the US Office of Management and Budget in 1997, represent the established boundaries for judging where products and services fit, and the definitions are highly misleading when it comes to capabilities fit. For example, motorcycles and bicycles are grouped in one SIC category, but they are produced in very different ways for very different customers; they require very different capabilities in product launch and marketing. The conventional view of grocery goods includes canned, frozen, and preserved foods together, but these require very different forms of production, distribution, and marketing.[17] If you aren't careful to look at capabilities, you risk falling into the "adjacency trap": expanding into seemingly similar products or services—for example, from canned to frozen foods, or from bicycles to motorcycles—without taking into account the very different capabilities needed to succeed in that new enterprise.

Growth, Change, and Identity

Most business leaders recognize the power of a strong identity. They understand how alignment between strategy and execution enables a company to win, and they recognize the role of distinctive capabilities in creating that alignment. They also see the level of focus this requires. Why then do they let their companies get distracted?

One big reason is the daunting pressure that many companies face: to seek growth in the face of uncertainty, increased competition, and relentless commoditization. They pursue many diverse growth avenues and organizational interventions. They do this in the name of agility or resilience or with the idea that if they try a lot of things or let a thousand flowers bloom, they'll be more likely to find a path that works. This saves them from having to make difficult choices in advance about their portfolio, and to allow them to hedge their bets. But it also diffuses their efforts, reinforcing incoherence. Inevitably, those multiple businesses will have to justify

TOOL

A Capabilities View of Your Portfolio

This exercise, conducted by a group of people with visibility across your enterprise, can help you evaluate the link between strategy and execution for each of your businesses. Consider the following questions for each product or service:

- How well does the offering fit your value proposition? Can you envision it as the basis for a sustained stream of attractive growth opportunities with the customers who matter most to your company?

- Is the offering core to your company's capabilities system? (Does it benefit directly from your most important strengths and thus provide scale to your efforts?)

- Does the offering reasonably provide its best possible path to financial performance in your company—or could a more profitable home for it be found elsewhere?

Concentrate your effort on the businesses for which you can answer yes to all three questions. These are the kinds of products and services worth keeping or acquiring. For a given offering, if you can't answer yes to all three questions, then it might be worth more to a different organization than it is to you. It is worth the most to the organization with the capabilities required to meaningfully advance its success.

their demands by growing revenues as rapidly as possible, even if that growth comes at the expense of sustained profits.

In practice, this approach leads companies into a growth treadmill: chasing multiple market opportunities where they have no clear identity, and not enough of a powerful capabilities system to compete with. They find themselves serving so many different customer groups with diverse offerings that it's impossible to define what the company is really about. Although such companies may have been great once, their lack of focus makes it hard to be truly excellent now.

Consider, for example, the story of Smith-Corona. In the 1960s and 1970s, it was the preeminent maker of user-friendly, portable typewriters for consumers: students, teachers, and people with home offices. The company's leaders saw disruption coming: electronic calculators had eclipsed its adding machine business and the company realized early that computers could do the same thing to its typewriter business.

So Smith-Corona hedged. In the mid-1960s, it acquired Procter-Silex (which made kitchen appliances), Glidden (paint), and Durkee (salad dressings and seasonings), all of which needed different capabilities than typewriters. It also bet heavily on electronic word processing machines, which seemed to represent a compelling extension of its existing product line. But the new R&D facility, opened in 1976, was located in Danbury, Connecticut, a four-hour drive from the company's headquarters near Syracuse, New York, where the mechanical engineers worked on "real" typewriters. The two facilities were treated as two different operations, with no regular opportunity to learn from each other or build a common identity and capabilities system.

In 1986, after five years of losses, the company was acquired in a hostile takeover. The new owners sold off most of the non-core businesses and focused the company on word processing computers, which succeeded at first; SCM (the new name of the company) led the market in 1989. But the company continued to distract itself. There was a series of failed products, including personal computers (a joint venture with Acer), daisy-wheel printers (which could not print pictures), label makers, electronic dictionaries, and a service that set up home offices. The company declared bankruptcy in 1995, and today it is a much smaller manufacturer of pressure-sensitive labels and thermal paper.

Smith-Corona never carved out a true identity for itself. You might question whether it ever had the right capabilities to become the purveyor of the next generation of writing machines, the kind that even Apple or Microsoft could not make. But because of the company's array of ancillary businesses and the accompanying distractions, it never got the chance to find out.[18]

It's understandable that businesses get caught in this growth treadmill, even when they are aware of its dangers. The treadmill is a natural response to a major dilemma in business today: the transience of advantage. Even the most formidable position in an industry, buttressed by assets and capital, can be vulnerable to rapid change: commoditization, technological upheaval, shifting capital flows, political and regulatory turmoil, and other facets of a chaotic and unpredictable world.

But there is a second reality, just as powerful: distinctive capabilities are inherently slow to change. The capabilities system in any large, coherent enterprise involves hundreds or thousands of people as well as embedded investments in technology and specialized skills. These capabilities have been built up slowly, decision by decision, and thus they are *sticky*: they take time to update and replace. If the capabilities system could be changed easily, it wouldn't be worth very much, because anyone could build something similar. It is impossible to shift identity and build new distinctive capabilities on a dime.

The answer is to treat the stable nature of your capabilities as a strength, not a weakness. The goal of being adaptive and resilient is admirable, and when you're in industries under disruption, you have to move quickly. But you can't move effectively unless you're willing to plot your expansion path in line with, not in opposition to, your existing strengths. Amazon's founder and CEO, Jeff Bezos, clearly agrees, as a 2012 video interview shows.

"I very frequently get the question 'What's going to change in the next ten years?'" he said. "I almost never get the question 'What's *not* going to change in the next ten years?' And I submit to you that that second question is actually the more important of the two. Because you can build a business strategy around the things that are stable in time."

Then he gave an example. "In our retail business, we know the customers want low prices. I know that's going to be true ten years from now. They want fast delivery; they want vast selection. It's impossible to imagine a future ten years from now where a customer comes up to me and says: 'Jeff, I love Amazon, I just wish the prices were a little higher. I just wish you delivered a little more slowly.' [When] you have something that you know is true even in the long term, you can afford to put a lot of energy in it."[19]

The core value proposition for Amazon—vast selection, low prices, and fast delivery—has remained intact since it began as an online bookseller in the late 1990s. It has also maintained essentially the same capabilities system since the beginning, combining distinctive approaches to online retail interface design, back-end supply-chain management, merchandising, customer relationship management, and technological innovation. Yet despite this high level of continuity, the company is clearly capable of rapid change. Many of its innovative bets, including auctions, cloud-based services, Kindle e-books, online media distribution, automated logistics, and its rapid delivery options, have paid off. Some bets, like the Fire Phone, have failed and have been criticized for overreach, but enough of them have been in line with the company's strategy that they fueled a consistently remarkable and long-standing growth rate.[20]

True agility doesn't come from pursuing growth wherever it may be located or somehow spotting trends and getting to those markets first. It comes from pursuing opportunities where your capabilities give you what we call the *right to win*—the ability to compete more effectively than your competitors could in the arenas where you choose to do business. Agility depends on having these advantages already in place. They give you the tools and engines to disrupt new markets, they focus your energy on staying in front of customers where it really matters, and they enable continuous innovation—not just in the individual products and services that you launch, but in your capabilities themselves, and thus in the ways you create value.

Amazon's Identity Profile

With headquarters in Seattle, Amazon.com is the world's largest online retailer, with retail websites around the world and a seemingly endless variety of products and services, including those from other merchants who sell through Amazon's system.

Value Proposition: Amazon is a super-aggregator of vendors and customers, giving people a compelling, one-stop online shopping experience with easy access to products, information, and friction-free delivery.

Capabilities System

- *Retail interface design:* Amazon creates and maintains digital pages that are elegant, seamless, and full of detail and have highly sophisticated search, comment, linking, and online payment features.

- *Back-end supply-chain management:* The company handles massive inventories through networks of specialized warehouses and the distribution networks of many partners, vendors, and suppliers.

- *Rapid and effective online merchandising:* A hidden source of value involves Amazon's ability to identify attractive products and feature them in the most appropriate places on its site.

- *Customer-relationship management:* Amazon uses data from past interactions to notify customers of potential affinities with other products and to solve dissatisfaction issues before they occur.

- *Advanced technological innovation:* This capability provides a platform from which the company can offer its one-click instant-ordering system, its Kindle e-book offering, and its cloud computing services— among many others.

Portfolio of Products and Services: Amazon offers just about any product that can be shipped through the mail or other delivery services, along with e-books, computer-based software through its cloud services, and a wide variety of downloadable and streamed content.

In suggesting a growth strategy, we suggest starting with your strengths: Use your capabilities system to grow. Our colleagues Gerald Adolph and Kim David Greenwood have developed a model for this that combines four complementary ways to grow, all making use of your advantaged capabilities system:

- *In-market growth:* seeking out new growth opportunities in your existing core market, as currently defined, and among your existing customers. These opportunities often include major growth prospects unexploited by anyone to date. Amazon's Prime membership offering is a good example. The company didn't change any of the products it sells, but offered free two-day shipping on all purchases in return for an annual fixed fee. This offering made powerful use of the company's distinctive supply-chain capabilities, generating both fixed-stream revenue and customer loyalty at once.

- *Near-market growth:* expansion into adjacent markets, but only those where your existing capabilities system will make a difference. Haier, for example, has used its capabilities to expand from refrigerators to other major appliances to air conditioners to air and water purification services. In 2015, Tesla Motors announced it would use its capabilities in lithium ion batteries to create a new line of batteries for homes and other buildings—an idea suggested in a Tesla Motors online forum by an automobile customer four years earlier.[21]

- *Growth through capability development:* evolutionary extension of your capabilities system, building one capability from another. This is sometimes known as "capabilities chaining," because each new form of proficiency, while fitting into your capabilities system, enables you to establish a chain of new businesses that in turn spur the development of other capabilities. The companies that we studied for this book are all expert at this: IKEA's and Natura's sustainability-oriented sourcing, and Haier's on-demand production and delivery, are examples of capabilities that these companies developed relatively late in their history.

- *Disruptive growth:* responding to dramatic change with new business models and new capabilities. You must be sure that you have a genuine right to win in this new venture, and that the circumstances warrant the significant investment involved. True disruption—the kind that merits disruptive growth—is rarer than many business people think. For example, biotechnology had a massive effect on the pharmaceutical industry, and the compact disk (CD) shook up the recorded music industry, but neither of those were disruptions. The basic business models and capabilities systems of those industries remained the same. People went on making and selling products in the same ways, with somewhat different technological parameters. On the other hand, biotech was truly disruptive to the agricultural chemicals industry, where every company had to redesign its business model; and online music thoroughly disrupted every aspect of the recorded music business. If you are facing disruption in your own industry, you'll know it because your capabilities system will no longer suffice and you'll need some fundamental change.[22]

Some industries are facing disruption now as digital technologies cross a threshold of integration. Cloud computing, electronic commerce, mobile payments, three-dimensional printing and other forms of digital fabrication, the internet of things, data analytics, broad-based activity monitoring, social media, and other digital innovations are indeed transforming business models and challenging old ways of working.

Why are some companies managing this transition well, while others get it wrong? The digital winners don't try to build a separate technological solution; they reimagine their existing capabilities, using digital technology to move their strategy forward. Starbucks, for example, has rapidly developed prowess with mobile payments and a strong online presence. It has invested both time and management attention in the capabilities needed to accomplish this. It has also taken advantage of its intensive cost-consciousness, investing heavily in digital while making sure that it doesn't waste money, for example, on overlapping IT vendors. Lego similarly incorporated digital design into its existing capabilities. Its computer-driven building block sets like Mindstorms are examples of staying true to its "play well" heritage while increasing its relevance to today's children and parents.

Natura has, in some ways, a tougher challenge. Its customers—particularly the young Latin American women who represent its future—will inevitably be regular e-commerce purchasers. If the company doesn't move rapidly to have more presence online, particularly with the internet and social media, it could lose these young customers. On the other hand, if it moves in a way that isn't congruent with its distinctive identity, the company could undermine its current value proposition, which is based on sales "consultants" who have traditionally sold to their neighbors in the physical world.

Their solution is to adapt their existing capability in relationship-building to the online world. "Natura is already a social network," Alessandro Carlucci, the former CEO, explains, "even though we have not been connected online. We have offline moments of truth, and we don't want to lose them; they are important. But we want to add the online moments of relationship." The new Natura system allows Brazilian women who spend significant time abroad to remain as Natura consultants even when they're out of the country, while embracing customers around the world who could not previously buy Natura products.

In navigating this change, Natura is deliberately not shifting away from its existing capabilities system. Instead, it is adding new capabilities by building on its existing system. Its online platform is one example of making fundamental changes, while remaining true to its core value proposition. "Some people ask why we need to keep consultants," says Carlucci. "But we know we need them, because they are the people who connect the company to its customers. They put a level of energy into relationships with clients that we could never match. And because consultants have these authentic relationships, they can use electronic platforms—and extend their relationships—in ways that would not otherwise be possible. If we do this right, we can create an online platform that is uniquely Natura."

The Triggers of Identity

It may feel daunting to think about defining your company's identity in this manner and making a full commitment to it—not for a quarter, but for years and maybe decades. You may feel it requires too great a leap. After all, you may have several value propositions at the moment, each based on a different product or service group. They may not be sharply defined enough to help you differentiate your company and lead your industry. The capabilities of your company may be pretty good, but they may not be embedded cross-functionally in the way they need to be. Your portfolio of products and services, if you're a large global enterprise, may have evolved in ad hoc fashion over the years. Their diversity may have provided a hedge against disruption in the past, but now it creates tremendous pressure on your functions—and, frankly, on your bottom line.

In that light, you may not think that your company has what it takes to become coherent, let alone to grow successfully. But look at how far Haier came. Even if your company, like Haier in 1984, only has the bare beginnings of a value proposition or capabilities system, you might be surprised to see how far you can come and how rapidly you can see results. (Haier was already winning quality awards within three years of Zhang's sledgehammer blow.)

Indeed, most of the companies we studied started at a point of relative incoherence. They all have stories to tell of the reasons they started down this path—and the rapid progress they made. When we ask executives to tell us about what stimulated their commitment, they tend to describe one of four triggers.

"We Can Do That!" [23]

Some companies start down the path to coherence when their leaders realize that they can excel at something. So they build a business around it. Mitchell Rales and Steven Rales, the founders of Danaher, had such a realization in 1986. They had recently acquired the first of their manufacturing enterprises, Chicago Pneumatic, which in turn owned a subsidiary business called the Jacobs Brake Company, which made brake components for diesel trucks. Jake Brake, as everyone called the company, was midway through a remarkable turnaround, led by its then president, George Koenigsaecker. A few years before, the factory had produced such poor-quality output, and the company had been so difficult to work with, that some of its largest customers were openly looking for alternative suppliers. Familiar with Japanese quality and lean production methods, Koenigsaecker had invited two former *sensei* (master teachers) of the Toyota Production System to come in one week every month for a year to help the company revamp its processes. "There's magic in that weeklong cycle," recalls Koenigsaecker. "It's long enough to study, make changes, and get the change semi-established." As one of the first American businesses to adopt Japanese production techniques, Jake Brake recovered rapidly, and it was soon producing high-quality output with high productivity and customer satisfaction.

The Rales brothers had bought the business just in time to benefit from the turnaround. "They came up to see what we were doing," Koenigsaecker recalls. "We thought they would kill our approach.

If they'd been manufacturing guys, it wouldn't have made sense to them." Instead, the brothers realized that they could apply similar techniques to buy and turn around other companies. Rather than selling the companies off, as a private equity firm might do, Danaher could hold them and profit from them.

It turned out that this approach to corporate turnarounds worked even better for companies that weren't in trouble. And Danaher, as we noted at the beginning of this book, had a knack for it. "Within a year," says Koenigsaecker, "we had established these practices as the beginning of the Danaher Business System." Every senior leader at Danaher still tells the story of saving the Jake Brake plant. It was the first step on a path that would take Danaher from less than US$400 million in market capitalization in 1990 to a value of more than US$62 billion in mid-2015.[24]

"We Have a Dream!"

Some coherent companies literally exist to change the world or at least their part of it. Ingvar Kamprad's statement of aspiration for IKEA, "Creating a better everyday life for the many people," is one example of this trigger. Another is Natura's slogan *bem estar bem* ("well-being, being well").[25] Others include Apple's "computer for the rest of us" and Walmart's vision of everyday low prices in categories that include not just consumer products but basic health care, eye exams, and financial services.

Probably the best-known example, among the group of companies we looked at, is Starbucks. When Howard Schultz took over a five-store Seattle coffee emporium in 1987 and began to transform it into a global retailer, he "saw Starbucks not for what it was, but for what it could be." He envisioned a convivial "third place" beyond home and work for people to gather, grounded in what he called "the romance of the coffee experience, the feeling of warmth and community people get in Starbucks stores." From the beginning, he set up health-care programs for his part-time employees and stock options for everyone who had been there six months. "We treat warehouse workers and entry-level retail people with the kind of respect most companies show for only high executives."[26]

At first, Schultz defended this aspiration as a way to earn employee loyalty and attract customers. But it went deeper, in a way he didn't fully articulate until 2007, when the company lost its way. He had resigned as CEO but remained board chairman, and his successors were caught up in a growth drive, opening as many as six stores per day. The supply chain was more efficient now, but overall quality was declining rapidly, in subtle but telling ways. Store managers were encouraged to boost revenue however possible, so they began selling products, like stuffed toys, that didn't fit with the coffee-bar atmosphere that had been so carefully cultivated. Hot breakfasts seemed like another good idea, but the stores began to smell like melted cheese. A new espresso-making machine that was introduced blocked the customers' view of the baristas preparing drinks. Other changes seemed less tangible, such as reductions in the quality of staff training, but they affected the store experience most of all. Each new misstep made the chain less distinctive, and by 2007, sales had slowed noticeably. Competitors like McDonald's and Dunkin' Donuts seemed likely to overtake Starbucks. The challenge of being a rapidly expanding global chain, without commoditizing the product, seemed insurmountable.

Schultz returned to the CEO seat and articulated a new aspiration: to "inspire and nurture the human spirit," in part by bringing the partners (employees) behind the counter to a new level of engagement and skill. In other words, the company would become a model of paying attention to the quality of life for employees, customers, and the community around each store. This change in aspiration occurred at the height of the global recession; while other retailers cut staff and dropped salaries, Starbucks invested in an immersive learning program that included coffee tastings and courses that ultimately qualified for college credit. (This was also the moment that Schultz wrote the "seven bold moves" described earlier in this chapter.)

The chain is always innovating and improving the capabilities needed to realize this goal, and it will never compete on price; that's not its value proposition. Yet it has more than rebounded from its 2007 doldrums. One of several books about the revitalized company, Michael Gates Gill's *How Starbucks Saved My Life*, recounts how partners can use the job to lift themselves from despair and remake their lives. That's the kind of thing that happens when a company reorients itself around a grand dream.[27]

"We're Going to Be in Trouble!"

Some companies are prescient enough to recognize trouble in advance. They see that the gap between strategy and execution renders them vulnerable to looming challenges. In the late 1980s, CEMEX had to face a new reality when discussions began about the North American Free Trade Agreement (NAFTA), which would remove commercial restrictions between the United States, Mexico, and Canada. The company had long enjoyed a protected status as a supplier of cement and other building materials within its home country.

The then CEO, Lorenzo Zambrano, recognized NAFTA as a strategic threat to the protected business model that CEMEX had relied on. A major global competitor could now enter the Mexican market and easily encroach on or undermine that business. Thus, during the few years remaining before 1994, when NAFTA would go into effect, Zambrano drove a transformation in CEMEX to turn the threat into an opportunity. This effort combined ruthless operational efficiency with a series of acquisitions throughout Mexico, Spain, and Latin America. Zambrano's resolve launched the company on a path to become one of a handful of global players in the industry, and the only one from an emerging economy—with its success directly related to its ability to be a solutions provider.

"We're Already in Trouble!"

Some companies get on the path to coherence when they see no other options. Desperation in a time of crisis triggers a change of attitude. A company could be in the midst of decline, facing imminent failure, or even confronting bankruptcy, and everyone knows it. The only possible responses are fight or flight—either build the capabilities the company will need for the long term while stanching the bleeding in the short run, or look for a niche where the company can defensively survive a while longer.

Lego was the world's most profitable toy maker in 2014. But just ten years earlier, in 2004, it was losing a million dollars a day and had a profit margin of negative 30 percent. The company's leaders suddenly realized that its survival was in doubt, unless it could turn itself around.

One problem was complexity. Though only thirty products generated more than 80 percent of the company's sales, Lego had a "long tail" of about fifteen hundred other products in inventory. The company's thousands of separate components included bricks of more than one hundred hues, sourced from an incredible eleven thousand suppliers (more suppliers than Boeing). Meanwhile, Lego's favored independent toy-shop customers were being replaced by big-box global retailers like Toys "R" Us, with which Lego did not have the same relationships.[28] And its efforts toward growth had included video games, clothing, and amusement parks, where it did not have the capabilities to succeed.

The board nominated a new CEO, Jørgen Vig Knudstorp, and charged him with rethinking both strategy and execution. He and Lego's other senior leaders set up a "war room" where they made a series of rapid decisions: choosing which products to cut and

Lego's Identity Profile

With headquarters in Billund, Denmark, Lego is the preeminent manufac-turer of building blocks and related toys and games for children and adults. It was recently declared the "world's most powerful brand." The largest toy company in the world and privately owned, Lego enjoyed an annual revenue in 2014 of DKK 28.6 billion (US$4.5 billion).

Value Proposition: Lego is a platform and experience provider focused on the "development of children's creativity through play and learning"; the company also fosters online and in-person communities of enthusiasts of all ages.

Capabilities System

- *Design of compelling blocks and sets for people of all ages:* Lego bases its designs on collaborative innovation among designers and the intensive study of how children play and learn.

- *Operations oriented toward complexity at reasonable cost:* Instead of fighting complexity or passing on its costs to consumers, Lego developed a facility for managing it. It manages the manufacture and packaging of thousands of precisely interlocking parts, all fitting together, arranged so the necessary mix of parts ends up in each build-ing set, and sourced and organized so that profitability remains high.

- *Management of a consumer-oriented platform:* Relationship-building with their network of avid customers, including online and offline activities (such as forums and clubs) that generate community-style engagement.

- *Learning-oriented brand development:* Promoting the benefits of cognitive development and associated skill-building through playing; linking those benefits to their toys and associated offerings, and posi-tioning model-making as a rich, cognitively sophisticated, creative and beneficial activity.

Portfolio of Products and Services: Lego offers building blocks and sets for all ages and Lego-focused community-building services such as video series, online communities, and theme parks.

debating how to fix operational weaknesses, including such detailed matters as resin costs and distribution center locations. Knudstorp himself visited the room frequently. Within two years, Knudstorp and other leaders brought the company's strategy and execution together. They rebuilt the company's logistics and supply-chain capabilities, making it profitable for the first time in years, but never losing sight of the company's identity—innovative, distinctive toys that pleased both children and their parents.

By 2006 the company had a stronger reputation and market presence than ever, and it was also profitable for the first time in years. In the following years, Lego continued to build its brand presence with tie-ins to movies, televisions, and video games, along with new kinds of digital capabilities in its building sets, while retaining enough simplicity in its operations to remain profitable. The company continues to thrive under the slogan introduced in 2009: "It's a new toy every day."

At some point, most companies experience at least one of the four triggers described above. These triggers are often the catalysts for change. In a coherent company, they are the catalysts for commitment. When your own company hits one of these triggers, the choice will be yours: Will you look for a rapid, expedient solution aimed at surviving the next quarter? Or will you look for an identity that will provide a long-term legacy?

3

Translate the Strategic into the Everyday

Most large companies are hotbeds of execution. Everywhere you go, you see people installing enterprise resource planning (ERP), implementing processes to support digital marketing, or redesigning parts of the supply chain. But when you look more closely, you often see that this activity is not aligned with the company's strategic intent.

Think back to the investments you've made in, say, upgrades to computer systems or new stage gate methodologies. Undoubtedly the new capabilities are urgently needed; a functional or business leader has approved the investment. If implemented successfully, a project of this sort will fulfill its stated goal: solving a significant problem, supporting income-generating products and services with some competence, or filling a gap in your company's practices. But how will it support your overall value proposition or advance your distinctive capabilities system?

All too often, the leaders of a company, including the chief information officer, have not considered that question. If they had, they might define, plan, and roll out their new software, training, or process implementations very differently.

This lack of connection between strategy and execution stems in part from the ingrained habit of not taking strategic issues into account when planning new implementations. With such habits in place, it becomes very challenging to build and develop distinctive capabilities. You may have to unlearn the old ways you put capabilities together and learn new ones that are linked closely to your strategy from the very first moment. In other words, now that you have committed your company to an identity, as we discussed in chapter 2, you have to translate that identity into everyday practice. Hence the title of this chapter.

Your new approach to building capabilities will be your own approach: bespoke to your company. You will not benchmark or copy it from anyone else—at most, you will borrow details and practices and convert them to your own way of doing things. This approach may also be unfamiliar. For all their experience in functional excellence, most companies have rarely built truly distinctive cross-functional capabilities in their own way. They follow a program created with generic business in mind. They end up with functional activity similar to every other company's functional activity.

The companies we studied, by contrast, have built their own bespoke capabilities, adapting best practices that suit their identity, inventing new practices of their own, and in the process learning to do something that no other enterprise has done before. One of the most compelling examples is Frito-Lay, the snack division of PepsiCo, with more than $14 billion in annual revenues.[1] For thirty-five years, this enterprise has defended its position as market leader by being better at what it does than any of its competitors. It introduces new varieties frequently and successfully and manages all of them in a way that meets the ever-changing tastes of snack consumers. The company also has consistently high quality, and, most importantly to a company whose products are often purchased on impulse,

Frito-Lay "owns the streets." It gets the right products to the right stores at the right time—all the time. As a result, the company currently owns seven $1 billion brands: Lays, Ruffles, Walkers, Fritos, Cheetos, Doritos, and Tostitos along with several other well-known snack brands such as Smartfood and Sun Chips.

Like many companies with remarkable capabilities systems, Frito-Lay makes what it does look easy. But its success is anything but an overnight story. The company has steadily invested its time, money, and—most importantly—executive and employee attention in building and improving its capabilities system.

Much has been published about this Frito-Lay story over the years, at least in technological circles, because the company revolutionized the way the entire consumer products industry thinks about its supply chain. As part of this process, the company invented the first handheld mobile computer, two decades before the smartphone. Frito-Lay remains on the leading edge today, incorporating robotics, analytics, location-tracking technologies, and a great deal of attention to staff recruiting and training. In effect, this system establishes Frito-Lay's capabilities system as the underlying grid of a powerful companywide network, with marketers, trade program designers, manufacturing and delivery experts, and other decision makers all plugged in. Productivity improvements from this and other innovations at Frito-Lay have been credited with generating $1 billion per year in bottom-line gains since the mid-2010s.[2]

Let's start by looking at Frito-Lay's capability in direct store delivery. In the eyes of a typical grocer, the Frito-Lay system may look expensive and inefficient. Most other food companies send their merchandise through giant sorting and distribution centers, sharing the facilities with many other producers and using economies of scale to save costs. Frito-Lay, by contrast, has its own overarching distribution system tailored to serve every kind of retail outlet. Its giant distribution centers have a highly efficient way of prepacking the bins delivered there. It also maintains a fleet of large and small trucks, each staffed with one or two "sellers" (as they're known in the company), who are recruited carefully, well trained, and well paid. They handle sales and merchandising as well as transportation and delivery.

The sellers' jobs are highly structured, with a detailed execution framework based on the idea of a "perfect order": an optimal product assortment for every store, oriented to consumer tastes. This is all reinforced by Frito-Lay's carefully-designed IT infrastructure. The sellers' handheld computers send sales and inventory data (including observations of how well competitors' products are doing) instantaneously back to the home office, where the data is analyzed and translated into new sales forecasts and specs for the next day's deliveries. The sellers, and the regional managers who supervise them, are thus equipped to make precisely the right moves in stocking the shelves.

This direct store delivery capability is just part of a larger capabilities system that Frito-Lay has parlayed into success. The delivery and sales information feeds directly into Frito-Lay's powerful flavor innovation capability, enabling the company to rapidly introduce new products that meet consumer demand. This capability has been prodigious for years, but it was enhanced in the mid-2010s through crowdsourcing and social media. Frito-Lay's "Do Us a Flavor" campaign, which started in the United Kingdom and migrated to the United States, invites consumers to suggest new chip flavors and vote on them, with a cash prize of $1 million for the creator of the winning entrant. The first year's American winner, cheesy garlic bread, became a market favorite; the second year's, wasabi ginger, heralded a new direction toward diverse and globally inspired flavors.[3]

Frito-Lay also has carefully developed capabilities in both quality production and local consumer marketing, with store displays and promotions tailored for each customer group. All of these capabilities together—flavor innovation, direct store delivery, manufacturing quality, and local consumer marketing—give the enterprise a tremendous advantage in launching new products. When

Frito-Lay's competitors introduce new products, these snack makers must pay significant slotting fees to grocers to feature them on the shelf. To reduce the risk of failure, other companies must test products carefully before launch—a process that adds cost and delays the launch. Frito-Lay avoids all these hurdles by managing the shelf itself. Using data analytics, the company can rapidly introduce a new product with confidence that it will sell reasonably well. Frito-Lay can further test a new product at low cost by introducing it in a few stores, then can roll it out rapidly across a region or a continent if customers like it. The power is in the capabilities *system*—in the way all of these strengths reinforce one another to give the company an unbeatable advantage. Indeed, this capabilities system has given Frito-Lay a 60 percent market share in US snack foods, a growing business in emerging markets, a productivity engine that gains savings of almost $1 billion per year, and an extremely high success rate in the introduction of new products.[4]

"The real benefit of this system is the energy it brings across the entire company," said Charles Feld, one of the prominent architects of the approach, in a recent interview. "It really tightens the link between every function involved in making, distributing, and selling the products."[5]

Building the Capabilities System at Frito-Lay

Now let's look at what Frito-Lay went through to put this capabilities system into place. The company had always been a relatively coherent enterprise; it was formed in the 1950s and 1960s through a series of mergers among several companies known for their facility with snack foods. (One of the founders, Charles Elmer Doolin of Frito Corporation, invented the cheese puff and perfected the corn chip.) But it wasn't until the early 1980s, about fifteen years after its

Frito-Lay's Identity Profile

With headquarters in Plano, Texas, Frito-Lay is the convenience-foods business unit of PepsiCo. Frito-Lay makes some of the best-known and top-selling savory snacks in the world.

Value Proposition: Frito-Lay is a category leader and experience provider, providing ubiquitous availability of a wide variety of impulse-purchase snack foods tailored to diverse consumer preferences.

Capabilities System

- *Rapid, highly successful flavor innovation:* This capability, particularly the innovation of new varieties, yields snack foods resonant with many diverse local markets and changing consumer tastes.
- *Development of local consumer and retail marketing programs:* Frito-Lay has an exceptional ability to monitor customer and market data and adapt its merchandising mixes and promotions accordingly.
- *Direct store delivery:* Its well-designed DSD system, skilled staff and technological prowess enables tailoring assortments to each store, providing unique flexibility, productivity, and influence over the shelf.
- *Consistent manufacturing and continuous improvement:* Frito-Lay products continually stand out in taste, freshness, and perceived value.

Portfolio of Products and Services: Frito-Lay excels in popular branded snack foods. In 2015, the company maintained countless varieties of snack foods, which are sorted into thirty brands. The best-known brands include Lays, Ruffles, Fritos, Cheetos, Doritos, Tostitos, Walkers, Smartfood, and Sun Chips.

---

merger with Pepsi Cola to form PepsiCo, that Frito-Lay's capabilities system took its current form.

The starting point was a desire to streamline direct store delivery. Though Frito-Lay's system outpaced the rest of the industry, the system was costly and inefficient. The paperwork used to track grocery shelf inventories, for example, was so complex that it took about ten days for the data to make it back to Frito-Lay headquarters.

In 1981, Frito-Lay recruited a new chief information officer away from the IBM team managing its account. Charles "Charlie" Feld had impressed Frito-Lay CEO Wayne Calloway with his view of IT as an enabler of company excellence, rather than as overhead. With Calloway's support, Feld and other top executives mapped out a plan for linking all the truck drivers and the head office in constant communication. As they tested their ideas with local prototypes, it became clear how much investment, innovation, and intervention would be required to build out this capability across the United States. They would need to combine sales, merchandising, and delivery, revamp their back-office processes, and build new relationships between the distribution, innovation, and marketing functions to ensure that all these functions would work together. Frito-Lay also had to invest in route design: picking the best vehicle for each delivery route, with the right frequency of visits and the right seller training, and the ability to change routes rapidly when circumstances called for it. In short, this would go far beyond the handheld computer and beyond IT itself; it would effectively transform the entire enterprise.

The project was such a complex and audacious endeavor that the company scrapped it more than once, but reinstated it each time. Pulling all this together, with so many leaders and functions contributing in so many ways, took everything Frito-Lay had, for almost a decade. It also required the support of three successive CEOs: Calloway; his successor, Michael Jordan, in 1984; and Roger Enrico, who took the reins as chief executive in 1990. (Their support also played a major role in the company's staying true to its evolving identity.) Jordan and Enrico, who were convinced of the project's value only when they saw how the prototypes increased profitability, became the capability's greatest champions. For example, when Jordan realized that the field sales organizations in each territory were resisting the new system, he required each organization to commit to a 1 percent reduction in the cost of sales each year. Like IKEA's annual price reductions, this was a forcing function. Jordan knew the only way the groups could hit that goal was to embrace the new approach.[6]

Frito-Lay rolled out parts of the new system starting in the mid-1980s. By 1991, seven years after the work began, it was in place throughout the enterprise. By then, the investment had already demonstrated the payoff. Frito-Lay managers knew more about their competitors' reach and costs than the competitors themselves knew about these factors. The company could also ask what-if questions about price cuts, advertising approaches, and other marketing initiatives, and simulations would calculate potential sales results. The managers could keep building each other's knowledge and putting it to work in increasingly sophisticated ways.

As with many great capabilities, the industry tends to catch up; a company like Frito-Lay must continually stay ahead of competitors and customer expectations. One important innovation developed in the 2000s was the Geographic Enterprise Solution (GES)—an automated logistics system with distribution centers equipped with robotics and sensors to track the flow of merchandise. Combined with advanced analytics to discern merchandising patterns, these innovations reduce inventory and lower the company's carbon footprint and energy use. (Environmental sustainability is a priority for PepsiCo.) These measures also help the sellers make the most of their limited time in each store, and ensure that the product on the shelf is fresh, often placed there just a day or two after manufacture. Much of the money saved through productivity gains is plowed back into further improvements.[7]

You can build similarly powerful capabilities in your own business. Like Frito-Lay, your company will start reaping benefits almost immediately—but the benefits multiply the more you keep improving your capabilities system. To get from here to there, you need to boil down your approach, as Frito-Lay did, to three main activities. First, *create a blueprint* of your capabilities system. Articulate the nature of the capabilities you need to develop: how they would interact and add value, what they would look like in action, and what would be required to make them work. Second, *build* the capabilities system you need. Use focused interventions, breakthrough innovation, continuous improvement, and, often enough, M&A to augment the capabilities you already have. Third: take it all to *scale*. This is a far more involved and participative process than many executives expect; it involves organizing activity across functions and finding ways to codify tacit understanding into explicit knowledge without losing the creativity of a small enterprise.

Blueprinting, building, and scaling capabilities may seem like familiar work, something that all companies manage to do all the time. But as we'll see throughout this chapter, a great deal of innovation, attention, discipline, and creativity is needed to bring distinctive capabilities to life. Because they are closely aligned with your value proposition, there is no gap between strategy and execution in this process; the process of developing strategy is intimately connected to the process of building the relevant capabilities.

Blueprinting the Capabilities System

Your first step is deductive. You start with a desired outcome: the value proposition you outlined in chapter 2 and the three to six capabilities that will add up to deliver on the proposition better than anyone else can. Your blueprint is the detailed design and architecture of that capabilities system, explaining how and why it will deliver the promised value.

A capability, as noted in chapter 2, is the combination of people, processes, technologies, and organization that allows you to deliver your intended outcome. The blueprint covers all of those components, but not separately: it determines how they will fit together. There is also an accompanying plan that specifies the people who will build pieces of the capability, the targets and incentives that govern their actions, and a timetable for implementation.

The CEO and the team driving the strategy must lead this effort in a hands-on fashion. They don't necessarily plan every detail themselves, but they generally handpick the people overseeing details, recruiting them from outside if necessary (as Wayne Calloway recruited Charlie Feld) and remaining closely involved themselves. Follow the example of Lego's CEO Jørgen Vig Knudstorp, who continually checked in on the "war room" at Lego, effectively creating a blueprint for the company's new supply chain and product development capabilities. You cannot simply delegate this job to functional leaders, especially given the numerous connections and trade-offs that have to be made.

Like an architectural blueprint, a blueprint of your capabilities system is not purely functional; it is artistic and it should evoke the identity of the company. It must meaningfully integrate diverse processes and technologies while preserving the strategic value of the enterprise. You may find yourself iterating these capabilities in detail in successive blueprints, each one a refinement of the previous version. At Apple, for example, the outsourcing of manufacturing processes is part of the company's product design capabilities. According to writer Adam Lashinsky, this can involve extensive iteration of blueprints for operations at local facilities in China. Apple's representative at the China factory will repeatedly "bring the latest beta version back to Cupertino for senior executives to see—and then get right back on a plane for China to repeat the process."[8]

You might benchmark what other companies are doing, because it's helpful to know the best practices of your industry. But be skeptical. You risk being drawn into practices that are not right for your company. Don't try to be great at everything, especially everything your competitors do. Don't feel pressure to keep up with their IT systems or supply chains, unless there is reason to do so. Focus on building excellence in the areas that matter the most for your company's success; be lean and merely "good enough" everywhere else.

Seek inspiration from companies that have successfully developed capabilities like the ones you're trying to build, even (or especially) if the firms are not in your industry. Apple famously adapted its Genius Bar design from the Ritz-Carlton concierge desk. Lego, in rethinking its supply-chain capability, drew on the experience of the electronics industry and ended up outsourcing some production to Flextronics, a Singapore-based supplier to that sector.[9] In the mid-2000s, Danaher developed its product innovation capability by looking beyond the boundaries of its tool and instrument sectors. "We sent a team of people to Procter & Gamble," recalls Steven Simms, the executive vice president (since retired) who led the effort. "Their concepts on innovation stretched our thought process. We [also] went to Starbucks several times to look at customer management."[10]

It is rare to see a company's capabilities blueprint because they often involve closely held competitive secrets. But one that we mentioned in our previous book, *The Essential Advantage*, is a good example of how to lay out a blueprint in detail. The story took place in the 1990s at the Automotive Systems Group (ASG) within Johnson Controls Inc. (JCI). (It was later renamed the Automotive Experience Group.) Based in Milwaukee, Wisconsin, this group makes motor vehicle interior components, including car seats. (The parent company, which also makes batteries, energy efficiency-related products, and heating, ventilation and air conditioning systems, announced in mid-2015 that this group may be spun off into a separate company.)[11]

Around 1991, the leaders of JCI-ASG began to recognize that their market had changed. During the previous few decades, car seats had become highly sophisticated appliances incorporating hundreds of components. The seats could adjust to drivers' body shapes, protect the lumbar region during extended travel, keep track of preset positions, convey warmth and ventilation, and, perhaps most importantly, help shield against danger in a crash. With unionized labor wages driving up the costs of designing and building car seats, major automakers began looking for suppliers that could help produce these complex mechanisms less expensively. A core group of ASG executives saw an opportunity to leap ahead of their competitors. They would abandon their current practice of building seats to specifications and competing on price. They would no longer underbid competitors to win orders and then make up the difference with relentless cost-cutting. Instead, they would adopt a new value proposition as a solutions provider. They resolved that ASG would be a consummate champion of what seat engineers call the *golden butt*: the customer's point of satisfaction. They would seek to understand the evolving needs of drivers and passengers; they would resolve automakers' concerns about ergonomics, functionality, and consumer appeal; and as they did all this, they would keep moving the technology forward.

The senior team set up a cross-functional steering committee to oversee the development of a capabilities blueprint. The committee began with what we have come to call *peeling the onion*: an intensive, deductive analysis of the capabilities needed to make a value proposition work. Only one of the capabilities that JCI-ASG needed was fully in place: just-in-time manufacturing, which the company had learned as a supplier to Toyota. The team members concluded they would have to build up four other capabilities significantly, in some cases almost from scratch:

- *Solution selling:* Dealing directly with product-launch engineers instead of the procurement functions, gaining credibility by demonstrating technical competence, selling solutions by providing innovative car seat designs, and managing the customer relationships that enabled this new approach.

- *First-time design:* Deploying engineering prowess to create innovative seats without waiting for guidance or specs from the automakers.

- *Shelf technology:* Creating a common design platform for all the seats the company made. This was the enterprise's name for a new and unfamiliar modular R&D management capability. Most project managers vehemently resisted the idea at first, on the grounds that it would constrain their ability to customize features and designs. (For Ford alone, JCI-ASG had nineteen separate seat designs.) But a shared design capability was critical for gaining scale, realizing the full potential of new innovative features, and making the technology cost-effective.

- *Extended enterprise:* Cultivating other suppliers for sub-components. JCI-ASG had not done this much in the past, but now, as it became more technically sophisticated, it had to outsource more parts of the car seat.[12]

Each of the practices in these capabilities had to be simple enough that all of JCI-ASG's business units could use them. They also had to be robust enough to make the company world-class.

It took months for the design teams—which included top management along with senior people from engineering, sourcing, manufacturing, legal (for contracts), and finance (for costing and pricing) working closely together—to build the blueprints. The teams articulated the processes, systems, skills, behaviors, and organizational changes that would need to be in place for each of those capabilities. For each capability, they developed a plan for reaching the desired goals, backed up with detailed databases of costs, design changes, supplier information, and insights about the automaker teams.

Together, the final blueprints laid out a detailed view of the company that JCI-ASG would become. Some new capabilities, like first-time design, required major investments in IT tools—for example, sophisticated computer-assisted design systems. Other capabilities required relocation or reorganization. To improve its just-in-time manufacturing capability, the company relocated the facilities that produced the seat frame and the foam padding, moving them closer together—while it offshored other activities, like the manufacturing of the trim covers. As part of the new extended-enterprise capability, JCI-ASG linked the procurement, research, and design functions more closely into product development. It also brought the list of regular suppliers down from hundreds to about thirty. This latter group were integrated into engineering and design, with dedicated communications links and new financing arrangements.

When bridging the strategy-to-execution gap in your own company you will need to build a similar blueprint. As you work through the details, you naturally test the concept you articulated in chapter 2. The first step is to bring together the right steering group: a cross-functional group of senior leaders with ties to every major line of business and function, ideally led by the chief executive of the enterprise. Then take a closer look at the capabilities system you identified at the end of chapter 2. For each distinctive capability in that system, ask yourself a series of questions. In the next few pages, we'll lay out those questions and show you how the JCI-ASG committee answered them for one of its new capabilities: solution selling.

1. *What is the capability?* The simple discipline of defining each capability gives you a much clearer view of what you are trying to build, and why it matters. For solution selling, the stated definition was: "To build long-term strategic relationships." They would communicate directly with the automakers' technical specialists, instead of just the purchasing staff, and build their own financial models of the products, so they understood the costs and potential revenues, before signing the contract.

2. *Why is it valuable?* It's important to understand what this capability does for your value proposition, and for your business in general. At JCI, this capability would enable a change that being a solutions provider required: from selling based on price to selling based on value. It would also

minimize the risk of commoditization, eliminate high-cost transactions and conflicts stemming from forced partnerships with other suppliers, and protect the company's proprietary technology from competitors. It would also be a major cost-saver, reducing the wasted time and expense of last-minute design changes or multiple alternative designs.

3. *How would it be different from what we have today?* Under conventional practices, suppliers were brought into platform development at too late a stage to influence the overall product. Now JCI-ASG would be part of its customers' vehicle platform development cycles from the beginning. They would design to match an overall concept rather than to specs selected by automakers. They would select their own technologies, suppliers, and production methods, instead of those specified by their customers.

4. *Describe a day in the life of this capability.* What does it look like in action? Which functional groups are involved? What kinds of things do they do? The JCI-ASG team laid out the way the work would look and feel. The many scenarios they described included meetings to set joint targets; new ways of batching design changes; and a program schedule managed collaboratively with automakers rather than being dictated by either side.

5. *What is required to make it work?* What processes, systems, and tools will be used in making it happen? They broke the capability down into a long list of new measures. Some were processes: for example, new ways of developing product specifications, managing programs, and integrating warranty and product liability information into the designs. They would need new IT systems for performance and cost tracking, financial models, and inventories of previous

solutions, along with a strategic sourcing supplier database. They would have to become more knowledgable in such areas as strategic sourcing, making performance trade-offs, calculating tolerances, and all the many aspects of developing mutually beneficial relationships with customers and their own vendors. And they would reorganize to be more effective solution sellers: strengthening support functions such as account, legal, and quality management.

6. *For the capabilities system, what does the business case look like?* Calculate the return on investment and other parameters that can help you justify this investment. The team estimated one-time costs and recurring expenses for each measure they had already specified: the IT systems, recruiting arrangements, payroll for new staff, and so on. They also estimated the value of recurring benefits: revenue from new customers, money saved by avoiding last-minute changes, and profits gleaned from more flexible value-based pricing.

7. *How does this capability fit with the others in the capabilities system?* Make sure that the logic holds: that every part of the capabilities system contributes to your strategy. Step back to think about how they fit together. Imagine metaphorical pipes, extending from one to the other. What would the outputs and inputs flowing through those pipes be? For example, one of the "outputs" of solution selling was JCI's demand for more autonomy in choosing its own suppliers. This turned out to be a prerequisite for the extended enterprise capability. Think through what each capability contributes to the others, until you have the complete system mapped out. All the outputs, when they are fully realized, should add up to deliver your value proposition.

(For an online template that leads you through these questions, visit www.strategythatworks.com and see "Capabilities Visioning [Peeling the Onion].")

Now consider the plan for creating that capabilities system. What steps do you need to take to bridge the gap between the capabilities you have and those you need? Strictly speaking, this is not part of the blueprint itself; it is more like the plan for building the house. But it is essential. Think about the types of people you need to recruit—especially for skills that are not normally associated with your industry. The earliest Apple Macintosh had a graphic artist and font designer on the core team. Some engineers belittled that talent at the start, but it turned out to be critical for the graphical user interface.

Which functional groups need to be involved? Who would be the right people to draw in from the various functions—first, to enhance what you have (or in some cases to design and build a new capability) and, second, to manage and maintain it?

You may face internal resistance. Some entrenched senior executives at JCI-ASG had to be convinced that building a new capabilities system was worth the trouble. Others questioned the investment—for example, the money spent on new computer-aided design to enable first-time design and shelf technology. But the steering committee persevered, addressing criticisms as they were raised, and gradually the company came around. As a forcing function, the committee tied all funding to these new capabilities, cutting costs in other parts of the business so that the company could grow stronger here. (We'll explore this approach further in chapter 5.)

In the end, hundreds of people changed their ways of working, the five capabilities came together, and JCI-ASG became the premier manufacturer in the auto-seat sector. Following its acquisition of Prince, another automobile interior supplier, the enterprise deployed the same capabilities system for a broader group of interior components. Revenues rose accordingly; JCI went from earning about

JCI-ASG's Identity Profile

Johnson Controls Inc. (JCI)'s Automotive Systems Group (later renamed the Automotive Experience Group) is based in Milwaukee, Wisconsin.

Value Proposition: JCI-ASG became a solutions provider, offering automakers complete seats for a wide range of cars along with continuous innovation in technology and other features.

Capabilities System

- *Just-in-time manufacturing:* With this capability, this group has seats ready just as automakers need them and avoids inventory costs.
- *Solution selling:* Building and maintaining long-term relationships with automakers, including direct contact with engineers and early involvement in projects.
- *First-time design:* Deploying engineering knowledge to create innovative seats without waiting for guidance or specs from the automakers.
- *Shelf technology:* Developing and maintaining a common modular platform for all the seats the company made, ensuring a wider range of products at lower cost.
- *Extended enterprise:* Fostering more collaborative relationships with key suppliers, to ensure quality, consistency, and innovation.

Portfolio of Products and Services: This group now produces auto interiors for all kinds of automakers, taking on the whole process from design through manufacturing.

US$300 million in annual revenues in the mid-1980s to more than US$41 billion in 2014, with ASG making a large contribution.[13]

Building Distinctive Capabilities

At this point, you have a blueprint containing explicit descriptions of your distinctive capabilities, and a plan for building them. You may already have teams of people assigned to building each capability. Now you are ready to bring them to life.

Creating distinctive capabilities systems is a multifaceted process. While this process may seem familiar to you—after all, every company builds capabilities—few companies tackle it with the requisite focus and creativity. But you can do better. You do it the same way Lego, Apple, Starbucks, and the other companies we studied build distinctive capabilities. You put your best people on the job, you give them the resources they need (more on this in chapter 5), you involve your top leadership closely in the task, and you keep your outcome—your value proposition—clearly in mind.

The effort usually combines three basic activities:

- Focused interventions that sharpen the capabilities you already have.

- Capability innovation that creates new practices that your competitors can't easily copy.

- A capabilities-oriented approach to mergers and acquisitions that enhances your prowess through the activities of the businesses you buy.

All of these efforts are cross-functional. Small teams of people from each relevant function—typically including operations, sales, marketing, innovation, learning and development, IT, and procurement—must learn to speak each other's language and work toward common goals. This cross-functionality will become even more important, as you'll see, when you scale up capabilities to the entire enterprise. No function owns a distinctive capability: each distinctive capability belongs to the entire company.

Focused Interventions

To develop the level of proficiency you need, you'll have to make meaningful changes to the capabilities you already have. Some of these changes will start at the core of the business. Others may seem to be on the periphery at first, and you'll need to bring them into the mainstream. Some of these focused interventions will be identified in the blueprint stage; others will become clear later. Ideally, you'll continue making focused interventions throughout the life of your enterprise.

In the early 2000s, Pfizer's consumer products division went through this exercise. (Then called Pfizer Consumer Healthcare, or PCH, it was sold to Johnson & Johnson in 2006. It is not the same as the current Pfizer Consumer Healthcare, which Pfizer acquired when it purchased Wyeth in 2009. We'll refer to it in this chapter as Pfizer Consumer). At the time, Pfizer (the larger company) had several household-name brands in over-the-counter (nonprescription) medicines, confectionary, and personal care. The products included Listerine mouthwashes; Hall's cough drops; shaving and hair care brands like Barbasol, Schick, and Rogaine; smoking cessation aids like Nicorette; Chiclets, and Trident chewing gum; and some common household medicines like Benadryl and Zyrtec for allergies, Zantac for heartburn, and Sudafed for cold and flu symptoms. Many of these brands had come to Pfizer through acquisitions; for example, Listerine and the chewing gums had been part of Warner-Lambert, a major manufacturer of pharmacy and grocery products that Pfizer had bought in 2000. Individually, many of these products were successful revenue generators, but because they had come together through various mergers and acquisitions, they were not coherent. No single value proposition or capabilities system applied to all of them, and together they were not nearly as profitable as they needed to be.

In *The Essential Advantage* we described how Pfizer Consumer developed its value proposition: to offer over-the-counter medications with clearly articulated claims of demonstrable health benefits. The company sold off the products that didn't fit this value proposition (razors, shaving cream, and chewing gum among them) and concentrated on the products that did. For example, Pfizer Consumer reoriented Listerine toward mouth-related health care, advertising that it reduced 52 percent more plaque and 21 percent more gingivitis than did brushing and flossing alone.[14] Nicorette, Sudafed, Zantac, Benadryl, Zyrtec, and Rogaine were marketed with proven, compelling claims. This approach worked. Within four years, the enterprise turned its scattered portfolio into a $4 billion business, which it sold to Johnson & Johnson for $16.6 billion in 2006. This number was a multiple of more than twenty times earnings, at a time when multiples averaged fifteen—a clear validation of the value of coherence to any company.

Pfizer Consumer could not have made this strategy work without its own strong capabilities system. The system was made up of six capabilities, each existing in some form within the company. Some were legacies of Pfizer's pharmaceutical roots:

- Launching and commercializing new over-the-counter products, generally through *Rx-to-OTC switches* (converting prescription medicine to nonprescription forms).

- Influencing regulatory management and government policy, so that claims could stand in many countries and jurisdictions.

- Innovating new "forms and formulations" (as pharmacologists call their products), oriented toward making specific health-related claims, so that the company could raise the overall value of its product portfolio.

Others had been inherited from Warner-Lambert:

- Effective retail execution (product positioning, claims communication, pricing, and promotion) in a wide set of retail formats, with increasing emphasis on pharmacies.

- Claims-based marketing translating product advantages into relevant succinct messages to consumers, highlighting the demonstrable health benefit.

- Focused portfolio management, bringing each of the high-priority products to a global market.

As part of the transformation program, each capability involved its own focused interventions to bring it fully in line with the new strategy. For example, to fully develop the innovation of forms and formulations, Pfizer Consumer redefined its stage-gate process (which approves investment at each stage of R&D) to prioritize claims-related projects. To build out the claims-based marketing capability, a global team developed a methodology for sifting through the masses of clinical data around products like Listerine and drawing out viable claims. This extraordinarily difficult task would never have been undertaken without the specific link to a critically important capability.

Another example was the regulatory management capability. It was already impressive, especially in mature economies. The regulatory team worked with governments around the world to negotiate and follow the rules governing what a pharmaceuticals company could say to consumers about its products. However, the capability was oriented to local governments, which made it difficult to scale to a global level. The division leaders reorganized its worldwide regulatory affairs staff members, connecting them in a virtual center of excellence. They now were set up to communicate regularly, advising each other on how to manage relationships with regulatory agencies. This focused intervention led to quick wins almost immediately. For example, Pfizer Consumer rapidly gained regulatory approval in Europe for its eye care and smoking cessation products. In addition, as one of the focused interventions, a regulatory group within the R&D function set out to develop the ability to influence policy in emerging markets. This meant recruiting and putting in place people who knew how to navigate the government's requirements in precise detail, document by document.

Pfizer Consumer's Identity Profile (2001 to 2006)

Pfizer Consumer, a division of Pfizer Inc., was sold to Johnson & Johnson in 2006 for $16.6 billion. It has since been fully integrated into Johnson & Johnson.

Value Proposition: Pfizer Consumer was a category leader, regulation navigator and reputation player, developing over-the-counter healthcare products for people around the world and marketing their therapeutic benefits using demonstrable claims.

Capabilities System

- *Launching and commercializing new over-the-counter products:* Especially non-prescription products with plausible health-related claims.
- *Influence on regulatory management and government policy:* Enabling claims to stand regulatory scrutiny in many countries and jurisdictions.
- *Claims-focused innovation:* Developing new forms and formulations that could support health-related claims.
- *Effective retail execution:* Product positioning and other promotional activities that could raise product awareness in the right shops, particularly pharmacies.
- *Claims-based marketing:* Featuring and communicating a demonstrable health benefit for many products.
- *Focused portfolio management:* Moving each of the featured products to worldwide markets.

Portfolio of Products and Services: This enterprise offered a broad range of oral health and skin care products along with over-the-counter medications, almost all with well-known brands such as Listerine.

Focused interventions are familiar activities in most companies. On any given day, you'll find business people upgrading their IT systems, tweaking metrics, promoting people, implementing new training, or reorganizing a functional department. Continuous improvement, which is standard practice at most manufacturing companies these days, can be seen as one point intervention after another. But how many of these activities are tailored to helping the company realize its value proposition? If you set out to translate the strategic into the everyday—to bridge the strategy-to-execution gap—then every intervention should be aligned with your value proposition. If it's not strategic, it's not worth doing.

A good example of the power of a focused intervention occurred at McDonald's in the early 1990s. Any fast-food restaurant must provide rapid, consistent service; it thus relies on its soft drink machines. Breakdowns can lead to long lines and angry customers, especially during hectic rush periods. Moreover, the burden of fixing broken machines typically falls on the local store manager, who must arrange service from local repair people—with inconsistent results. Unsatisfied with this piecemeal approach, McDonald's operational leaders decided to augment their already-powerful capabilities in restaurant processes. They convened a group of franchise owners and operations experts, considered the problem, and ended up borrowing an idea from the emerging call-center business in the high-tech computer industry.

Today, in every McDonald's restaurant in the United States, there is a single point of contact for soft-drink machine repair. When that phone number is dialed, the call is immediately answered by a trained professional equipped with a list of diagnostics. That first encounter solves the problem for 80 percent of the callers. The rest are quickly directed to a "level two" expert technician, who immediately takes accountability for fixing the problem and guides the manager through another set of diagnostics and tailored processes by phone. Should these efforts fail, a local, prequalified service technician, contracted and trained for rapid response, is dispatched. The technician can typically resolve most of these rare instances within a few hours of the initial call.

The solution saved so much expense (relying less on costly local repair people) that it changed the rest of the industry. Deciding that its primary beverage supplier, Coca-Cola, could manage this new beverage repair service more effectively than it could, McDonald's turned the whole burden over to the beverage company. Coca-Cola then used it for competitive advantage with other restaurants.[15]

As digital technology advances, the "internet of things," data analytics, cloud computing, and mobile devices will provide many new opportunities for point interventions. Industrial companies will follow the example of shared-economy start-ups like Uber and AirBnB, using digital technology to make their operations much more flexible and responsive; their products and services will be customized to a degree that was never possible before. In China, for example, the color and feature set of every appliance that Haier sells can be tailored to the specifications of its purchaser, who arranges this in advance on a Haier company website. The point intervention, in this case, was not the design of the website or the factory's customization ability; those already existed. The intervention involved bringing these two activities together, making this level of customization standard for new sales, and incorporating them into Haier's on-demand production and delivery capability.

These technological changes are happening so rapidly that most companies have not yet taken advantage of the opportunities they provide. Every company still has a great deal to learn through prototyping and experimentation. But when translating the strategic into the everyday, be careful not to experiment for its own sake. The most successful companies link their technologically driven interventions closely with their strategy. They apply technology in their own way to their own distinctive practices, instead of taking on the same technological solutions that everyone else is attempting.

One company that uses digital technology effectively this way is Under Armour. Founded in 1996 by Kevin Plank, a former college football captain who found cotton T-shirts too prone to getting wet and heavy during sports and exercise, the company sells athletic clothing made from a synthetic fabric that wicks moisture away from the skin and stays light and dry. Plank's T-shirts first found a small following among other college athletes after he assiduously built up the capability of marketing to them and with them. Since then, the company has grown into a full athletic outfitter with over $3 billion in revenue in 2014.

The use of digital technology is embodied in the company's athletics-oriented value proposition, where they continually claim their clothes add to an athlete's comfort and performance. Under Armour has been a pioneer in computer-assisted fabric design, creating water-transmitting materials that allow people to feel dry instead of soggy and sweaty after a workout, and water-repellent sweatshirts that keep people as dry as a raincoat would. It was also one of the first companies to integrate its clothing with data from fitness trackers. In 2013 the company acquired MapMyFitness, a company that aggregates data from a range of fitness trackers and allows athletes to monitor their exercise and eating. The point in all this is not the improvement of any particular product, but the continuous improvement of Under Armour's distinctive product development capability. Like Natura, Apple, and Qualcomm, it has developed a group of followers who expect innovative new products will emerge from the company on a regular basis.[16]

The next time you discuss the threat of technological disruption to your business, try turning it around. What technological changes can you make to your capabilities to ensure that you can advance your mission, and better deliver your value proposition? Don't think of this as a request for more IT investment per se. Few IT infrastructure projects are designed to differentiate a company, instead, a certain amount of functional delivery is demanded against the cost. Think of your IT investment instead as a point intervention: a move to improve your current capabilities, working with other functions to do something better than you did it before, or to do it at a larger scale.

Capability Innovation

One of the great moments in IKEA's history came in 1956. Gillis Lundgren, the designer of the three-legged, leaf-shaped Lövet end table, was trying to figure out how to fit it in the trunk of his car. He took the legs off and then figured out that the table could be sold that way and be reassembled by purchasers. He is credited as the creator of the IKEA flat pack, a critical element of the company's price-conscious and stylish product design capability—and something that, to our knowledge, had not been done before with mass-manufactured furniture.[17]

This innovation paved the way for another: the creation of the IKEA self-service warehouse. It happened in 1970, after a fire nearly destroyed the flagship store, which was then located in Stockholm. During the reopening days, founder Ingvar Kamprad and a retail manager climbed up one of the warehouse racks to get a better view. "From that spot," recalls Peter Agnefjäll, who like many IKEA senior executives has worked at the company for his entire career, "they could look into the shopping area which was completely crowded with people . . . [Then they looked] into the warehouse area, where there were four or five workers running around, trying to collect the products for the customers. They thought: What would happen if we take this wall away, and instead let the customers enter the warehouse?"[18] That was the origin, to our knowledge, of the first warehouse-style retail outlet. As a result, IKEA was not just a business with a capability in customer-focused retail design. It had transformed that capability into a new outlet-format approach, which engaged customers in picking the furniture off the shelves as a prelude to assembling it themselves.

The advantage that comes from an innovation of this sort is not limited to a product or service. It gives you a sustained capability applicable to everything you offer. The companies we looked at are all remarkable capability innovators. They push the boundaries of their own ability to do new things, and then they apply that new capability to a wide range of activity.

The impetus for innovation may start at the blueprint stage—when people consider the problems that need solving to create the capabilities they need. Often, however, innovation doesn't stop there. All through the development of capabilities, the building of new processes, practices, and technologies becomes a way of life. "A lot of times we don't yet know quite how we're going to solve an engineering challenge," said a senior Qualcomm leader we talked to. "But we told the customer we would provide it by a deadline. So the engineering teams have to figure out the answer as they go along. It's typically a problem that no one has solved before, but that's what inspires people."

Some breakthrough innovations in capabilities are so powerful that they become entirely new ways of doing things, at the heart of a company's identity. One of the best-known examples is Zara, the flagship brand of the global apparel company Inditex. Zara's distinctive achievement was summed up eloquently by Amit Bagaria, the founder of the India-based fashion retail research group ASIPAC: "Zara comes up with 36,000 new designs every year, and it delivers new products as many as 2–6 times each week to its 1900+ stores around the world. Store orders are delivered in 24–48 hours. It takes the company only 10–15 days to go from the design stage to the sales floor."[19] One part of Zara's business model is a consistency grounded in changing fashion. Customers know that they will always find fashion-forward garments at Zara, at a reasonable price, usually within a few weeks after similar designs appeared on runways. They know that the clothing will be well manufactured and durable. And they know that if they don't buy those clothes when they first appear, they may not ever find them again.[20]

Inditex was founded in 1963 as a local dressmaking enterprise in La Coruna, a Galician port city on Spain's northern coast. The company is now a global apparel industry leader with more than sixty-six hundred retail stores for all its brands.[21] The roots of the company's innovative capabilities system go back to 1975, when founder Amancio Ortega opened a complementary business—a women's apparel shop—with the idea of selling affordable fashion that didn't seem cheap. He realized that by making the garments himself, paying close attention to the items his customers selected, and then quickly adjusting his line to match, he and his family-owned company could produce clothing faster than anyone else did and sell it at relatively low cost. As the business grew, he used innovative technological and process design to take this capability to a larger scale, in a way that no one had done before. This capability makes Inditex relatively immune to the inventory problems of many apparel retailers, which buy from overseas, often months in advance, and therefore must guess what clothing will be popular. Inditex avoids the cost of storing and discounting clothing that didn't sell and, more importantly, avoids the opportunity cost of missing trends.

Zara designers watch catwalk trends, fashion blogs, television shows, and the style choices of college students for early signs of customers' next apparel choices. In parallel, the company's retail employees are trained to serve as the company's frontline eyes and ears, tracking data, observing customers, and gathering informal impressions. The stores compile information about the choices that customers make, their inquiries about missing items, and their conversations. Are shoppers looking for skirts or trousers? Bold or subtle colors? These impressions are sent directly to a group of designers and operational experts at headquarters, who are charged with translating them immediately into new products for the racks.[22]

To make decisions based on all this data without being overwhelmed, Inditex created its own clear, and scalable, process for cross-functional communication. "We have a triangle of information,"

Inditex's Identity Profile

With headquarters in Arteixo, Galicia, Spain, Inditex is a Spanish clothing company with a global following. It pioneered the fast-fashion industry and had nearly 18.1 billion euros (US$19 billion) in revenue in 2014. Inditex is often called by its main brand name, Zara.

Value Proposition: As a customizer and innovator, Inditex provides on-trend clothing at reasonable prices.

Capabilities System

- *Deep customer insight:* Inditex analyzes trendsetters, fashion shows, and market reaction to its own products to design clothes that appeal to its target customers.
- *Fast, fashion-forward design of products:* The company rapidly translates consumer insights, including those from store observations, into apparel design, incorporating manufacturability.
- *Rapid-response manufacturing and operations:* Inditex moves products from design to stores in as little as two weeks and with highly variable capacity. This capability relies on a fast-moving, seamlessly integrated logistics system, and smart staging of production phases to increase flexibility (for example, color dyeing later in the process).
- *Globally consistent and pervasive branding:* The company approaches branding so that everything, from products to locations to merchandising to staffing, is structured to offer a trendy, high-quality experience. This approach allows the company to increase traffic in its stores, provide an on-trend environment, collect more customer feedback, and accentuate sales.

Portfolio of Products and Services: Inditex specializes in women's, men's, and children's apparel. The company sells about 85 percent of its stock at full price, far above the industry average.

---

chief communications officer Jesús Echevarría Hernández told a Harvard researcher. "The store managers, the [regional managers], and the commercials [who oversee sales figures for about forty stores each]. The commercials receive sales figures daily and communicate with the store managers and the [regional managers] every day to capture trends and interpret those figures. Store managers often ask to change a model (for example, changing colors and sizes), introduce variations (such as adapting short pants from long pants), or even design new clothes from scratch. If a lot of stores ask for similar changes, the commercials communicate these to the design team who will try to design the item and send it to all the stores."[23] Zara has successfully expanded its online sales and its global geographic footprint in recent years, always continuing to gather information about what customers look at and what they buy. Its net sales grow steadily year after year, putting it solidly among the category leaders in this sector.[24]

Qualcomm has also built capabilities through breakthrough innovation. This includes the licensing proficiency which generates much of the company's revenue. As journalist Dave Mock recounts in his history of the company, *The Qualcomm Equation*, this capability was oriented to "[help] licensees get up to speed fast on the technology and quickly introduce it to the market."[25] It goes beyond conventional licensing approaches, incorporating not just managing patents and intellectual property, but also in-depth consultation and building relationships with a broad group of telecommunications companies.[26] The pricing model was part of the breakthrough: the company steps up its fees when its licensees become successful.

The licensing capability was developed with as much intensive originality as any of Qualcomm's technological innovations. The story began in the early 1990s, when the mobile phone industry was establishing itself in the United States. Qualcomm commercialized a mobile phone transmission format called code-division multiple access (CDMA). Unlike other mobile standards of the time, which relied on specific bands of radio frequency, CDMA could travel on any part of the available electromagnetic spectrum, providing higher capacity and stronger quality on the same transmission signals than had been previously available.

But Qualcomm faced an uphill battle; at first the company was the only purveyor of its technology, which required a great deal of innovation investment without a clear market. When the company first proposed CDMA, the technology was more of a concept than a deliverable technological platform. At the time, many technical challenges prevented telecoms from accepting CDMA. Most companies had already committed to other standards. "Nobody believed [CDMA] would work," recalled former Qualcomm executive Bill Davidson, who had been active during that era. "[Others in the industry] absolutely disparaged the company. They said that we were selling vaporware. [Cofounder and then-chairman] Irwin Jacobs was called a crackpot."

Qualcomm's engineers and physicists were certain they were right. But to persevere, they had to simultaneously solve the technical challenges and figure out a viable business model for an emerging technology. This meant designing a fee structure low enough to attract business partners, but high enough that it would continue to subsidize Qualcomm's innovation. They had to establish themselves as impartial honest brokers, attracting handset manufacturers and mobile network operators without giving any of them preferential treatment—a departure from many conventional industry practices. Unlike AT&T in the old Bell System, they had to do all this with no government-sanctioned monopoly, little experience in licensing, and comparatively few connections in the mobile phone industry.[27] Instead of delegating the design of this new licensing system to legal and finance departments. Qualcomm focused senior management attention to it and combined it with customer service: bringing together engineers, patent attorneys, license negotiators, and business-to-business marketers to design it.

Since the mid-1990s, of course, CDMA has been eclipsed by other technologies and Qualcomm has often found itself in a recurring role: investing in the next generation of mobile communications technology (such as 3G, 4G, and, most recently, 5G transmission standards) and then using its licensing model to attract the rest of

Qualcomm's Identity Profile

With headquarters in San Diego, Qualcomm is a global leader in designing and licensing designs for semiconductors that support mobile communications and, more recently, internet servers. It is driven by the desire to deliver the world's most innovative wireless solutions and to connect people more closely to information, entertainment, and each other. The company had revenue of US$26.5 billion in 2014.[28]

Value Proposition: Qualcomm is an innovator and a platform provider, developing and providing infrastructure for advanced communications.

Capabilities System

- *Scientific conceptualization and realization:* Qualcomm develops unique product concepts from advanced theories and shows how they can be brought to reality.

- *Focused, "sprint"-style innovation:* By bringing teams of engineers to work together intensively on each new technological challenge, the company bypasses the conventional stage-gate approach and brings products and services online quickly and effectively.

- *Solution support and viability demonstration:* Qualcomm offers this capability for complex technologies—for example, through dispatch and service centers geared to work with its highly specialized B2B clients or through prototype manufacturing plants designed to show that the technology is feasible.

- *Robust network licensing:* Through robust licensing, the company derives income from its patented technologies.

Portfolio of Products and Services: Qualcomm sells a range of hardware and software to enable advanced mobile communications and networking. It also licenses its technologies across the telecom industry.

the industry. As Davidson puts it, "While it didn't feel fortunate at the time, it turned out to be fortunate that we were doubted in the beginning. It gave us a really scrappy culture." Qualcomm's technological audacity is unusual, but every company that has built distinctive capabilities has its own analogous structural innovations, enabling it to stand out in its field.

We could offer many other stories of capabilities system innovation. Apple, Lego, Amazon, and Starbucks—these companies are known for stepping outside the boundaries of conventional practice in highly successful ways. Some of their breakthrough innovations are small but telling. For example, Apple's checkout practice, in which retail clerks rove through the store with portable computers taking care of the payment, ensures that no one in the store ever has to wait at a checkout counter. This practice is a bigger deal than it appears to be; it removes a nagging irritant that consumers may feel, and reinforces the store's informal retail environment.

Just as with point interventions, the advent of digital technology will transform capabilities innovation in ways that have only begun to be imagined. For example, banks are just beginning to develop apps that play a much more active role in counseling and guiding people to financial health. In one future scenario recently developed by our firm, a young professional woman, after sending her monthly $1,650 rent payment, asks an app whether she should keep renting. "Great question," the app replies. "Let's discuss how to build equity over the next ten years." This introduces her to a suite of programs and services that guide her to appropriate neighborhoods, estimate the costs of purchase, design a savings plan with her, prompt her every day to stick to that plan (for example, by bringing her lunch to work), and ultimately find the moving company that carts her belongings to the new address. The process takes years, and the bank is with her, in her pocket or on her wrist, every step of the way. The capabilities for accomplishing this are technologically enabled, but technology isn't the critical innovation element. The bank must reimagine its business model and create an entirely new, cost-effective way to play the role of behavioral influence and guide, with the mobile device as its gateway. Few financial services firms have yet developed that kind of capability, or the trusted advisor identity, worthy of a customer's loyalty, that is needed to go with it.[29]

Capabilities-Oriented Acquisitions

Capabilities should be high on the strategic radar for dealmakers in companies. But all too often, they are treated as relatively minor factors, not as fundamental vehicles for creating value. Yet if you can look at prospective acquisitions as Starbucks, Danaher, and Amazon do, with an eye toward building capabilities, you are likely to be far more effective at M&A—and at value creation in general.

During the past few years, our firm has conducted a series of studies on the relative success of mergers and acquisitions (we referred briefly to the studies in chapter 1). The most recent iteration, conducted in 2015, analyzed more than 540 major transactions from around the world, all announced between 2001 and 2012. These were the 60 biggest deals in each of nine sectors: chemicals, consumer staples, electric and gas utilities, financial services, health care, industrials, information technology, media, and retail.

In the strategy-to-execution context, we have generally found that there are three types of deals. They can often be identified easily from the statements of intent that the acquirers make to investors, the press, and regulators. *Leverage deals* draw in products and services that make use of the acquirer's capabilities system. Danaher is well known for these deals, buying companies that will thrive when its Danaher Business System is applied to them. Starbucks also has a history of leverage deals; it often expands by buying chains, like Seattle Coffee, which can be converted to the Starbucks brand. CEMEX is a third example: It acquired Mexican competitors such as Cementos Anáhuac and Cementos Tolteca in the 1980s, the Spanish cement makers Valenciana and Sanson in 1992, several South American cement companies in the later 1990s, and two US-based cement companies in the early-to-mid 2000s.[30] These companies were integrated into the CEMEX enterprise, sharing the solutions-provider value proposition and all the CEMEX capabilities.

Enhancement deals draw in companies that fill in gaps in the acquirer's capabilities system. For example, when Starbucks paid $100 million for the La Boulange bakery chain in 2012, the acquisition was not just a matter of introducing high-quality breads and cakes. It raised the chain's ability to serve distinctive foods (without a grill, which ruined the ambiance with its odors). Amazon's 2009 purchase of the online shoe store Zappos brought expertise in customer service; its 2012 acquisition of Kiva Systems, known for its robot-driven warehouses, led to step-change improvements in its automated distribution logistics.[31] Under Armour's purchases of MapMyFitness in 2013 and Endomondo and MyFitnessPal in 2015 allowed it to build its digital capabilities in alignment with its core fitness-gear capabilities. Enhancement deals can be risky if they are not well managed; their success depends on a company's ability to integrate the people and technologies that it is acquiring. Many of these deals involve a long buy-and-hold period, which gives the two companies time to figure out how to assimilate the incoming capabilities and set up an environment where the acquiring company can learn from the acquired one.

Limited-fit deals are typically oriented toward diversification, often for higher growth rates, and may have little to do with capabilities at all. These deals tend to be far less successful. Our firm's studies have consistently found that the most immediately successful deals—as determined by total shareholder return in the two years after the deal was announced—are leverage deals. On average, they outperformed limited-fit deals by 14.2 percentage points. Enhancement deals also outperform limited-fit deals, by 12.4 percentage points. The return on the best enhancement deals is greater than that of leverage deals, but their success depends on the quality of postmerger integration. In all our studies, deals with a good capabilities fit outperform other deals by a significant and consistent margin.[32]

Capabilities fit helps explain why the Danaher group of businesses, which was largely assembled through acquisitions, works so well. At first glance, the firms in the conglomerate barely seem to fit together. Danaher does business in a variety of categories, including industrial products (Kollmorgen, Pantone); test and measurement instruments (Fluke, Tektronix); dentists' supplies (Kavo, Kerr); life sciences (Radiometer, HemoCue); environmental measurement and control (Hach Instruments, Gilbarco Veeder-Root); and science-focused enterprises (Leica, Beckmann Instruments, Pall, Videojet). This mix is not a coincidence. Danaher chose the companies it acquired carefully, sometimes spending years deciding to make an acquisition and following through. The rationale has always been the same: Danaher looks for companies that have a scientific or technological customer base, that have been languishing financially, and that could be revived with Danaher's capabilities in operational and business discipline. The company's pending 2016 split is being set up to enable the two new capabilites systems to be more tailored to each group of companies.

Our firm's M&A team has analyzed Danaher as a serial acquirer. We found that the thirty-one transactions (worth 72 percent of its market capitalization) that the company conducted between 1995 and 2011 were almost all classifiable as leverage deals. In each of these acquisitions, the company applied its capabilities system to a new product or service area—often keeping the acquired company and its brand names intact, but always applying the Danaher Business system and other key practices. This highly focused M&A program helped raise the company's share price fifteen-fold over that sixteen-year period, a performance far superior to that of the S&P 500 and many of Danaher's competitors.

Once Danaher acquires a company, as we'll see in chapter 5, it spends months onboarding the incoming executives. It also routinely moves top business leaders from one company to the other, making sure that the incisive, distinctive business knowledge inherent within Danaher is available to all the companies. And Danaher backs up these practices with other cross-platform and cross-boundary training. In this context, it shouldn't be surprising that Danaher is so coherent or that its coherence extends into every business it enters. Moreover, while Danaher is known as a leverage-deal company, most of its deals are also oriented to enhancing its capabilities system at the same time. Some of its extraordinary success may well stem from its ability to use its deals for both leverage and capabilities enhancement—in a consistent way that routinely bridges the gap between strategy and execution.

"As we buy companies, we learn new things," says Danaher executive vice president Jim Lico (who is slated to become CEO of the new industrial components spinoff company). "The dental businesses had great sales management practices that were new to us. When we acquired Fluke and Hach we learned better product management. When we bought Tektronix and some of the life sciences businesses, we learned more about technology development, advanced R&D, and software development. And those learnings were incorporated into all Danaher businesses. One of the most important things we can say about the Danaher Business System is that it improves and changes as our portfolio evolves."[33]

In the long run, enhancement deals may even be more lucrative than leverage deals—if you invest the time, attention, and capital needed to integrate incoming capabilities with your system and apply them to your portfolio of products and services. You can either acquire an entire capability or acquire part of a capability that you combine with something else. Better still, any deal that leverages or enhances your capabilities can play a profound catalytic role; the right acquisition can jump-start your efforts to innovate, continuously improve, and make powerful, focused interventions.

Finally, some parts of your business may be worth selling to other companies that can make better use of those capabilities. For example, in 2013 Qualcomm divested Omnitracs, a maker of satellite-based tracking and messaging systems for transportation and logistics management. This business had been part of the company since its beginnings in 1985. Qualcomm sold Omnitracs to Vista Equity Partners in 2013, telling reporters that they believed the company would do better with a different corporate parent.[34]

For most companies, an overall approach to building capabilities will include a mix of focused interventions, capability innovations, and capabilities-oriented acquisitions, all in sync. With each step, you'll be making your capabilities stronger and your company more coherent. People will rehearse and repeat the new routines and practices you put in place, paying close attention to what works and what doesn't work. Once your capabilities system is working effectively where you piloted it, or where it may have naturally existed, you'll be ready to bring it to scale.

Scaling Up Your Capabilities System

Distinctive capabilities are expensive. They involve significant fixed costs and enormous managerial attention. To unlock the potential value from your investment in them, you must focus on only a few, and instill them throughout your enterprise, everywhere you do business.

Yet it is tempting to fall into a Skunk Works or special-forces mind-set. That's when you think of distinctive capabilities as a kind of artistry performed by an elite corps of high-potential talent: the elite players work long hours and deliver unusual results, while the rest of the organization struggles along in its usual incoherent fashion. This approach rarely leads to success, especially if you have coherent competitors that have brought their capabilities to scale.

Thus, building scale for your distinctive capabilities must be at the top of the CEO agenda. The best approach will vary from one company to the next, but at its heart lie two common challenges. The first has to do with transcending functional boundaries—a difficult achievement in itself. The second has to do with balancing two forms of knowledge: tacit (held in peoples' habits and behaviors) and explicit (codified and formal). This means centralizing and systematizing activity throughout your company while still fostering participation and experimentation. In the end, whatever your industry and whatever your enterprise's size, scaling up your distinctive capabilities is one of the most difficult and yet essential things you can do.

Let's explore these two challenges in more detail.

Transcending Functional Boundaries

When we began the research for this book, we expected to hear a lot about organizational design. We thought that creative, capability-rich companies would have paid a lot of attention to the way they organized and the value that restructuring gave them.

Instead, our interviews found a willingness to let organizational forms and structures evolve naturally, developing in line with the identity of the enterprise. This makes sense, given what we know about organizational design: the best designs, as our colleague Gary Neilson has pointed out, are those which are "fit for purpose": designed to reinforce the distinctive capabilities of that particular company.[35]

We only uncovered one recurring pattern in organizational design, and it was closely related to the ability to bring distinctive capabilities to scale. The companies we studied, each in its own way, had transcended the limits of functional boundaries.

In other more conventional companies, work on capabilities takes place within separate specialized departments. You'll often find customer relationship management within marketing, budgeting within finance, supply-chain management within operations, outsourcing within procurement, training within HR, and new product development within R&D. You'll find some capabilities sitting in multiple versions in parallel functions: IT, HR, and operations will all have their own version of an outsourcing capability, with people sometimes only dimly aware of their counterparts in other functions.

The functional model of organization dates back to the 1850s. Some of the first business functionaries were railroad telegraph operators who managed schedules. Then came sales forces, finance departments, and R&D labs—including the original labs of Thomas Edison and Alexander Graham Bell. As companies grew steadily, the "corporate staff" (as it was originally called) grew accordingly. The functional model has been ingrained ever since, so much so that it is rarely questioned. Business units come and go, but finance, HR, marketing, IT, legal, and R&D seem to last forever.

We are not proposing the elimination of functions. Their value is undeniable; no company could do without them. They perform the essential task of marshaling people with important skills to manage crucial activities. But functions as they exist in many companies, without a clear link to distinctive capabilities, tend to drive incoherence and widen the strategy-to-execution gap.

On one hand, functions are treated as sources of expertise within the enterprise, which gives them an incentive to emulate world-class functions in other companies—to whom they will inevitably be compared. On the other hand, they are set up as cost centers and service bureaus, mandated to meet the needs of all their constituents as rapidly as possible under the ceiling of their budget. As we'll see in chapter 5, the entire budgeting process often facilitates and reinforces this—with functional leaders often incented and driven to protect and extend their functional reach just to maintain the resources they need. Meanwhile, as they juggle an endless list of (sometimes conflicting) demands from line units, they become skilled at solving the problems of the moment. They focus their attention on expedience, not on the most important distinctive capabilities. Aligning the functions to capabilities, which is often the only strategic way to resolve these pressures, may not even be considered.

The functional model of organizations is an important reason why so many companies struggle with the gap between strategy and execution. It makes a company good at many things, but great at nothing.[36] When functional boundaries prevail, there is no construct for managing capabilities. It isn't clear who owns the capabilities, how to track spending on them, or how to connect them to the strategy or to each other.

Much of the task of scaling up capabilities depends on resolving this issue—on transcending the limits of functions. For distinctive capabilities are inherently cross-functional. The most important capabilities systems do not fall neatly into groupings designed many decades ago. Indeed, much of the distinction in a powerful capabilities system stems from the sparks created when people with different backgrounds, skills, technologies, and perspectives build practices and processes together. Frito-Lay's direct-store delivery capability brings together IT, marketing, logistics and distribution, and financial analysis. The IKEA product design process involves design, sourcing, shipping, manufacturing, and customer insight. Apple's distinctively intuitive product and user interface design similarly involves customer insight, engineering, manufacturing, marketing, and distribution. In all these cases, the teams work collaboratively rather than sequentially; they think together, rather than throwing projects "over the wall" to each other.

The most common organizational solution is the cross-functional team: a committee of people drawn from the relevant departments to solve particular problems. Unfortunately, many cross-functional teams fall far short of delivering effective and efficient solutions. They rarely have the time they need to resolve their different ways of thinking. They are also limited by their conflicting functional priorities and sometimes by a lack of clear accountability. What's more, many of these teams are temporary; they will dissolve once the project is over, and their members may not work together again. There are also far too many of these teams, and the more there are, the more they tend to proliferate. When all cross-functional teams are temporary, an organization has little incentive to overcome these hurdles.

Permanent cross-functional teams tend to fare better. A grow-ing number of long-standing innovation groups, for example, bring together disparate functional skills (typically R&D, marketing, cus-tomer insights, and IT) to facilitate the launch of new products or services. Some of these teams are relatively informal, whereas others involve major shifts to the organizational structure. In one case, to develop its portfolio management capability, Pfizer Consumer set up communities of practice: semi-formal ongoing networks that included lawyers, health professionals, and marketing experts. These communities helped spread key ideas and best practices to brand and product groups around the world.[37]

From permanent cross-functional teams, it's only a small step to having formal capabilities teams. These operate outside the func-tional structure entirely, led by top executives with newly created job descriptions: Chief Digital, Risk, or Innovation Officer. Mem-bers of these teams, no matter how specialized their skills, follow a cross-functional career, reporting to people who may not share their background but who have a common commitment to the capability and all the projects associated with it. The functional departments, instead of managing projects, focus on learning and development and specialized guidance for the relevant staff assigned to capabil-ities. Examples include the IKEA sustainability team and Natura's supply-chain management council, whose purview includes sourc-ing, manufacturing, logistics, and aspects of the relationship with sales consultants. The capabilities team model can be likened to a symphony orchestra; the conductor is responsible for the whole work, but if a soloist needs help, he or she will turn to masters of the particular instrument for guidance.

The most farsighted functional leaders are not just waiting for these changes to affect them. They are taking the first step by help-ing evaluate the current state of their company's capabilities system and suggesting ways to bring it closer to its potential. This is part of the functional leader's new mandate as a strategic partner for the enterprise: delivering not what individual constituents demand, but what the whole enterprise needs.

Balancing Tacit and Explicit Knowledge

In their classic management book *The Knowledge-Creating Company*, management writers Ikujiro Nonaka and Hirotaka Takeuchi argue that the operating knowledge used to run distinctive capabilities in most companies is tacit.[38] In other words, it is held within the minds of people doing the work, is habitually followed, and is passed on through on-the-job training. This tacit knowledge is rarely written down in any systematic way. Because this knowledge is learned on the job, often within a function or business unit, it varies across different parts of the enterprise, often with some parts of the organization being far more capable than others.

To bring that knowledge to scale, you must take it beyond the purview of the elite "special forces." It must become *explicit*. It must be captured systemically, with clear instructions—like recipes and routines—or must be embedded in processes and technological setups, like algorithms and blueprints, that anyone could use to execute well. These codified routines and practices must be treated as standard practice: repeated at every level, in every location. Otherwise, the company loses its consistent value, and its distinctive capabilities are lost.

(Codifying the capabilities is not the same as creating a blueprint. The blueprint describes the capability and how it works, including the need for codification. The codification is embedded instructions: knowledge used to put it into practice throughout the company.)

Tacit knowledge should be gathered selectively. You must consciously focus on the knowledge that makes you distinctive. When people are asked what they do at work or what others should learn from them, the first things they say are probably not the most important. You need to probe more deeply, to get past their ordinary perceptions, and to codify not just what people consciously recognize as their work knowledge, but what has been ingrained into unconscious habit. You may end up discarding 75 to 80 percent of what people think is important, because it doesn't quite get to the heart of what makes you distinctive.

You must also resist the temptation to codify too mechanistically. You want to create step-by-step recipes and routines, often embedded in technology, that make it possible for a wide number of people to learn to do things the same way. Yet your goal is not to standardize everything or hamstring creativity. Rather, as people get used to these recipes and routines, they adapt them to their own circumstances while remaining true to the identity and capabilities that the entire organization needs. You want to promote ownership of the knowledge embedded in the capability, to encourage innovation while operating at scale. Give your recipe-followers opportunities to become master chefs, practicing the steps until they no longer need the recipes; the knowledge has become tacit again and second nature. If you can make it work, you have a whole enterprise of people who are skilled enough to make their own valuable variations; who understand how they fit the value proposition, see their place in the capabilities system, and continually learn from each other.

Or as organizational learning specialist Robert Putnam puts it, "The learning of skills begins with recipes. Without practice, the concept won't be second nature. But until it's second nature, you can't practice with it effectively. So you short-cut the dilemma by following a set of rules"—at least at first, until you don't need the rules anymore.[39]

Having a capabilities-oriented structure (a chief capability officer) can make it easier to balance explicit knowledge (centralized codification) and tacit knowledge (decentralized creativity). Whatever the structure, there needs to be a process for continually improving the work of your distinctive capabilities. People need to feel free to comment on the recipes, routines, and other standardized practices they are following. They need to know that their comments will be heard, and that the recipes and routines will rapidly be adjusted if the suggestions are right. They need opportunities to share information and learn from each other. And this needs to be tied to every aspect of codification, including the metrics that have been agreed upon to determine if a project is successful. Then they need the autonomy to act on what they have learned.

Frito-Lay, for example, has strict routines and metrics built into its direct store delivery capability. There are clear routes, and required steps in sending back data from the field. But regional managers are continuously involved in improving those routines and metrics, and in making sure the company continues to learn from its experience in the field. Danaher has regular review sessions at every level, and a culture in which anyone is encouraged to raise questions about the effectiveness of the Danaher Business System or any metric, practice, or rubric associated with it.

Once you have a capability that is codified and brought to scale, it will be available to you thereafter—even if you lose your way. In the mid-1980s, the sports apparel manufacturer Adidas learned this in a very striking way, and recovered a nearly bankrupt business as a result. Based in a small Bavarian town near Nuremberg, Germany, the company had been led since its founding in 1949 by the original managing director, Adolf ("Adi") Dassler, a dedicated designer of athletic shoes for high performance. For example, he designed football shoes (or, as they're called in the United States, soccer shoes) that were only two-thirds as heavy as those of his rivals. The company became famous after the 1954 World Cup, which its shoes were credited with helping the West German team win. Drawing on Dassler's direct contact with athletes and insights about their needs, Adidas became known for its expertise in developing shoes tailored to competitive sports.

While little of that knowledge was written down in instructions or processes, it was codified in artifacts: a small museum of shoe prototypes and other design experiments. But after Dassler died in 1978, the company lost interest. Instead, according to management researchers Nicholas Ind, Oriol Iglesias, and Majken Schultz, Adidas tried to compete against Nike and Puma on fashion and price. The subsequent decline in profits led to near bankruptcy and a takeover in 1989. René Jäggi, a judo enthusiast and marketer from Duracell, was hired to turn the company around. He in turn hired two former Nike managers, Peter Moore and Rob Strasser, to visit its operations. "It only took about five minutes in the museum," Moore recalls, "before I realized that these people had a gold mine in their hands, and that they really had no idea what they had had."[40]

The tacit knowledge from the past, brought back to life as the old shoe prototypes were unearthed, rejuvenated the company. "[Adidas] started to rebuild its archive," Ind, Iglesias, and Schultz explain, "buying back shoes and clothes from collectors and asking for donations [of old Adidas items]. Managers were also asked to think about their current work and what they wanted to save and document. They re-created the company's archive—which [as of 2014] had 90,000 items and 10,000 images," along with many of Dassler's notes.

It wasn't enough to capture the old experiments, of course; Moore and Strasser had to encourage and support a new group of researchers to carry on, building a broad-based capability for athlete-friendly design rather than just a winning product or two. Adidas soon began producing new shoes in the Dassler tradition of experimentation in collaboration with athletes. One such line, called Equipment, focused on lightweight design and authenticity. Later renamed Performance, the line represents more than 75 percent of the company's current sales. Another shoe produced through this revitalized innovation capability, the Stan Smith tennis shoe, has sold more than sixty million pairs.

Your company may not have what Adidas had: a founder's forgotten museum linked to your value proposition. But your organization no doubt has a body of tacit knowledge highly relevant to your business. Much of it is probably not yet captured; it takes the form of conversations or behavior: "how we do things around here," conveyed to newcomers when they join the enterprise. Your goal is to find this knowledge—often sitting behind your most successful businesses—and scale it so that hundreds or thousands of people are thinking together, as if they are all owners and not just following instructions. As you'll see later in the book, this way of operating—*collective mastery*—becomes an inherent part of a coherent company's culture.

If you can balance tacit and explicit knowledge successfully, the result is a paradoxical, but very effective, combination of people marching in step but thinking for themselves. Starbucks masters this balance. Its codification of practices and methods, from its retail store design principles to its use of reward cards and mobile-phone payments, has allowed it to scale up its distinctive look and feel around the world. Yet there is always enough local autonomy to cater to local tastes and interests. No two stores are exactly the same; they have varied menus and prices, depending on their location. Their promotions often involve community action, which is managed by the local store leaders.

The IKEA organization is similarly good at managing the balance between explicit and tacit knowledge. Every IKEA staffer around the world follows the same basic guidelines, almost to the letter— because the employees are convinced that it is the right thing to do in service of their value proposition and capabilities system. Even so, everyone is encouraged to speak out when they see a reason to change, and they know their insights will be heeded.

"One of our core values," says Torbjörn Lööf, the CEO of Inter IKEA Systems B.V., "is to be entrepreneurial. Everyone takes initiative to improve the IKEA concept. But of course there are areas where we're very strict and structured. If you look at the description of our concept, [you'll see] what a store should look like, how it should be built, where people come in, how the flow goes, where they exit, where the restaurant should be and how it should be, what range we offer, what style we should have, what the price ladders are. A lot is almost set in stone. People don't resist it. They know it's been extensively tested [and] they know we're constantly trying out new things, and if they prove out to work, they'll become part of the concept."[41]

Beyond Business as Usual

Though the specifics may vary from one company to another, the three activities described in this chapter—creating a blueprint of a capabilities system, building those capabilities, and bringing the capabilities to scale—are relevant to all enterprises. The activities require a disciplined focus that goes beyond business as usual.

When you follow this path, then people who work with you will internalize their capability-building activity as a form of engagement and creativity. People see themselves as what they do, so as they see their direct connection to the capabilities of your company, and as these capabilities become ingrained in day-to-day activities and habits, you will tap into a great deal of emotional energy. Indeed, the essentials of your capabilities system, as we'll see in the next chapter, will become core elements of the culture of your company.

Put Your Culture to Work

What's your company's biggest asset? We often asked this question in interviews we conducted with leaders of companies that had closed the strategy-to-execution gap. These leaders nearly always named their culture.

At CEMEX, human resources chief Luis Hernández said the culture "produces the behaviors that reinforce the capabilities that will make us successful."[1] Haier's CEO Zhang Ruimin said that "the main factor enabling [the difference between Haier and other companies] is our culture."[2] Peter Agnefjäll, CEO of the INGKA Group at IKEA, said, "Our culture is very difficult to copy. You could copy our Billy bookcase or the retailing format or our warehouses, but how do you copy our culture?" We could quote similar remarks from leaders at Danaher, Lego, Natura, Qualcomm, and Starbucks. These cultures may not always be friendly; they can be tough on people. But they are always seen as a source of strategic strength.

To be sure, executives at most companies talk frequently about their culture. But all too often they describe it as something to overcome: an impediment to performance. They launch "culture change" initiatives to eliminate negative cultural attributes and build new ones. These efforts prove futile; a culture does not change easily or rapidly.

An organization's culture is a multidimensional, complex, and influential thing. It is the reservoir of behaviors, thoughts, feelings, values, and mind-sets that people in an enterprise share. Culture influences the most common practices of an organization, many of which are more informal than formal, especially those practices which people take on themselves and which may not be consciously recognized or talked about explicitly. Like tacit knowledge, a culture can't be managed by controlling it; but its impact is concrete. "Cultural forces are powerful," writes Edgar Schein, the MIT professor who first articulated the concept of corporate culture, "because they operate outside of our awareness."[3]

In most companies, the culture manifests itself in the way people look at things and talk to each other; in the way they compliment and criticize one another; in the posters on the wall and the knickknacks on the desks. Most of all, it is evident in the stories people tell each other, about what matters at this company or why some people fit in while others don't. Thus, closing the gap between strategy and execution often involves telling new stories that are deliberately chosen to reinforce coherence: stories about the capabilities that make this company special, the reasons why we do the things we do, events that have challenged the enterprise, the things people did to meet those challenges, and the evolution of the company's capabilities and attitudes. (Indeed, these are the kinds of stories that came up repeatedly in the research for this book.) It isn't necessary to become a good storyteller to lead a company in this direction; but it is necessary to become aware of the prevailing stories, and how well they fit the identity of the enterprise. If there are serious contradictions, then it may be necessary, as we'll see later in this chapter, to find the stories that fit better, and bring them to the surface.

Your culture is a valuable resource. Learning to work with your culture can make the development of differentiated capabilities much easier. In a relatively coherent company, when strategy and execution are closely aligned, the culture provides the support that individuals within the enterprise need to find their own personal connection with the overall strategy. It helps break down the barriers that separate strategy from execution, such as the boundaries between functions. A culture that is in tune with your most distinctive capabilities can also draw people to accomplish amazing things.

Most business leaders understand the power of a company's culture. But it's not always clear how to harness that power. To do so, you must understand the way that culture evolves as you close the gap between strategy and execution, and how it can help you move further down that path. This chapter has three main points. First, we explore the way a company's identity shapes its culture. Then we look at three facets of culture that all of the companies we studied seem to have in common: emotional commitment, mutual accountability, and collective mastery. Finally, we describe a focused "critical-few" method developed by Jon Katzenbach that you can apply in your company to accelerate the cultural evolution already going on there. Coherent companies use their cultures this way to truly differentiate themselves by bringing their strategic identity to life.

Fostering a Distinctive Culture

Peter Agnefjäll hits on an important point when he says IKEA's culture is difficult to copy. Like almost everything else about them, the cultures of coherent companies are unique and hard to replicate. No other retail chain can adopt the practices of Starbucks or Zara and expect the same result; the people in these companies behave the way they behave because a culture has grown up, over time, which reinforces this behavior.

Many very capable people are drawn to work for companies with distinctive capabilities. Although they might not think of it as an emotional connection to the company's culture, that's what attracts them. They want to be part of something distinctive. Thus, at companies that close the gap between strategy and execution, you don't typically find people trying to leave their culture behind. They celebrate the bespoke attributes that make them special, and they keep bringing those elements to the forefront. In a coherent company, the elements of the culture, often dismissed as merely personal, reinforce what the company is trying to be.

Consider, for example, how Natura's culture expresses and reinforces its identity. Every artifact, from the product designs to the architecture of the buildings, is a testament to the company's shared purpose and values. Even the annual reports open with this statement: "Life is a chain of relationships. Nothing in the universe stands alone."[4] The culture goes a long way toward reinforcing the relationship with sales consultants at the heart of Natura's value proposition. You can also see its impact in the company's relationships with rain forest suppliers, and its intent focus on keeping promises. The culture is also reflected in the way people talk about the company. "We are driven by language," says brand director Ana Alves. "We tell stories. This comes partly from the Brazilian culture; you understand things in part by feeling them." And it is manifest in its architecture. Visitors to Natura's headquarters in Cajamar, a suburb of São Paulo, encounter a six-story glass-and-steel building, with the upper three stories built on stilts to promote airflow and a bowstring bridge that encourages people to linger and look at the forest around them. The company has been regularly planting seedlings to recover the native biome on the site since 2009, when the building opened.[5]

Some forty-seven hundred miles to the north is Danaher—an equally coherent company with a completely different culture, one that centers around operational effectiveness, ruthless execution, and no-nonsense candor. It's a necessary culture for an enterprise assembled from other companies who must all operate as high achievers, helping one another continually do better. There is no room for slack or indecisiveness. When you run a business at Danaher, it's understood that your performance might drop sometimes, but you'd better be prepared to explain what happened and what you are going to do about it, with lots of data and no embellishment. "If you're touting pabulum, that's an unsafe place to be," says Steven Simms, who spent eleven years at Danaher and is now CEO of another manufacturing company. Danaher's global headquarters occupy an unpretentious floor in a building in downtown Washington, D.C. "We are nonpolitical and nonbureaucratic," says the company's culture statement. Executive vice president Jim Lico adds, "We have the soul of a small company. We still remember the day when we all pitched in to ship product on Fridays if the warehouse was full, or we took a tech support call even if we were top executives. Though those days are long gone, we remember and long to keep that culture."

We could paint a similarly compelling portrait of every company that we credit with closing the strategy-to-execution gap. Apple, Amazon, and Starbucks are famous for their idiosyncratic cultures, and you'd find a similarly distinctive sensibility in Frito-Lay, Inditex, Lego, and Qualcomm. They don't take their culture for granted. Moreover, the cultures of these companies are directly linked to their capabilities systems. Natura doesn't just have a commitment to environmental and social sustainability; its people know how to achieve it because it is one of their distinctive capabilities. The culture reflects not just what people believe, but what they do exceptionally well. Behaviors lead to stories; stories engender new behavior; and everything ties in with the value proposition and capabilities system. That's why these cultures are so different from each other.

You may think of your company as having a standard, nondescript business culture, just like everyone else's, but it too is unique. It has come to life over time through the accumulation of many factors: the background of your company's founders and key leaders, its geographic roots (companies founded in Silicon Valley tend to be different from companies founded in the Netherlands or in Singapore), its prominent functions, its history of mergers and acquisitions, and its structural constraints (highly regulated industries lead to cultures different from those in more freewheeling industries). Your company's culture is unlike any other, and that distinction is a strength.

Now that you are moving to close the gap between strategy and execution, it is time to celebrate and use that distinction. You can foster commitment with it; you can bring your value proposition to life. Think of your culture as the "intrinsically cool" part of your identity—the part that engages people. When you talk about your company's culture, articulate the ways in which it reflects your capabilities system and the value your company creates.

If you've already begun to work on the first two of the five acts of unconventional leadership as outlined in chapter 1—namely, committing to an identity and translating the strategic into the everyday—then this articulation has probably already begun to happen. Your effort to build capabilities and bring them to scale have already highlighted the amazing things your people can do. People naturally identify with their capabilities, especially if shared by an elite organization full of highly skilled colleagues. Companies that define themselves by their capabilities, instead of by their financial results or an abstract mission statement, thus enjoy a huge cultural advantage.

Finally, while the distinctiveness of your culture is a strength, coherence does seem to bring with it three common cultural elements: emotional commitment, mutual accountability, and collective mastery. These will tend to emerge as you practice the five unconventional acts enumerated in chapter 1. Most companies are familiar with these elements—but only in places. As you close the gap between strategy and execution, you will increasingly be able to rely on them. Let's look at these three elements, the natural outcomes of those unconventional acts, in more detail.

Emotional Commitment

Suppose, then, that you are on your way—that you are following the first two acts, and your company has a clearer identity and a stronger capabilities system. One of the first changes you will notice is a rise in the level of emotional commitment. When people understand the identity of the enterprise, and when they feel aligned with that identity, they are ready to give more of themselves to the enterprise, because they see its success as their own.

Emotional commitment is impossible to measure precisely. It may not even show up reliably in employee engagement surveys. But people who are attuned to it can generally tell when it's present. "You can walk into [any type of retail store]," CEO Howard Schultz is quoted as saying, "and you can feel whether the proprietor or the merchant or the person behind the counter has a good feeling about his product. If you walk into a department store today, you are probably talking to a guy who is untrained; he was selling vacuum cleaners yesterday, and now he is in the apparel section. It just does not work."[6]

At some companies, the emotional commitment begins with devotion to some aspect of the company's identity, such as the product. Michael Gill, author of *How Starbucks Saved My Life*, first connected with the company through a love of coffee. Many are drawn to Natura, Lego, and Apple because of appreciation for the elegance of their products. Other companies, such as Danaher and Qualcomm, generate emotional commitment through appreciation for the skill of their employees. And some companies, such as Inditex, inspire commitment when employees understand how their role fits with the company's way of working. Whatever the initial connection may be, when a company is coherent, that commitment expands to include a strong affinity for the company, its people, and its community.

The experience of Natura shows how emotional energy changes a company's perspective. As we noted earlier in this book, the company's slogan, *bem estar bem*, translates to "well-being, being well." When asked what's important to the culture, people talk about two things: the products and the company's relationships with people. The products themselves are designed and packaged to evoke long-term vitality, cherished relationships, and other aspects of personal commitment. A fragrance is scented to remind people of the Amazon rain forest (from which its ingredients are sourced); a skin cream is designed for grandchildren to give their grandparents; a moisturizer called Tododia ("Everyday") deliberately evokes the pragmatic pride of a professional on her way to work. Featured among several seductive fragrances for men and women is one called Brasil Humor, which is intended to encourage "a more humorous take on life."

Conspicuous by their absence are performance-oriented claims. Natura's anti-aging creams and moisturizers never promise to reduce wrinkles by a particular percentage. Such claims don't fit with the products' value proposition, which itself is grounded in emotional commitment—the commitment people make to their relatives and close friends. There are also practical reasons for avoiding these claims. "Some of our business units have asked for products where we can claim better performance than a competitor," says R&D director Alessandro Mendes. "But if we tried to play that game, we could only afford to launch three or four new products per year." Instead, Natura launches more than a hundred.[7]

Natura's emphasis on the rich, multi-faceted, relationship-driven nature of daily life reinforces its emotional connection to the people who sell its merchandise. Within Brazil, the company maintains a network of 1.5 million "consultants," as they're called: individual representatives who are commissioned and trained by Natura. They show the products regularly to their friends, neighbors, and acquaintances—mostly door to door, although some operate small shops out of their homes. They take orders, distribute the products, and collect the payments. The company must therefore give them a reason to get in touch with their customers every twenty-one days: a hot-off-the-press product catalog, containing a few new products and seasonal specials (e.g., for Christmas or Mother's Day) along with the company's mainstays. Unlike most direct-sales companies, which have multilevel hierarchies of sales representatives and concentrate wealth at the top of the pyramid, Natura is directly connected to most of its consultants. They know that it is committed to their success, and therefore they return that sentiment.

The company proves its emotional commitment through its actions. For example, it makes heroic efforts to avoid shipping problems. Rather than outsource distribution, the company has invested millions in a state-of-the-art supply chain that delivers orders within two to four days, even to extremely remote parts of Brazil. Natura maintains very high flexibility in its supply chain because a well-liked new fragrance or cosmetic can suddenly take off, selling at one hundred times the average sales volume of other products. The company also maintains high reliability. In 2011, when the percentage of lost or damaged deliveries rose from near zero to about 1 percent, the company paid no bonuses. The following year, the failure rate fell back to zero. People at headquarters spoke of this measure as not just pressure for performance—but as a sign of the commitment they had made to its consultants.

In the early 2000s, Natura deepened its commitment—to employees, consultants, and customers—by broadening its capabilities system. It embraced a management principle known as the *triple bottom line*, that is, accountability for financial, environmental, and social success.[8] This required types of proficiency the company had not had before: a new capability in sustainability-related management. The development of this capability began in 2000 when Natura launched a line of products called Ekos, using plants collected or harvested from the biodiverse Brazilian Amazon region. Denise Alves, the company's sustainability director, recalls, "We decided that Ekos would only use ingredients from the Amazon region that would be extracted from fruits cultivated or collected in an organic way, in a quantity that would not hamper that region's ecosystem."

The sheer complexity inherent in this capability has become a barrier to entry for competitors and a differentiator for Natura. When its buyers collect ingredients from rain forest villages, they demand that the plants be grown and harvested sustainably. Natura compensates villages with long-term investments and has created a unique financing system to foster this approach. The company also works diligently to reduce air and water pollution at every step of the value chain, publishes data on its carbon and recycling footprints, designs sustainable packaging, and creates job opportunities for disabled people in its warehouses and factories.

One important moment came in the mid-2000s, when Natura ran out of an ingredient called *pitanga*, which is needed for one of the company's most popular products. Other companies might have looked for less sustainable sources. Natura announced that it was stopping production until it could be sure that its procurement didn't compromise company values.

With this move, Natura found itself embracing sustainability wholeheartedly. Since then, it has used triple-bottom-line reporting so consistently that if Natura doesn't meet goals in all three areas everywhere in the company, Natura doesn't pay bonuses. The company also energetically seeks to make its practices transparent to outsiders. Alves explains, "We pioneered an environmental table on our packaging that describes the product content and how much of the packaging is recycled, even when the numbers aren't flattering to us." Natura's social programs have also expanded well beyond the typical level you might find in other companies. Executive vice president João Paulo Ferreira (who oversees sales, sustainability, and customer relationships) describes Natura's approach:

> If I go to the board and I say, "I need a new distribution center," they say, "Okay, maybe." But if I go as I did [in 2012], and say, "We should have a new factory, but I think we should make it an eco park with symbiotic industrial flows in the middle of the rain forest to increase our impact in society, and by the way I don't have a clue how to do it," the board will definitely accept, as they did. . . . If I say, "[We should design our next distribution center] to make sure that we can have a workforce of up to 30 percent mentally or physically disabled people, including autism and Down syndrome," they say, "Okay, we want this. Go." That's the sort of thing we do.

Some of the other companies we looked at, such as IKEA and Starbucks have developed similarly deep commitments to environmental or social responsibility. The critical factor, all too often overlooked, is the link between that emotional commitment and the capabilities that support it. When a company voices this commitment and then cuts corners or hides data—as some do, with visible and extremely damaging results—the problem generally seems to be insufficient attention to the required capabilities. They just can't figure out how to deliver. By contrast, its capabilities make Natura trustworthy. Customers who care about the rain forest or developmentally disabled people know the company keeps its promises. That emotional commitment has become part of Natura's culture.

Natura's Identity Profile

With headquarters in São Paulo, Natura is the leading cosmetics company in Brazil, with revenue of US$2.6 billion in 2014.

Value Proposition: Natura is a relationship-focused experience provider and reputation player, selling products that promote well-being, relationships, and connection to nature.

Capabilities System
- *Direct-sales distribution:* Natura maintains a uniquely powerful model of sales through qualified representatives ("consultants").
- *Rapid innovation:* The company develops and markets a steady stream of new products that create an emotional connection with customers, consultants, and employees.
- *Operational prowess:* Managing the complexities in a company that manufactures and delivers more than one hundred new products each year, ensuring that consultants can reach out to customers every few weeks and enhance relationships.
- *Creative sourcing:* Natura builds and maintains a supplier network that gives the company unique access to rain-forest products and helps build Natura's reputation as a sustainable company whose employees and customers believe in the value of relationships.
- *Sustainability-related management:* Natura makes environmental responsibility an integral part of operations and expresses those ideals in everything it does.

Portfolio of Products and Services: Natura develops, produces, and sells personal-care products, mainly in Latin America.

Mutual Accountability

When everyone in an enterprise is working together toward the same goal, they tend to strongly identify with each other. People think, "We're all jointly responsible for fulfilling the goals we've set, or we will let each other down." A differentiated capabilities system depends on this quality. People have to recognize one another's contributions and how they can rely on these contributions, or they will be vulnerable themselves.

In their book *The Wisdom of Teams*, Jon Katzenbach and Douglas R. Smith report that mutual accountability is the clearest indicator of what they call a "real team"—a team whose people share goals and work interdependently, as opposed to merely being assigned to the same projects.[9] This type of team-based collaboration is particularly important for distinctive capabilities, which are inherently cross-functional. When the culture reinforces the attitude that people are responsible for the success of the enterprise, not just for their functions, it is much easier to bring a distinctive capability to life.

Where there is mutual accountability, there is trust. Even in relatively harsh cultures, like Apple, there is a clear sense that people can be relied on to pull their weight. Adam Lashinsky quotes an unnamed Apple executive who explains the "culture of excellence," as the executive calls it: "There's a sense that you have to play your very best game. You don't want to be the weak link. There is an intense desire to not let the company down. Everybody has worked so hard and is so dedicated."[10]

In companies with mutual accountability, management doesn't need to rely on command and control to get things done. "I was to learn," Michael Gill writes of his experience as a barista, "that nobody at Starbucks ever ordered anyone to do anything. It was always: 'Would you do me a favor?' or something similar." There is generally a culture of open experimentation in firms with mutual accountability, because people know that the full team will support anything that credibly leads to better long-term results. Everyone is invested in each other's success, interested in making sure it goes right. That in itself enables everyone to be more adventurous.

The IKEA culture fosters this kind of accountability. Montserrat Maresch, global marketing and communications director at the INGKA Group, says, "We're not an organization of superstars and divas. We're much more tolerant with C performers than with C behaviors. If I'm not good enough but I have the right attitudes and the right values, I will be helped by the organization. In the same spirit, we don't celebrate a high-performing store. We celebrate when that high-performing store helps a weaker store."

The extent of mutual accountability can provide a clear test of your company's coherence. Many companies have diverse business units and functions, each with its own budget or profit-and-loss statement, and the units or functions have never worked closely together before. As companies build distinctive capabilities and bring them to scale, they set up teams and conversations in which people have to engage more effectively with specialists from other parts of the enterprise. The conversations are illuminating: "I never realized what you did or why it mattered to me."

Moreover, the mutual accountability of your enterprise can help overcome the short-term orientation and unproductive internal competitiveness that pervades many organizations and prevents them from doing amazing things. Once people feel responsible for each other's success, they are more likely to take the time to understand each other's perspectives. IKEA has used its high level of mutual accountability in precisely this way. Søren Hansen, the CEO of Inter IKEA Group (which includes Inter IKEA Systems B.V. along with independent property and finance operations), describes how mutual accountability works for his enterprise:[11]

> One might think it would be easy for people to say, "No; this is not my responsibility," and go off and paddle in their own pool, handling only their own tasks. But that's not the way it is here. Everybody feels more responsible than they actually are on paper. As soon as there is an issue somewhere, people jump in, help, support. This creates checks and balances throughout the system. Indeed, there is no clear demarcation between functions, and you

therefore feel responsible for the company and the end result.[12]

People who have worked in a culture of mutual accountability tend to remember it all their lives. They are in an environment where everyone is dedicated to everyone else's success. At its best, the purpose of the company becomes the fulfillment of its members' potential. This is not just because the company expects a return on its investment, but because it knows that the accountability of key employees is critical to distinctive capabilities.

Collective Mastery

Think back to the great teams you have known: where you and your colleagues seemed to sense what each other was thinking, where you all understood how your work fit into a common purpose, and where you recognized how to accomplish great things together, without needing to follow a script. Now imagine an entire global organization operating more or less this way. That is what a culture of collective mastery feels like. In the companies that we studied, collective mastery is prevalent. It is a high level of shared proficiency, visible across the enterprise, where people at the top of their individual games continually practice collaborating across functional boundaries to raise the overall quality of what they do together. They grow accustomed to thinking together: solving problems, minimizing formal rules that block progress, and experiencing the intrinsic joy of working with other high-caliber people.

A culture of collective mastery can lead a company to great achievement. The companies we studied, to the extent they have that culture, get there through the direct involvement of the senior executives of the company. They're not just involved in the blueprinting of capabilities systems, but also in their implementation, including (as we'll see in chapter 5), the details of resource allocation.

Most of all, they're involved in the capabilities system of the enterprise: paying constant attention to its successes and failures, and routinely moving people to the positions where they can make the greatest contribution. Top leaders take a fresh look at every significant practice and ask, How well is it working? How can we improve it? What have we learned from it? In turn, they glean direct insight about the day-to-day business of delivering the enterprise's strategy. Participating in this sort of capabilities-building work requires a great deal of effort, and few companies have the discipline to make it stick. Yet all the coherent companies do.

Consider, for example, Danaher's approach to executive teaching and learning. The company's Danaher Business System was directly influenced by the tenets of lean management and the quality movement, to the extent of learning directly from some of the Toyota leaders who developed that approach. But Danaher's leaders were closely involved, from their first use of this system in the mid-1980s, in adapting and adjusting it to make it their own. They also devoted themselves wholeheartedly to the tools and methods.

"[Most managers] have a mind-set that if you apply a tool, you've done it and you're done," recalled George Koenigsaecker, who implemented the first version of the Danaher Business System in the 1980s. He said a single application of process improvement might yield 40 percent productivity gain. "But to get the 400 percent gain you have to pass it at least 10 different times. You must restudy the process over and over."[13] Over time, as you continue to apply the techniques of capability improvement—the point interventions and innovations that we described in chapter 3—this way of life becomes embedded in your culture. "Whether you're in a strategic plan review, an operating review, a growth initiative, or walking the plant floor," says retired executive vice president Steven Simms, "all the questions and challenging come back to some aspect of 'How do we get better?' It leads to great, rich discussions everywhere."

The result is a company where not just practices, but attitudes and habits, are geared toward fostering collective mastery. Danaher's culture evolved this way in part because, as a serial acquirer, the company has had to continually onboard new people and increase the reach of its capabilities system. "We have been learning how to extend the Danaher Business System to larger and larger scale for more than a decade," says Danaher executive vice president Jim Lico. "In 2003, I was running the DBS office and [founder and board chair] Mitchell Rales asked me how I was going to teach DBS to twenty-four thousand people in the next three or four years. I said, 'We only have twenty-four thousand people in the whole company.' Mitch said, 'Yeah, but we're going to double in size in the next three or four years and that's our task.'"[14]

The emphasis on collective mastery is evident in the way Danaher recruits, onboards, and develops people. It can take months to get a new executive onboarded, and the process frequently involves immersion in several businesses temporarily—with the explicit idea that both Danaher and the newcomer will learn from each other. Danaher also conducts a cascading series of meetings and initiatives, with top management involved, where the DBS methods are practiced. For example, the top twenty Danaher executives get together regularly to talk about tools and techniques related to key capabilities. "We quickly pick up everything we can from each other," senior vice president Henk van Duijnhoven explains. "Not every operating company has to implement every tool; they choose the tools that will enable them to achieve their strategic goals, fix quality issues, or improve delivery or other operating company objectives."

Regular meetings are not just devoted to decisions, but also consideration of how well the capabilities are working. "In each business," CEO Tom Joyce says, "we have a disciplined cadence of monthly operating reviews: eight-hour face-to-face meetings with a standing agenda. It's very data-driven. We focus on things that are not going well and what we're going to do to improve them."

The Danaher Leadership Conference is another organizational construct that reinforces scale and improvement at the company. It consists of a series of forty or fifty presentations highlighting best practices over three days for the top 100 to 150 leaders at the operating companies. "One [session] could be a story about how the water quality platform has captured customer insights for accelerated product development," Simms says. "Another could be, 'We finally learned to do policy deployment right after fifteen years.' Each one explains the problem, the root cause of the issue, the countermeasures taken to solve it, what they'd do differently in retrospect, and what they'd advise you to do—with an email address and phone number. [The implied message is] 'Call me, and we'll talk about some ideas and people to help get you started.' . . . Senior managers were actually rated every year on our proficiency with [the Danaher Business System] tools."

Other companies we looked at have similarly involved top leaders as teachers and learners. During its most energetic efforts to develop new capabilities, JCI-ASG conducted meetings known as stake-in-the-ground sessions. Every few months, executives convened to report on cost-cutting measures they had identified, along with other measures designed to improve and focus on capabilities. The committee decided which ones to implement.

Starbucks takes this idea one step further. By establishing that every employee is a partner (reinforced with stock options), it also enlists every employee in developing collective mastery. The education of a Starbucks employee is an intensive, ingrained affair, with a great deal of one-on-one apprenticeship. It takes time and attention to learn the ins and outs of the espresso machines, the varieties of coffee, how to treat customers (including lengthy scripts that role-play different types of encounters at the register), and the ethics of community engagement. All of this is necessary, founder Howard

Schultz suggests, because of the inherent complexity of the Starbucks system. The company must therefore give employees a deep and shared understanding of the underpinnings of the enterprise.

It is on-the-job practices like these, which may or may not involve formal training, that generate collective mastery. When enough people at a large enterprise participate in distinctive capabilities, paying close attention to what matters most about the work itself, they gain a collaborative proficiency that is greater than their individual skill. As we noted in chapter 3, they codify their tacit knowledge, processes, and practices into recipes that get rolled out to the entire enterprise. But, like master chefs, as people gain proficiency, they use the recipes less rigidly, more as launching points. They develop the confidence and sheer skill that comes from long experience and practiced creativity. Since they are working with other master chefs, they also gain a common frame of reference; they can act together with a range and scale that no individual artisan can match. "At Apple," writes Lashinsky, "thirteen out of fifteen topics get cut off after a sentence of discussion. That's all that's needed."[15]

Not surprisingly, one of the most tangible benefits of collective mastery is the ability to attract higher-caliber people. An organization that defines itself by what it does better than any other organization resonates with individuals who can contribute something significant. The ability to be an engineer or physicist at Qualcomm, a product designer at Apple, a platform leader at Haier, a customer-relationship manager at CEMEX, or a barista at Starbucks is more compelling than doing similar things elsewhere. On the companies' side, the cultural clarity created by collective mastery makes it easy for them to see who fits and who doesn't: Is a prospective Natura employee energized by relationship building? Does a prospective IKEA employee value frugality? If not, whatever the prospect's other professional strengths are, he or she won't be effective in that company.

In many business circles, mastery is seen as heroic and hierarchical. Junior people or functional specialists are told to pay their dues by doing whatever is necessary to meet an impossible deadline. But the goal of collective mastery should not be to lean on the efforts of the young and the dedicated. Instead, collective mastery should ultimately allow the organization to achieve its remarkable outcomes by spreading the genius to a broader base of activity. If you can accomplish that, in a sustainable fashion, then you have a truly extraordinary culture.

Deploying Your Critical Few

The temptation is great to blame your culture when the organization resists change. For not every aspect of your culture is positive. Indeed, the same attributes of your culture can have beneficial effects but also hold your company back. Figure 4-1 shows a few cultural traits that some companies have and the ways in which they manifest themselves.

FIGURE 4-1

Advantages and disadvantages of an organization's cultural traits

KEY CULTURAL TRAITS	POSITIVE IMPLICATIONS	NEGATIVE IMPLICATIONS
Engineering orientation	Technical excellence	Lack of commerciality
Command-and-control foundation	Effective and disciplined execution	Siloed thinking and limited speed to market
Pride in company's legacy	Confidence and dedication	Arrogance and complacency
Company as caretaker	Loyalty and sense of community	Sense of entitlement
Importance of personal reputation	Consensus and compliance	Excessive risk aversion

As we suggested earlier in this chapter, many executives mistrust their culture. You may not believe that your company has the kind of culture it needs. Chances are, it has several subcultures operating simultaneously, often at cross-purposes. Sometimes, these are legacy cultures from acquisitions. Other times, the subcultures are tied to specific functions, with the mandates, priorities, and cultural values associated with a profession like IT, organization development, or sales. The enterprise's overall value proposition may not have been clearly articulated, and people may not understand how their work fits with it.

If this sounds like your company, then your situation probably seems daunting. You can't live with your culture, you can't ignore it, and you can't completely change it. What, then, can you do? You can find the parts of your culture that work in your favor and bring them to the fore. There may be more value in your culture than you realize at first. One way to accomplish this is through what we call the *critical-few* approach. It was developed by a team of people at our firm, led by long-standing culture expert Jon Katzenbach.[16] The critical-few approach involves a small number of cultural elements:

- *A critical few informal leaders:* These people have the behavior you want to see more of, and you can enlist their help in spreading coherence through the company. They tend to be quietly influential, they can be strong allies in gaining coherence and guides to aspects of the system that you would not otherwise see.

- *A critical few emotionally resonant traits:* These traits are touchstones tied closely to the identity of the company. We've already mentioned many examples throughout this book: people's dedication to "insanely great" products at Apple, to customer experience at Amazon, to relationships and products at Natura, to continuous improvement at Danaher, and to frugality and leadership by example at IKEA. Behind each of these few traits, there is a story that, like many of the stories recounted in this book, exemplify your company's identity and why people should care about it.

- *A critical few behaviors that you want to spread throughout the organization:* These behaviors are ways of operating that, if everybody followed them, would help the company move forward. At CEMEX, one such behavior was the emphasis placed on closing the books on the first or second day of every month. "A lot of managers initially wondered why it was so important to do this," recalls Juan Pablo San Agustin, executive vice president of strategic planning and new business development. "They thought nothing would be lost if they did their closings on the seventh or eighth day. But we believed that having that information readily available would increase the likelihood that managers would make the right decisions. And the practice had a very high-level overseer: [then-CEO Lorenzo Zambrano] into whose email inbox all of these reports flowed."[17]

  Other behaviors might include keeping all memos to a page; eliminating the formal committee meetings where the decision was already made in the corridor beforehand ("Let's just have the 'real meeting' instead"); the inclusion of leaders from at least two separate functions for every decision made about a distinctive capability; or as former Campbell Soup Company CEO Douglas Conant once did, putting on running shoes and taking a slow walk around the grounds every day, always at different times. Knowing that he might be passing by, people got in the habit of striding along with him and raising candid questions. The critical behavior he wanted to encourage, after all, wasn't walking; it was open conversation.[18]

TOOL

Identifying Your Own Critical Few Elements

For each of these three questions, identify a critical few elements that you will bring to bear from your culture. Look for elements that line up with your identity: reflecting your value proposition and supporting the capabilities system you are building.

1. ***Who are your critical few informal leaders?*** There are two categories of people. Exemplars are role models, visibly exhibiting the set of key behaviors you want the organization to adopt. "Pride builders" are internal guides, helping you understand the culture. Both groups together should number no more than 5% of the total population of your enterprise. They are your advance guard: people who see the value of your company's move toward coherence and who are prepared to help others make a commitment. They can also help you identify the attributes and behaviors in questions 2 and 3.

	Exemplars	Pride builders
Where to find them	In roles identified as critical to building distinctive capabilities—especially those who have worked across functions to innovate or make point interventions that have added value	In roles "close to the work" with frequent opportunities to observe and influence colleagues—not necessarily through formal management positions
What they provide	Experience in translating tacit knowledge into concrete, everyday actions in ways that can be emulated by others	Insight into the reasons why people will come on board and ways to enlist their commitment
How they can serve your transformation	They act as visible role models, informally coach colleagues in similar roles, and participate (or lead) in blueprinting, building and scaling capabilities	They share practical ideas and provide feedback on the impact of the new capabilities system and the reactions of the culture

(continued)

2. *What are the critical few traits you want to highlight?* Identify a few key attributes that exemplify the best of your company's culture. (These are often the distinctive qualities as described earlier in this chapter.)

How to find them	What to look for
Ask people: conduct interviews with exemplars, pride builders, and leaders about the traits that characterize your company.	Pick traits that support the distinctive capabilities you are trying to build. For example, "empathy" in a health care or financial services company could support a new capability for designing support services that would help customers make better decisions.
Listen for stories: in formal gatherings or informally, seek out people who can recount the experience of building the new capabilities.	Pick stories of challenge, in which the company faced a difficulty in developing the capabilities it needs—and overcame that challenge.
Go back in time: surface historical perspective that is relevant now.	Look in your company's history, as we saw Adidas doing in chapter 3, for antecedents to the capabilities you are building now.
Look for artifacts: find objects that represent the aspects of culture you seek to promote.	These artifacts can include architectural features (like Natura's building), memos, product prototypes, old machines, reports, photos from key events, or anything else that symbolizes the link between strategy and execution in your company.

3. *What are the critical few behaviors that you want the organization to exhibit going forward?* These are things that a few people do regularly now; and if everyone did them, they would help close the gap between strategy and execution. Assemble a list of ten to twenty behaviors and use the following checklist to winnow them down to three or four. Pick the behaviors that give you the most "yes" answers:

Supporting the strategy	<ul><li>Is the behavior related to the value proposition or capabilities system? Will it add to their effectiveness?</li><li>Does it lead to tangible business results, especially the results you want from your capabilities?</li><li>Is it effective at or near the front line (the interface with customers)?</li></ul>

Signaling	• Is the behavior highly visible?
	• Does it require people to act in unconventional ways that will catch others' attention?
	• Is it instigated at the top leadership level?
Multiplying	• Can the behavior spread? Will it inspire others to act in similar ways?
	• Does it trigger other related behaviors?
	• Does the behavior involve networks and teaming?
	• Is it applicable to the middle ranks of the hierarchy?
Ease of implementation	• Can you describe the behavior in plain language?
	• Do people, once they're aware of this behavior, find themselves naturally falling into its practice?
	• Does the behavior fit well with one or more of the cultural traits you identified in question 2?

Having identified a critical few informal leaders, traits and behaviors, put them together with your capabilities system. For each capability, identify one or two behaviors that would make a difference. (The same behaviors can be used on more than one capability.) Create a rationale for each of these behaviors, using the attributes as a way to articulate them. Enlist your informal leaders to exemplify these behaviors and to help you convey their value to others throughout the enterprise.

Zhang Ruimin followed the critical-few approach at Haier when he introduced the idea of open innovation. He identified a trait: the company was full of people who spoke openly and candidly, especially when compared with managers at other Chinese companies. Or as he explains it, "A few people who have gone from Haier to work for other companies have written to me telling me that the biggest difference between Haier and their new company is Haier's transparent interpersonal relations." He knew therefore that at least some managers at Haier could handle it when he brought customers into their R&D process around 2012.

"When we started requiring that products be developed in cooperation with users participating in the front-end design . . . some [employees] flatly refused. Some were [passively] unwilling," he recalls. So Haier started conducting design sessions with consumers with the Dizun and Tianzun air conditioner series, where there was a stronger interest in making this new type of customer engagement work. "We told our employees in these groups that it wasn't a big deal if they failed," Zhang says, "that it was meant to be a process of trial and error." The groups turned out to be a great success, leading directly to several innovations, including smartphone-based controls and units that change color depending on the air quality in the room. This type of conversation is now becoming standard practice at Haier.[19]

The critical-few approach may seem simplistic, but its power comes from simplicity. It starts with the premise that you already have everything you need in your culture—it's just not evenly distributed. Some people are already living the right behaviors, some traits are already taking you in the right direction, and some people are already worth cultivating. With the critical few methodology, you can accelerate your company's movement to coherence. The resulting culture—a culture of emotional commitment, mutual accountability, collective mastery, and a number of other attributes unique to your company—will become a source of strength, if it isn't one already.

5

Cut Costs to Grow Stronger

Ever been to the Danaher Open? Watched the Danaher 500 on TV? No, you haven't. Industrial conglomerate Danaher doesn't sponsor big-time sporting events. That's not who they are. Nor does it conduct corporate or image advertising of any sort, and its PR is handled by investor relations. It also does without some other things you might expect to find at a company its size—like expensive office furnishings, even for its top executives.

Danaher doesn't bother with activities that don't directly support its unique value proposition—its "way to play"—in the market. Instead, it invests where its identity is, as a science and technology leader comprised of well-run businesses in selected specialized industries. It pours money, time, and management attention into building up its differentiating capabilities. For example, incoming executives, whether recruited from the outside or joining as part of an acquisition, go through an extensive onboarding program, including an elaborate introduction to the Danaher Business System and stints in several businesses within the Danaher system. This onboarding can last several months—a significant investment, especially when multiplied across many new leaders. But it ensures that when they finally take the reins of part of a business, they are equipped to handle it in Danaher's way.

Outside of its capabilities system, Danaher watches its funds carefully. It spends only what is necessary to compete in the industry sectors where it does business: scientific and technical devices, instruments, life sciences equipment, and industrial tools and components. (As we noted earlier, Danaher announced that it is spinning off this latter line of business to a separate company in 2016.) And it spends even less on everything else.

Danaher's thoughtful, disciplined use of resources is ingrained in everything it does. Like IKEA's executives, Danaher's executives treat the company's money as a precious resource over which they have stewardship. This will likely strike you as something all companies do, and of course, most companies recognize that cash is a precious resource, and most companies strive constantly for cash savings. But they manage costs separately from strategy. In fact, only rarely does a company link its expense tracking and budget process directly to its value proposition or consider the budget's effect on distinctive capabilities. If your costs are not fully driving your strategy, then what chance will you have to execute it successfully?

The answer is to place intensive interest in differentiating the costs that don't matter from the costs that do. This important distinction is a way of life in most of the companies we looked at closely. Amazon, Apple, Frito-Lay, Inditex, Lego, and Starbucks have all garnered comments about the tightfistedness of their top management. Yet all of them are willing to spend money if they think it will distinguish them. And all of them have prospered as a result.

To close the gap between strategy and execution, you need to learn to allocate costs in a different way than you have in the past. Making this transition will often be a game-changing, breakthrough experience for you. To be sure, it may be triggered by desperation. You might be in financial trouble; if you don't rapidly stem the

Danaher's Identity Profile

With headquarters in Washington, D.C., Danaher is a group of companies that produce industrial components, instruments, and other devices for scientific and technological industries, including life sciences. Since 1980, its annualized returns to shareholders are three times higher than that of the S&P Industrials Index.

In 2015, Danaher announced a forthcoming split into two companies: a focused science and technology company (which will retain the Danaher name) and a diversified industrial growth company.

Value Proposition: As a "company that builds companies," this consolidator adds value through M&A and operational excellence. These capabilities enable its member companies to be B2B category leaders, consistently offering high-quality, reliable products and solutions in what otherwise would be a diverse group of professional, medical, industrial, and commercial enterprises.

Capabilities System

- *Acquisition and integration:* Danaher succeeds by acquiring and integrating companies that will thrive with its business system, building a long pipeline of potential transactions to ensure that incoming companies fit with its capabilities system.

- *Leadership development:* Through this capability, the company engages people in learning sophisticated management practices.

- *Intensive continuous improvement (the Danaher Business System):* Applied across product and company boundaries, this capability drives operational improvement of quality, service, reliability, and cost.

- *Scientific and technical innovation:* Danaher's innovation capability is specialized for the development of precision instruments and similar products.

Portfolio of Products and Services: Danaher has grown since the mid-1980s into a conglomerate with almost $20 billion in annual revenues and forty-one businesses spanning five manufacturing sectors: dental; environmental; industrial technologies; life sciences and diagnostics; and testing and measurement.

bleeding, your survival could be in doubt. But it might also be triggered by an aspiration. You might sense that your company could do something powerful, something that you've never done before, if you deploy your cash more deliberately.

Either way, you are probably already aware of the dangers of across-the-board cuts. You have seen first-hand how they weaken companies. This time will be different. Instead of seeing growth and frugality as opposing imperatives, where cutting costs means giving up the chance to grow, you will treat every cut as an opportunity to channel investment toward building advantage.

You now begin an exercise in strategy and cost management that will empower you to bring your capabilities system to life. You will judge the value of each business, function, or project according to how it lines up with your company's value proposition and capabilities system. Distinctive capabilities will get the resources they need to realize their full potential. Everything else is up for reconsideration, as if it's a new expense. You'll gain an in-depth awareness of the expense of building, maintaining, and extending distinctive capabilities systems. You'll pay for them by taking the money from everything else. Cutting costs to grow stronger will become an essential part of your company's culture. Aligning your internal investments with your strategy will help you overcome the habits of mind built into your existing budgets, and to build up your critical capabilities, even as many of your competitors weaken themselves by cutting costs across the board.

During this exercise, you'll assemble working teams from every part of the company to identify the expenses that need to be cut. They will appreciate that they are freeing up money for reinvestment. But no working team should have the authority at this stage to spend that money. A central steering committee will be needed to oversee the decisions. The executive committee or the CEO will need to approve them, on behalf of the capabilities system of the whole company. Investment capital is precious, and there will never be enough to go around. The organization must make the best use of its funds as a whole, and that can only be done from the core.

This exercise will give your enterprise the freedom to make the right choices over the long term, choices that are required to close the gap between strategy and execution. You will make a transition from pro forma annual budgeting to strategic resource allocation. This may not be easy for you—it is very difficult for many companies. But it can be done—and the rewards are immense.

How Frito-Lay Found Funds for Growth

When Roger Enrico took the helm as CEO of Frito-Lay in 1991, the company was still developing its remarkable capabilities system, including the innovative and distinctive approach to direct store delivery that we described in chapter 2.[1] At the same time, however, its growth had stalled and it was facing strong competitive threats. Eagle Snacks, after ten years of efforts to compete with Frito-Lay, was steadily gaining market share and approaching profitability. They had just launched a successful knockoff of Doritos, one of Frito-Lay's most profitable brands. Eagle Snacks had also poached some of Frito-Lay's sales executives and was beginning to leap forward in its merchandising skill and its own effective distribution system.

Worst of all, other Eagle Snacks products were, for the first time, outperforming their Frito-Lay counterparts in blind taste tests.[2] Some observers saw this as a slap in Enrico's face. He had been the PepsiCo executive who had pioneered blind taste tests to beat Coca-Cola under the banner of "The Pepsi Challenge." He may have seen it the same way; in any case, he reacted decisively. He temporarily shut down a poorly performing plant to demonstrate how seriously he took quality issues. Like Zhang Ruimin's refrigerator-smashing at Haier (see chapter 2), this was a symbolic gesture, to make sure everyone at Frito-Lay understood that the company's reputation was at stake.

Enrico explicitly stated how the company would regain its dominant position in the industry. First, Frito-Lay would "make quality a reality": it would invest in brand-building and improving the value of its products. It would also "take back the streets": use its DSD capability to outmaneuver Eagle, stopping it in its tracks. And the company would "empower the front lines," reconfiguring the field organization to aim directly at Eagle Snacks and its nascent relationships with distributors.

But how would Frito-Lay fund the expansion of its capabilities system to do this? Enrico resolved to start by cutting US$100 million in annual general and administrative costs. This cut represented 40 percent of the expenses in these functions. Several external cost-cutting experts were invited to help, and each said that this plan was impossible. Cuts of 15 to 20 percent would be more realistic, they said. Enrico shook his head and decided that Frito-Lay would do the cuts itself. Indeed, to ensure that everyone at the company understood how serious he was, he put Charlie Feld, the developer of the merchandising handheld computer and a company hero, in charge of the effort.

As part of the cost reductions, the company laid off eighteen hundred managerial and professional people in just one day. The transition was, of course, highly traumatic for everyone involved, including those who stayed.[3] But it was also liberating for the company. The cost reduction wasn't just a layoff exercise; it removed layers of management and many unnecessary practices—enablers of incoherence—and led to a much higher level of responsiveness and effectiveness. The action also freed up money to invest in Frito-Lay's distinctive capabilities: its direct store delivery, rapid-cycle flavor innovation, consumer marketing, and high-quality manufacturing, all of which needed continuous upgrading and development.

One marketing executive from that era remembers helping a brand manager, just before the layoffs, try to make a case for adding a new factory to make Rold Gold pretzels. The category was growing and there were product shortages: "The [brand manager's proposal] for new capacity was a no-brainer. Even the guys in the finance department thought so." A meeting seeking the necessary approval from about a dozen managers went smoothly, with no questions asked. Yet the next day, the proposal was rejected, apparently for purely bureaucratic reasons. It contradicted the established schedule for new factory construction, which was laid out years in advance.

After the layoffs, the brand manager convened a repeat meeting, inviting the same group. Only a handful were left at the company. The approval processes were instantly streamlined. The request sailed through.

"While the transition felt terrifying," the marketing executive recalls, "we were all blown away, not by how little went wrong after that, but by how much went right. Eliminating 'sacred cow' initiatives was suddenly easy. Nobody had the time or the people to do anything except the top strategic priorities." Another big change was directly related to empowering the front lines; suddenly, Frito-Lay could tailor programs to specific markets and work with store managers much more easily. "We had all been held back by our own controls. Those were replaced with a sense of purpose and freedom that no one will ever forget."

Within two years, Frito-Lay's quality was back at the top of the sector, its brand equity scores were climbing exponentially, and Eagle Snacks was on its way to oblivion. Frito-Lay's other leading competitors were also hurt: Borden was forced into liquidation and Keebler withdrew from the salty-snacks category. In 1996, with no other competitor willing to buy them, Anheuser-Busch sold four out of its five Eagle Snack manufacturing plants to Frito-Lay for a fraction of their investment.[4] Frito-Lay grew its US market share from about 50 percent in 1992 to more than 60 percent in 2000, a share it has maintained or exceeded to this day. None of that would have been possible with the old cost structures, and the incoherent management practices they engendered, in place.

Where to Find Funds

Having made the important decision to connect cost to strategy, you now begin to rethink your investments in capabilities. These were probably hidden in the past within an array of functional budgets. You need to unravel those costs and sort out the implications of your current spending patterns. That is the purpose of what we call the "parking-lot" exercise. In this exercise, you list all the expenses related to the activities of your enterprise. You move them to a metaphorical parking lot. One by one, you're going to decide whether or not to let them back into the building.

As shown in figure 5-1, this spending should be broken down into four categories, depending on the type of activity and its relationship to your distinctive capabilities system.[5]

Because this analysis divides your cost by capability, rather than by division or function, it allows you to see how closely your spending is tied to your strategy. The analysis will not be easy, because most conventional expense-tracking systems don't assign costs to capabilities. Your new approach will probably raise some cultural and operational issues that, as we'll see throughout this chapter, require direct leadership attention.

The first of the four categories is *differentiating capabilities*. All these activities are related to the few things you must do better than anyone else to excel at your value proposition. They should get as much investment as they need—enough to fund the point interventions, capabilities innovation, and acquisitions needed to build them, and to fund the costs of scaling them up across the organization as well.

FIGURE 5-1

Expenses by capability type, for a hypothetical company

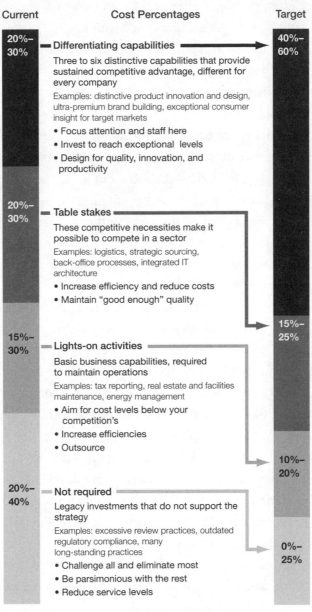

Current   Cost Percentages   Target

20%–30% ■ **Differentiating capabilities** → **40%–60%**

Three to six distinctive capabilities that provide sustained competitive advantage, different for every company

Examples: distinctive product innovation and design, ultra-premium brand building, exceptional consumer insight for target markets

- Focus attention and staff here
- Invest to reach exceptional levels
- Design for quality, innovation, and productivity

20%–30% ■ **Table stakes**

These competitive necessities make it possible to compete in a sector

Examples: logistics, strategic sourcing, back-office processes, integrated IT architecture

- Increase efficiency and reduce costs
- Maintain "good enough" quality

15%–25%

15%–30% ■ **Lights-on activities**

Basic business capabilities, required to maintain operations

Examples: tax reporting, real estate and facilities maintenance, energy management

- Aim for cost levels below your competition's
- Increase efficiencies
- Outsource

10%–20%

20%–40% ■ **Not required**

Legacy investments that do not support the strategy

Examples: excessive review practices, outdated regulatory compliance, many long-standing practices

0%–25%

- Challenge all and eliminate most
- Be parsimonious with the rest
- Reduce service levels

Note: Cost percentages are illustrative, based on extensive client experience.

Sometimes this high level of resource allocation doesn't seem fair to other parts of the company. But such outsized investment is justified by the strategic importance of differentiating capabilities. Inditex, for example, sometimes pays to air-ship its clothes to stores in line with its capability in rapid-response manufacturing and operations. CEMEX, in the midst of a financial crisis after the meltdown of the global housing market, still invested in its knowledge-sharing platform to support operational efficiency, sustainability, and innovation. And as discussed earlier, Frito-Lay's entire direct-store delivery system is much more expensive than traditional distribution methods for consumer packaged goods. But all these expenses are more than paid back in revenue and profit growth.

And then there's Starbucks. It invests in the well-being of its partners (employees) because it sees the company's relationship with them as a differentiator. Indeed, recruiting and managing a cadre of dedicated employees is one of its distinctive capabilities; it ensures that the high turnover and inattentive indifference of other retail chains will not be evident at Starbucks stores. "Why didn't every company work that way?" Michael Gill asks in his memoir about working as a Starbucks barista after losing his job as a J. Walter Thompson executive. "Because, I had to admit, it cost money. Most companies didn't want to really give their people decent health benefits . . . It cost too much money. No other company I knew gave part-time people such incredible benefits. And stock . . . The company's respect was backed up by costly investments in me and every [employee]." He says that because he didn't want to risk losing his job, he would not treat his work at Starbucks casually. The interest the company takes is an investment paid back by most of the people there.

The second category, *table stakes* (sometimes called competitive necessities), includes the activities that aren't related to your differentiating capabilities, but that you need to stay viable in your industry. Every industry has its own table stakes, which are recognized by insiders and are often unseen by outsiders. In the auto industry, if

Starbucks' Identity Profile

Based in Seattle, Starbucks is a coffee roaster and a retailer of coffee and other beverages, known for the ambience in its retail stores.

Value Proposition: Purveyor of the "third place" for conviviality—a center for human activity after home and work—this experience provider and category leader has one of the world's most iconic brands.

Capabilities System

- *Stewardship of a globally available consumer experience:* The company offers a consistently comfortable and welcoming ambiance, embedded in the store design and in practices for welcoming customers and providing amenities.

- *Distinctive delivery of product and service:* Starbucks marshals and orchestrates every element of the value chain, down to the finest detail, in its delivery of the brand promise, while customizing some elements to fit different store requirements.

- *Design and development of a premium product line:* With this capability, the company maintains its own stringent taste and quality for coffee, tea, and related food, beverages, and products.

- *Recruiting and managing a cadre of dedicated employees:* Starbucks uses a variety of means to build loyalty with its employees to ensure the store experience is delivered as promised.

Portfolio of Products and Services: Starbucks manages retail stores; sells coffee, tea, and related food and beverages in a variety of forms; and continually innovates new products for its own stores and for groceries.

---

you're not already proficient in lean manufacturing production and the implementation of digital features, even in the least expensive vehicles, you won't survive. In the chemical industry, sophisticated prowess in sourcing and procuring raw materials is a condition for entry. The same is true for specialized recruiting in the oil and gas industries, where there are recurring cycles of oversupply and undersupply of petroleum engineers.[6] User interfaces that work seamlessly across multiple platforms constitute the table stakes in the media industry, whose audiences routinely tune in through mobile phones and tablets. In health care, the table stakes include the ability to forecast demand, as the number of people needing medical attention fluctuates with various factors. Appendix D describes table-stakes capabilities in more detail for the biopharmaceutical, retail, and technology industries.

When thinking about table-stakes allocations, make sure you target the right level of proficiency: All too often, companies underinvest in some table-stakes capabilities and overinvest in others. There is always a temptation to overspend in some of these areas because your competitors do or because you always have. But while table stakes get you in the game, they do not differentiate you. Don't assume you have to spend as much as your competitors spend. Your goal is to increase efficiency and stay in the game without draining investment or attention from your differentiating capabilities.

This temptation is especially difficult to resist in rapidly evolving industries, where the list of potential table-stake activities continually grows longer as companies compete. They get caught up in an arms-race-like melee, trying to match each other's investments and prowess. In these industries, all companies start to look the same.

When Qualcomm first began to develop its CDMA technology for licensing, the company ran up against a table-stake requirement. Without semiconductor design and manufacturing capabilities (which its leaders called infrastructure), it could not sell its platform. At that time, in the 1980s, the existing computer industry was not equipped for outsourced manufacturing. So the company built its own fabrication plants, making the specialized integrated circuits needed to connect to CDMA, thus demonstrating that the manufacturing was feasible. A few years later, Qualcomm built additional factories to make handsets for digital mobile phones.

"Qualcomm essentially had to bootstrap its own industry," Dave Mock says in his book about the company, "hoping that at some point in the future, partners or joint ventures would relieve it of this necessity."[7] The company increased its factory footprint from seventy thousand square feet in 1994 to more than two million square feet in 1996.[8] The costs came directly out of earnings growth—which undermined shareholder confidence.

There were benefits, to be sure—Qualcomm controlled the product, learned from production, and got its wares quickly to the phone companies—and the company leaders considered establishing a permanent manufacturing capability. But other companies that were better equipped for this job were now emerging. The pace of change in fabrication was exhausting, and Qualcomm began losing bids to manufacturers that could handle the fabrication better. Thus, in 1998, Qualcomm's leaders decided to spin off manufacturing altogether. They sold off the last factories, which made handsets, to Kyocera in 1999.

Thereafter, Qualcomm invested in manufacturing when it had to, but always with an exit strategy. As with any table-stake activity, the company's goal was always to make the transaction as cleanly and inexpensively as possible, saving the greatest investment for capabilities that mattered more.

The third category is *lights-on activities*. These basic business costs are required simply to operate. Legal, administrative, and facilities costs often fall in this category. Lights-on activities should receive just enough cash to keep things going (which will typically be less than competitors spend and proportionately less than table stakes). These costs should be subject to strict scrutiny, constant pruning, and a continuous search for greater efficiency.

The final category is simply costs that are *not required*. These costs do not contribute to the business in any tangible way, but nonetheless show up on the income statement. There is generally more in this category than you'd expect. In extreme cases, we have seen such spending constitute as much as 40 percent of a company's budget. Almost every company will have some obvious candidates for this list: a layer of management that was once important, an internal approval process that is no longer needed, upkeep on several buildings in a country where no one is willing to decide which offices to close, or an underused corporate jet.

There may also be an array of legacy functional projects that are often created with great intentions and backed up with elaborate IT infrastructure but that no longer serve any clear purpose except perpetuating themselves. They may have come into existence to support a part of the business that required different capabilities from the rest. These initiatives may have been funded for years, fostering incoherence. This analysis gives you an opportunity to reclaim those funds for more strategic purposes.

The not-required costs are pernicious enemies of success and growth. Not only do they drain financial resources, but they also fund activity that distracts from the core work of the company and drives a wedge between strategy and execution. Realistically, no enterprise, not even the most coherent, will reduce this category to zero, but you should reduce it as much as possible. The only way to do that is to go back to your identity—and test whether each set of costs will further any part of your strategy. If the answer is no, then you may have to let go of a part of the enterprise, even if it has historic or sentimental value.

Out of the Parking Lot

The parking-lot exercise allows you to break free of the budgetary practices of the past. Year after year, in many companies, annual budgets are determined in relation to those of the previous year. They typically represent the same trajectory as in past spending, with only slight variations. Now all this is going to change. You are using this exercise to rethink your costs from a capabilities perspective, in light of your strategic priorities.

Conduct this exercise at the business unit level. In many companies, you'll need to divide the costs into subgroups, ideally organized according to the broad capability the costs seem to fit best. Assign a working team to each group, with the mandate to develop a rationale for each expense in light of its strategic relevance. Until all the working teams have made their recommendations, the senior core team can't create a holistic picture of the investments being allocated and their larger impact on capabilities. If you are a member of one of these teams, you will have to challenge everything based on your understanding of the overall company's identity and strategy, not the priorities of your part of the company. Is the activity critical to your company's value proposition and capabilities system? If so, it's part of a distinctive capability. If not, do you have to be somewhat proficient at this activity, given your industry (a table-stakes capability) or business necessities (a lights-on capability)? And if not (a capability that is not required), how close can you come to zero spending on it?

Take the time to come to an accurate view of the connections between these expenses and your strategy. Adidas' old museum of discarded shoe experiments might have seemed superfluous, but it was critical, as we saw in chapter 3, to the company's revitalization. Putting it in the not-required category might have been disastrous. On the other hand, we've seen projects occasionally defended as critical to a company's distinctive capabilities; but when examined closely, the link turns out to be mostly wishful thinking.

After cataloging all the expenses related to your differentiating capabilities, you'll bring them back in from the metaphorical parking lot and begin developing plans for their further development (like the blueprints in chapter 3). You'll usually find that your capability-building efforts have been starving for investment because so many resources have been channeled elsewhere. Then look at your table stakes. Ensure they are at necessary levels only and nothing more. Do the same for the lights-on activities. Everything remaining in the parking lot is not required: it is subject to dismissal or, at least, significant rethinking.

Occasionally, one of the table-stake or lights-on activities—and the costs that go with it—could suddenly acquire strategic importance; for instance, a telecommunications company moving into providing internet service might suddenly find that regulatory relationships demand much more attention and investment. No matter what investment you assign, however, the basic principle remains the same: the largest percentage of spending should be on your differentiating capabilities.

Coming to a final set of recommendations will undoubtedly take a bit of iteration. Each working team in turn must be prepared to help the members of the central steering committee (the core team) understand the risk or trade-offs of their cost-cutting recommendations. This information will also help the core team understand the benefits (or disadvantages) to the whole. The core team keeps track of all the ideas, maps them against the capabilities the firm needs, and makes adjustments accordingly. For example, if one working team suggests an investment in the marketing capabilities for the Far East region, the core team asks whether the company can take advantage of the scale of that capability for all product lines and perhaps for other places around the world.

Your old conversations about cost cutting were probably only loosely connected to strategy and largely focused on being fair. Your top executives worried about distributing the cuts evenly across the board so that no single group would have to change dramatically. Big cuts were made only under duress, and usually in the most visible (or immediately addressable) areas rather than the areas where there was a strategic rationale.

Now there are explicit conversations about relevance and purpose. You understand why each investment adds value, and you can thus look at all your expenses holistically and free up capital in a way you never could before. The tool "Spending Alignment" offers specific questions to help you close the gap between your company's strategy and its budgetary practices.

Spending Alignment

How close are your company's current spending practices to those the most coherent companies follow? The following questions can help you close the gap between strategy and execution:

- Are your company's current initiatives and major projects aligned with its strategy?

- Does your company avoid giving underperforming or lower-value initiatives, products, and departments funding or support that appears unjustified?

- Is your company's budgeting process well aligned with its strategic planning process?

- Does your company have clear mechanisms (e.g., the parking-lot exercise) to align its budget with its strategy?

- Does your company have funds to build the differentiating capabilities it needs to win in the market? Are these funds assigned at the center, by the entire global enterprise? Are they diverted from less critical areas?

- Does your company use clear mechanisms and criteria for channeling funding to critical initiatives or differentiating capabilities between budget cycles?

- Does your company seek cost reductions continually as part of everyday practice, rather than waiting for some major event (e.g., an acquisition) or shareholder pressure?

- When cutting costs, does your company set priorities at the enterprise level and ask business leaders to design cost reductions in line with your capabilities system, rather than using a "haircut approach" (e.g., everyone gives up 10 percent) or letting business units and functions come up with their own priorities and targets?

At www.strategythatworks.com, you can find an interactive tool that allows you to assess your company's *Fit for Growth** index, a

(continued)

quantitative measure of the strategy-to-execution gap: how clear your company's strategy is, how well its resources align with its strategy, and how supportive its organization is. You will also be able to compare your *Fit for Growth* index with that of other companies in your industry and get a sense of the areas that need most improvement.

Fit for Growth is a registered service mark of PwC in the United States.

The parking-lot exercise has other, perhaps unexpected benefits. First, it provides a tremendous release of emotional energy. Many business leaders dread the discussion of "not required" costs, but such a discussion can create much new energy. As in the Frito-Lay story earlier in this chapter, people experience the release as an escape from bureaucratic shackles and unnecessary constraints. By tackling these costs head-on and explicitly guaranteeing that you will reinvest the money in the capabilities system that you need most, you make it clear that you are not just making cuts. You are making it easier to create sustainable value.

To be sure, you'll probably spark emotionally laden resistance from the organization at first. Some executives will have to consciously stretch their comfort zones as you go through this cost-analysis process. After all, nearly every activity, whether strategically relevant or not, has a rationale behind it. Some of these sessions represent a first step in a major overhaul that could lead to the departure of colleagues.

Yet executives also recognize the value of freeing up cash. When you raise awareness of the potential of investing more in distinctive capabilities, you can catalyze a massive change of attitude. We have seen increased awareness foster a climate of mutual accountability of the sort we described in chapter 4. People become willing to look anew at reducing costs, because they know a fresh assessment will enable a more effective strategy and make the entire enterprise feel like a better place to work.

One CEO opened a parking-lot exercise by putting up a slide and saying, "Look at all these departments that are not essential to executing our strategy. Many of you are in those groups, and I'm sorry about that, but we have to be clear minded and clear thinking in what we're about to do. You can still be a hero, if you're in one of these less important groups, by creating the leanest operations possible."[9]

Another benefit of this exercise is the movement of cost allocation from functions to capabilities. As you decide where one activity ends and another begins, think outside your functional definitions. That in itself brings clarity to your decision making. When costs are tied to established functional areas, then functional leaders have an incentive to treat any cost management as a challenge to their department's value. Who can argue with sales costs, marketing costs, or costs for ensuring quality? The trade-offs between expense and strategic value are almost invisible in the functional context, and the true value of each expense is masked.

For example, in many companies, all of the investment in improving employees' skills and proficiency is consolidated within a single budget line called learning and development, which is attached to the human capital function. Seeing training as a single cost center in this way will make it hard for you to differentiate between the training that really matters to your capabilities and training that is less important. If you allocate those costs by capability, you'll know which training deserves the attention of senior leaders. They may get directly involved, as Danaher's top executives do in the company's Danaher Business System training. Other training, such as that of support staff in how to use ERP software, will be relegated to the lights-on category.

You will find that this new approach is ultimately much better for functional leaders as well. It takes them out of the familiar budgetary trap common to incoherent companies, where the leaders never get enough cash to provide what the businesses ask of them, yet don't have the time, capital, or support to innovate capabilities in the way that the business requires. In chapter 3, we described the trade-offs that functions must make in this situation, trying to meet multiple demands. Now, instead of forcing the functions into this impossible situation, the enterprise can have an open discussion about priorities, gaining insight into the way incoherence drives complexity in their company. These conversations can provide a huge relief for functional leaders who previously had to manage this problem on their own.

The parking-lot approach also replaces the conventional practice of pitting functions against each other in a pro forma way. In some companies, budget exercises routinely shortchange internally focused functions like HR while giving market-facing functions money according to last year's results. With the parking-lot exercise, there is more opportunity for mutual accountability. The rationale for cost allocation is clearer; it is expressly articulated by the management team with the overall strategy in mind. Whatever is needed to create value is more likely to gain support.

This exercise may also prompt you to look at outsourcing in a new light. Outsourcing becomes a strategic vehicle for rationalizing (and often improving) your table-stakes and lights-on expenses. In make-or-buy decisions after you've conducted the parking-lot exercise, you're not just looking for cost reductions; you're looking for a long-term relationship that will enable you to deliver these functions more effectively. When it comes to distinctive capabilities, outsourcing can still play an important role if access to talent, knowledge, or tools will be easier to gain that way. However, if you have proprietary advantages in this area, make sure your distinctive capabilities are carefully managed and protected.

Finally, the parking-lot exercise makes some use of benchmarking. In chapter 3, we discussed the perils of benchmarking. When you benchmark what other companies are doing, you risk setting yourself up to borrow practices and processes that erode your differentiation. But once you have divided your activities into these four categories (differentiating, table-stakes, lights-on, and "not required" capabilities), benchmarking becomes helpful. You can learn a great deal from the experience of other enterprises that have reduced the costs of table-stakes and lights-on activities. In particular, look for examples from companies that, like Frito-Lay, reduced their operational expenses dramatically under stress while becoming stronger in the process.

Benchmarking may also be useful for targeting where each category of costs should land financially. With differentiating capabilities, either there should be no similar examples in your industry at all or they should fall near the high end of the cost range—unless you've found your own way to deliver the capability at lower cost. Table-stake capabilities should cost no more than the industry average and hopefully less. And of course, lights-on capabilities should be at the bottom end of the cost range. Since few companies classify expenses according to their capabilities (which is why traditional benchmarks can be so misleading), it's unlikely that your competitors do. Your benchmarks will come back with functional classifications, dividing the expenses related to a single capability among, say, marketing, operations, sales, and R&D. You'll have to recategorize them so that you can translate those costs into the capabilities meaningful to you, or close-enough proxies.

A New Way of Life at Lego

There are plenty of examples of this kind of parking-lot exercise among companies that have closed the strategy-to-execution gap. One compelling example was Lego's war room, which we described earlier in the book. CEO Jørgen Vig Knudstorp set up the room in 2002, and he and a group of top managers met there daily to work through issues, redesign their operations, and figure out ways to cut costs. The give-and-take was instrumental in putting Lego on a profitable course.

One important factor was the decision to suspend growth plans until the managers had rethought their expenses. "Many of us found it very difficult," Knudstorp told *Bloomberg* reporter David Tweed, "but I thought it was fantastic because growth is like a sugarcoating on your problems. You don't see them so well when you're growing. When you're not growing you really have to drive productivity."[10]

The Lego story is worth exploring in more detail because it shows how many costs have become habitual over time and how a bit of awareness can revitalize a company. The account that follows comes from a close observation of the Lego case by our colleagues Keith Oliver, Edouard Samakh, and Peter Heckmann.[11] (Oliver is also known for being the operations expert who coined the term "supply chain management.")

There were indeed costs directly related to Lego's superior capabilities. The costs included the "Kitchen," the company's product development lab and a point of corporate pride. But not every aspect of product development was distinctive; in fact, the most costly aspects of product design were detracting from Lego's differentiation.

As a pilot program to show the value of sharp cost management, the company started with sourcing. This was linked to a distinctive capability, but primarily as a means to an end. Customers recognized the quality of Lego bricks, but did not care where the resins came from. More importantly, sourcing was not managed strategically.

> Each engineer had his or her own favorite vendors, and the company's lack of procurement compliance procedures allowed the engineers to form ad hoc relationships with suppliers—a practice that grew more problematic as the group expanded into new businesses . . . A new design might call for a unique material, such as a specially colored resin, that sold in three-ton lots. It might take just a few kilos of the substance to produce the new toy, but the company would be stuck with €10,000

($13,500) worth of resin it would never need. Ordering so many specialized products at irregular intervals from a large number of vendors left the Lego Group's procurement staff powerless to leverage the company's scale in dealing with suppliers.

As Oliver, Samakh, and Heckmann describe, chief financial officer Jesper Ovesen took charge of the sourcing pilot project:

[Ovesen's assignment was] a clear signal that this initiative was of the utmost importance. Ovesen's team believed that rationalizing the cost of the company's materials would yield savings immediately. Not coincidentally, the initiative went right to the heart of the Lego Group's innovation capability: the resins that gave the bricks their distinctive colors . . .

The price of colored resins, always a major expenditure for the company, was highly volatile. The sourcing team analyzed the prices of the raw materials and worked with a narrowed roster of suppliers to stabilize pricing. The resulting contracts made production much easier to plan. More importantly, the success of the sourcing project created a sense of optimism and the momentum to move ahead with other changes. At each cost center along the supply chain, the transition team applied its new insight: Constraints don't destroy creativity or product excellence, and they can even enhance them.

Once the benefits of the sourcing change were clear, then the new initiative had credibility, and Lego moved to a more fundamental issue: raising the creativity of product design through awareness of cost trade-offs. Designers were encouraged to recognize that extra features had to be considered part of the cost of the overall package. "Yes, you can give sparkling amber eyes to your new Bionicle space alien action figure," Oliver, Samakh, and Heckmann write, "but it may limit your choices on its claws." The new proficiency in navigating cost trade-offs was a major change for the company's product development center (the Kitchen) and was treated as a great source of pride. It was also accepted as a strategic move. Designers began to use existing elements in new ways, rather than devising new elements requiring new molds and colors.

Added interoperability in toy design now became one of Lego's distinctive features. "The best cooks are not the ones who have all the ingredients in front of them," a senior manager wrote in a memo to the Kitchen. "They're the ones who go into whatever kitchen and work with whatever they have."[12] Knudstorp says that the Lego designers "initially saw reducing complexity as pure pain, but gradually they realized that what they had seen at first as a new set of constraints could in fact enable them to become even more creative."[13]

Previously, the manufacturing function had been considered sacrosanct; its chaos was seen as part of the company's history. Oliver and his coauthors say that Lego had previously run "one of the largest injection-molding operations in the world, with more than 800 machines, in its Danish factory, yet the production teams operated as hundreds of independent toy shops. The teams placed their orders haphazardly and changed them frequently, preventing operations from piecing together a reliable picture of demand needs, supply capabilities, and inventory levels. This murkiness led to overall capacity utilization of just 70 percent." Now, however, manufacturing was treated as a table-stakes activity: essential but not distinctive. With the teams rationalizing production cycles, reorganizing the assembly lines, and outsourcing some production, the results were immense cost savings and improved manufacturing effectiveness.

Distribution was even more of a table-stakes activity—or in some cases, a liability. Lego's sales were moving online, and its delivery priorities were outmoded. Oliver, Samakh, and Heckmann explain: "The company spent a disproportionate amount of time and effort serving small shops, which drove up the costs of fulfillment substantially. Sixty-seven percent of all orders consisted of less than a full carton—an incredibly costly proposition that demands labor-intensive 'pick-packing' at the distribution center." The company cut the number of its logistics providers, immediately saving 10 percent of its transportation costs. It standardized its contracts with retailers, provided discounts for early orders, and refused to ship partial cartons.

In retrospect, all of this may seem like an obvious set of moves, but at the time, it represented a remarkable exercise in collective change: moving an entire resistant organization to a better operating model. It took tremendous management attention, and a willingness on everyone's part to confront the realities of their cost structure. The company had no choice; it had to shrink costs in these areas or it could not survive, let alone win.

Many of Lego's most innovative moves since then were made possible by these changes. Cost savings aside, the company could never have developed its Lego community or narrative skills if its leaders were still struggling with logistics and sourcing. The new approach "allowed us to again focus on developing the business, on innovation, and on developing our organization to become a much more creative place to work," says Knudstorp. "Those are luxuries we didn't have when we didn't make money and we had a supply chain that was ten to fifteen years behind the times."[14]

Rethinking Next Year's Budget

Once you've gone through the parking-lot exercise and done the blue-printing described in chapter 3, you're now set for the next quarter or the year. But you have to look to the long term as well: you need to reconsider how your enterprise conducts its annual planning and budgeting.

Within most big companies, few things are as universally loathed as the annual budgeting process. Every year, each business unit and function adjusts the previous year's budget by a few percentage points, up or down, across the board. People think about the best practices they are trying to develop and the selling, general, and administrative overhead that they need. Their efforts are not integrated into the strategy, and people typically give little or no thought to the capabilities that span functional boundaries.

Finance typically approves the budget—or doesn't—according to revenue and profit projections, not according to strategic priorities. The result of the exercise is the assignment of a percentage increase or decrease for the firm as a whole. The company might adjust the figures by taking into account new projects or imperatives, but essentially everyone uses last year's budget as a baseline. Every business unit and department thus has an incentive to show that it deserves the same budget it had before, and sometimes more. This budgeting approach orients the whole company toward repeating (or at best making incremental changes to) the often distorted spending patterns of the previous year.

Our parking-lot exercise, in itself, frees you from the tyrannical mind-set of the end-of-year budget. In that sense, it is similar to the management trend of zero-based budgeting, in which every allocation must be evaluated every year and not just carried over from the past. But zero-based analysis considers costs only in terms of functional or short-term relevance, which, as we noted earlier, can often be misleading. It doesn't distinguish distinctive capabilities from other activities, and it may shortchange critically important expenses that might take more than a year or two to come to full fruition.

Our exercise goes further. It links annual budgeting directly, and transparently, to your value proposition and capabilities system.

You reconsider your funding, every year, in light of how your priorities need to change, how your teams are innovating what they need to do, and as we'll see in the next chapter, what new funding you might need in order to shape your future.

Start this process well before the usual period—perhaps halfway through the fiscal year. Instead of asking for the usual projections and adjustments from each budget from each business unit and function, ask the groups to conduct an exercise similar to the parking-lot exercise. In this version, ask them to look closely at each line in the budget. How does this activity contribute to the company's distinctive capabilities? How does it contribute to table-stakes or lights-on activities? To what extent is the activity draining resources?

Then look ahead: How will this business unit realize its growth aspirations this year? Which capabilities will it require most? Where are the gaps between the capabilities that already exist and the capabilities it needs? What risks would the business run if it made the cuts and other changes you are suggesting?

If a capabilities-oriented budget exercise is conducted with skill and proper attention, it can often put 20 to 40 percent of a department's general and administrative costs back into play for redeployment. (You may want to target that level of savings, as Frito-Lay did, to fund your capabilities system.) It also leads each team to prioritize its activities and costs—and to drop or diminish activities that take up people's time without adding much value. Finally, the top team should consider all the requests and prioritize investments accordingly, just as they did with the original parking-lot exercise.

Over time, as you regularly conduct this exercise, it becomes a habitual aspect of your company's continuous improvement. You may want to explicitly say that the budget for each department will depend, as it never has before, on strategic alignment; therefore, if people can make a case for funding their activities as contributing to distinctive capabilities, their budget may actually increase. But they must also demonstrate how they expect to deliver. In some companies that have closed the strategy-to-execution gap, executive bonuses are tied to their ability to design, defend, and execute these investments.

You can use these budgets as guidelines for executing necessary changes. Continue to operate with your new focused mind-set, with senior team members as ambassadors throughout the rest of the enterprise. They will need to explain the rationale for cuts (and for reinvestment where that is taking place) and to listen to concerns and suggestions. You will undoubtedly continue to be challenged by events; every plan will require adaptation to meet changing realities. But those changes in allocation will henceforth be made in the context of a clear identity and rationale. You are cutting costs to grow stronger, holding and building the capabilities that support your right to win, and creating and supporting a more coherent portfolio. You start to see all your costs as investments in your future.

With facility in cost management, you have more room to maneuver. You can open the door to greater aspirations—and begin taking your company to new, more proficient levels. That's the subject of the next chapter.

6

Shape Your Future

Suppose that you are an executive leader in a highly coherent company—one that has successfully closed the gap between strategy and execution. After a few years, your company achieves sustained success. It crosses a threshold and becomes a mature competitor. Your customers, employees, suppliers, distributors, contractors, and investors are loyal to your company; you have ample reason to believe it is special. You internalize that perspective. Even though you know better, maybe you even start to believe that you can do no wrong.

You and your company are about to be tested.

Just about every successful, coherent company we studied for this book has gone through a daunting episode of self-discovery, where the organization realizes that, despite its success, it is falling prey to distraction and incoherence. Sometimes the companies have an existential crisis. Apple almost went bankrupt in 1997, Lego in 2002; CEMEX narrowly avoided insolvency in 2008, after the global financial crisis. And Starbucks, after two years of intensive growth, faltered dramatically in 2009. Each of these organizations recovered; each took its value proposition and capabilities system to new levels afterward.

If your company is mature, your aspirations are likely to grow. You are likely to see new opportunities for growth, and new ways to make an impact at a larger scale. At the same time, you are likely to face new challenges. Your size, visibility, and success make you more vulnerable to competitors—especially those with new value propositions that can disrupt your existing sector, or those that deploy different capabilities from your own. If your customers shift their preferences and patterns of behavior, the value of your own value proposition may erode. Sooner or later, every successful company reaches this point.

In chapter 2, we argued that companies can only be successful at adapting to change if they remain true to their identity—and grow from their strengths. When they reach this stage of success and maturity, many companies are tempted once more to abandon those strengths and to look for new markets or sectors. But the companies we've studied, the companies that close the gap between strategy and execution, take a better approach. Instead of reacting to change, they get out in front of it. They leverage their advantaged capabilities system, not with a string of random growth plays but by using their capabilities to sustain new kinds of growth. Like these companies, you can shape your own future in at least three distinct (and complementary) ways:

- You can recharge, innovate, and extend your capabilities system, becoming more proficient than you were before, building on your existing differentiation and making it stronger.

- You can create demand by making use of the insights you have about your customers, creating products and services that define their needs, and in the process disrupting the businesses of your competitors.

- You can step out in front of your industry and realign it around your own strengths, becoming a supercompetitor: a company whose value proposition and capabilities system define a business ecosystem around it, to its advantage.

The path from incoherence to coherence to supercompetitor status is clearly staked out. Not every company will get that far, but many will. In the rest of this chapter, we'll look at the benefits from moving along this path and how companies do it: how they recharge their capabilities system, create demand in their markets, and realign their industries.

Recharge Your Capabilities System

Why do some companies seem to know when the world is going to change? Why did Apple put cameras in every smartphone it created, while Kodak hedged its bets on digital photography and invested both in digital technology and a digital-film hybrid? Why do Zara's lines of clothing remain popular, while other apparel merchants struggle? It's not because there are smarter geniuses in the companies that win. It's because these companies adopt the discipline of looking ahead. They challenge themselves to seek out early warnings of changes that could affect their value proposition, and they adjust their strategies accordingly. When they see a challenge coming, they prepare for it in advance, before they are under duress.

They do this forward-looking activity in the context of their capabilities system. They explicitly try to anticipate changes that they might need to make in their capabilities. These changes are deliberately robust: rather than tailored for any particular prediction of the future, they are designed to be ready for any of several futures that might emerge. You could think of this approach as a coherent company's version of agility. As we noted in chapter 2, this approach avoids incoherence by grounding your changes in the strengths you have built up over time.

Apple made one of these moves when Steve Jobs returned as CEO in 1997. It cut costs to grow stronger, bringing its product line from dozens of models down to four. Jobs could not have known exactly what the future would hold—but no matter what happened next, slimming down the product line was a good move. It also had the immediate benefit of improving cash flow, a desperate need at the company.

Recharging your capabilities system is not just a matter of launching new products or services. It is a matter of expanding your ability to launch, again and again, with consistent success. Starbucks learned how to package and sell food successfully without grilling it; since gaining proficiency in that area, it has introduced many popular snacks. IKEA has learned how to create a better online presence, which represents an ever-increasing part of its business. Natura developed a new capability, incorporating environmental sustainability into its day-to-day practices, and is using its reputation for responsible rainforest commerce as a springboard for sales outside its home country. CEMEX also introduced sustainability, in a very different industry, as a way of solidifying its role as a solutions provider.

All these company leaders realized that a value proposition is never fully achieved; a capabilities system is always open to advancement. If your strategy is grounded in a pure market play—for example, you want to gain market share in a sector or expand around the world—then once that strategy is accomplished, there is no reason to move further. But if your identity is expressed in terms of what you do, and the value you create, then there are always better ways to achieve that value. You continually have reasons to advance and improve.

One company that has continually taken this principle to heart and embedded it in daily life is Haier. As we saw earlier, the company has developed an identity as a solutions provider, but has continually improved its capabilities system and the reach and scope of its value proposition: first to consistent quality, then to niche products, then to global reach, and now to digitally driven innovation and services. Each of these moves has been coherent and logical, and while Haier has occasionally stumbled (e.g., with quality problems at times in the United States), its efforts have largely been sure-footed. Its culture resolutely steers clear of complacency.

"We have felt a sense of urgency at Haier ever since we began to rebuild the company in 1984," says Zhang Ruimin. "From the start, we've felt like there was an extremely large gap between us and more established international companies, a gap we would have to overcome. The only way to survive was to pursue a path of constant self-improvement . . . That's why we have a culture of self-questioning. Everyone is always challenging their own ideas and continuously surpassing themselves."[1]

About once a decade, Haier explicitly sets out to reinvent its processes, practices, and organizational structure. The most recent such move occurred in 2013. At that time, Zhang and other Haier leaders decided that the company should be restructured as an internet-based company, assuming customers would first seek access to all its products and services online. To Zhang, this also meant that every product line should be treated as an entrepreneurial enterprise—a platform sharing Haier's capabilities and tied closely to its value proposition as a solutions provider, but open to the world in unprecedented ways.

The first step was to reshape Haier's retail operations, starting in China. Every appliance that Haier sells there is customized, with the purchaser specifying the look, feature mix, and other aspects of functionality and design, either in the store or on the web. The next move was to change the company's structure. Business platforms were unmoored from restrictions on hiring or recruiting. Half the senior executive positions were eliminated, and the rules about who could work on a platform, or share information, were dramatically loosened. Anyone overseeing a product had the authority to decide who else to involve, including people outside the company, as if each platform were a start-up. "As part of this change," Zhang says, "more than four thousand employees who worked for the company were unemployed." Many of the newly unemployed were quickly invited to reapply, but this time for entrepreneurial positions where they could build businesses under the Haier brand. "We know of no other Chinese company of our size that has done this," Zhang says.[2]

To Zhang, this dramatic experiment is a way of overcoming the company's own complacency about its capabilities. Instead of managing and controlling product development, the goal is to become more openly creative and innovative: to invite opportunities from anywhere and everywhere. "Some [of our collaborators] aren't interested in joining [as staff]," says Zhang, "preferring to stay outside in society, partner with the company, and use our platform for pioneering work." To him, this level of openness is a starting point for creativity. A platform leader is now like an impresario, inviting great craftspeople, from inside and outside the company, to participate in designing Haier's next line of products and services. Among the first products to be developed this way were the successful Tianzun air conditioners described in chapter 2.

Your company may not want to go as far as Haier has gone, but you can emulate the most important thing Haier did: To allow your distinctive capabilities to evolve repeatedly without losing your focus. Most of the other companies we studied have similar stories to tell. IKEA expanded its capabilities system as it expanded around the world. Danaher expanded its capabilities system to fit the scientific and technical businesses that became the heart of its enterprise starting in the early 2000s. The opportunities for growth increase as your companies mature, but only if you can figure out ways to expand your capabilities system: to make it accomplish more, and handle more, while staying essentially true to the same identity.

Create Demand

Nearly all companies strive for growth and expect to find it in the world outside. Coherent companies can become skilled at creating demand from the insights they generate themselves. These are the companies that created online music and video stores (Apple), the self-serve retail format (IKEA), and wireless broadband (Qualcomm)—all at mature stages of their company's evolution. Like any successful company, they pay close attention to customers. But they don't limit their efforts to providing what customers ask for, or figuring out what customers are going to ask for and providing that. Instead, these companies also provide what no one will ever ask for, until it exists. They do this by looking closely at their capabilities system and asking themselves something that all companies should ask themselves when considering growth: "What is needed in the world at large—that only we can offer?"

The IKEA slogan for this continual growth effort is "Staying Relevant. Staying Ahead."[3] The enterprise has continually adopted anthropological methods for understanding the people who shop in its stores, particularly the stores far from its home in Northern Europe. In mid-2015, IKEA announced that it was dramatically increasing its "home visits"—house calls made by staff for research purposes—from six hundred or so per year worldwide to about a thousand per year in the United States alone.[4] "The more far away we go from our culture, the more we need to understand, learn, and adapt," says Mikael Ydholm, who heads research at IKEA of Sweden.[5]

As an extension of these methods, IKEA has put cameras (with permission) in people's homes in Stockholm, Milan, New York, and Shenzhen. The IKEA identity gives it privileged access; its employees are trusted to enter people's homes or even to install video cameras there, because customers feel that IKEA has their interests at heart. A company with less privileged access would be regarded as an intruder. It is also significant that among the visitors are store managers and senior executives; this is a visible demonstration of the depth of IKEA's interest.

One product that came out of IKEA's new research is the Knapper: a freestanding mirror with a rack for clothes and jewelry, making it easier to put together an outfit the night before work and avoid stress in the morning. In China, another change involved new sample rooms consistent with the local custom of sitting on the floor, with sofas as a backrest. However, the enterprise didn't redesign its sofas for the Chinese market. "The IKEA model, remember, is volume, volume, volume," writes Beth Howitt in a *Fortune* article about the enterprise's global expansion.[6] "It needs vast economies of scale to keep costs low, and that means creating one-size-fits-all solutions as often as possible."

The company continually refines its means of understanding customers—not through conventional market research, but by improving its access to people, placing itself in the same frame of mind and developing a better feel for the customers' wishes, frustrations, and attitudes. In recent years, for instance, the chain has developed more sensitivity to the needs of young adults and single adults of all ages. People who grow older without children tend to live in small urban apartments, and their social lives and homes are very different from those of the families and students who constituted IKEA's original core market.

This activity—creating demand—doesn't replace recharging your capabilities system. The two activities complement each other. But they place different demands on your company. In recharging your capabilities system, you set out to learn more about your capabilities—to see how you might expand your horizon. In creating demand, you set out to learn as much as you can about your customers' potential, and how you might contribute to expanding *their* horizon.

CEMEX, the global cement manufacturer and ready-mix concrete provider from Mexico, has done a great deal to expand its customers' horizons. This is a specialized group of customers: construction companies, municipality leaders, and do-it-yourself homebuilders throughout the world. At first glance, it might seem that CEMEX's opportunities to create demand with them are limited. Cement is a commodity product if ever there was one. It is a bulky raw material, delivered in giant bags to construction crews, and it all looks roughly the same. It is a popular product—the key element in concrete, by far the most widely used building material in the world. Three tons of concrete are poured each year for every person on earth.[7] In a literal sense, cement and concrete form the foundation of civilization. Whoever can provide it at the lowest price would seem to have an unbeatable edge.

To distinguish itself, CEMEX began to delve into the reasons people use cement in the first place. For example, thousands of people of modest means throughout Latin America build their houses one concrete room or story at a time. Their flat roofs often have black metal bars, called rebar, sticking up as anchors for the next vertical addition, while the homeowners save up enough to pay for the construction.

In 1998, CEMEX introduced its Patrimonio Hoy program. (The name means "Property Today.") The program helps lower-income families build homes in relatively little time by arranging credit through microfinance loans, selling building materials at low prices, storing the materials safely, and guiding customers through regulatory hurdles and basic architecture. Nobody had done this before at such a scale, and the program opened up an idea among Mexican homeowners and owners of small businesses; they could aspire to a more rapid improvement in their way of life.

A few years later, CEMEX made a similarly creative move on behalf of its independent retail distributors. It introduced a new franchised retail brand called Construrama, which transformed a string of dusty outlets frequented by bricklayers into stores with consumer appeal; the new stores could better compete against foreign market entrants. The first Construrama stores opened in 2001, offering bagged cement, bricklaying tools, rebar, and other ancillary products for builders, contractors, and do-it-yourselfers. The stores, which shared marketing practices and an orange, blue, and white store logo and design, became local gathering places for people interested in home improvement.

. CEMEX applied the same logic to another major customer group: local city and town officials across Latin America. Their communities needed highways, ports, and airfields, but the officials didn't always know how to plan, organize, and manage major infrastructure projects. This challenge led the company to establish many innovative programs, like the design of entire rapid-transit bus systems. "Our capabilities helped us orchestrate infrastructural offerings in a way that others cannot," explains Luis Hernández, executive vice president of organization and human resources. "For example, you might have a municipality with good tax revenue, but they don't know how to structure a project, get the permits or make a good decision about where to put in a road, a bridge or a public housing project. If we can help orchestrate all this, then we can provide value."[8]

No customer asked for any of these solutions. CEMEX came up with them through its privileged access to its customers, and its attention to their interests. For instance, the municipal consulting practice was based on the realization that leaders of communities in emerging markets are eager for help but not sure whom to trust. They are more likely to pay attention to guidance from a company they know, rather than a commodities-oriented company or a global development agency like the World Bank.

In the past, CEMEX had moved managers rapidly around its territories to share their experience and help them advance. Now, it encourages managers to stay in one location longer, to build stronger relationships with local customers. The customer relationships that CEMEX has built, starting in the late 1990s, became a primary source of stability for the company during the extremely difficult years between 2008 and 2010, when the financial crisis particularly affected construction industries around the world. In short, rather

CEMEX's Identity Profile

With headquarters in Monterrey, Mexico, CEMEX is a global leader in the building materials industry.

Value Proposition: CEMEX is a global solutions provider, offering builders and municipal leaders a portfolio of cement and concrete products and guidance on how to use these products effectively.

Capabilities System

- *Industry-leading operational effectiveness:* CEMEX continuously improves its logistic and operational practices—a critical capability in managing and moving building materials.
- *Sophisticated knowledge sharing dedicated to customer problems:* Backed up by technological innovation and a highly supportive culture, this capability gives CEMEX the information it needs to disseminate solutions in diverse locales.
- *Building of long-term customer and community relationships:* Through in-depth consultation and relationship building, CEMEX obtains unique insights into customer needs and erects barriers to entry for competitors.
- *Solutions-oriented innovation:* The company excels at launching new products (e.g. energy-efficient cement), services (infrastructure maintenance and 24/7 load delivery), and design offerings (new forms of concrete pavement) that address customer concerns.
- *Proficiency in sustainability-related building materials:* This capability lowers costs and creates new opportunities for environmentally conscious construction.

Portfolio of Products and Services: CEMEX provides cement, aggregates, ready-mix concrete, specialty concrete products, and building and infrastructure solutions to individual customers, institutions, and communities worldwide.

than seeking to increase its market share as a commodity producer, selling largely on price, the company created new demand that it was uniquely positioned to capture.

The essence of creating demand was famously expressed in 1971 by Alan Kay, the former chief scientist of Xerox Palo Alto Research Center, who pioneered the Smalltalk programming language. "Don't worry about what anybody else [meaning any of your competitors] are going to do," Kay said. "The best way to predict the future is to invent it."[9] That maxim was updated recently by Kevin Plank, the founder of Under Armour, who has a sign in his office saying, "[The] best merchants are the ones who dictate cool, not those who try to predict it."[10] This level of confidence comes naturally in companies that put capabilities first, because they gain privileged access to customers, and just as importantly, they develop the acumen to make sense of what they see.

Realign Your Industry

The ultimate payoff for becoming and staying coherent is a position of market leadership. Companies that close the strategy-to-execution gap can become the centers of their own ecosystems, changing the structure of the industries around them to advance their own position. When companies accomplish this, they become what we call supercompetitors.

A supercompetitor is a company that gains an insurmountable advantage by realigning a broader group of companies around its own value proposition and capabilities system. You can recognize a supercompetitor by its influence over customers, talent markets, competitors, other companies in the industry, and shareholders. For example, Amazon has realigned the book publishing industry. Any individual can now self-publish a book with almost the same physical quality and reach that a conventional book publisher has.

This newfound capability is changing the basic value proposition in the book trade; publishers now compete primarily on editorial and marketing skill, where Amazon has inferior capabilities, rather than on access to audiences. McDonald's in its heyday inspired dozens of other restaurant chains. Starbucks is doing the same today. Qualcomm's innovations realigned other telecommunications companies around the standards it fostered. Supercompetitors are not studied and copied because of their capabilities alone, but because of their influence on other companies around them.

As Thomas Hubbard, management professor at Northwestern's Kellogg School of Business, has pointed out, supercompetitors are particularly successful in industries where capabilities systems are scalable: where they can be applied to more and more products and services.[11] For example, Starbucks and IKEA benefit from their ability to replicate their distinctive capabilities in locations around the world. By contrast, a high-end premium restaurant, founded by an artisanal chef, may thrive in one or two places. But its capabilities, which include procuring local ingredients, creating menus that change from day to day, and personalized marketing and service to a local clientele, cannot be scaled as easily.

At any time, in any given industry, there may be one, two, or several supercompetitors. Just as beavers and earthworms—species known as ecosystem engineers—transform their environment to better meet their needs, these new market leaders act, bit by bit, to turn industry dynamics to their advantage. As they grow larger and yet more differentiated from other companies, their value proposition becomes more successful. Their success allows them to invest more heavily in their capabilities system, enhancing what they do well and expanding into new markets successfully. Other companies find it difficult to compete with them directly, so they become the only company competing in their industry with their particular value proposition and capabilities system.

This momentum is often accelerated through mergers and acquisitions. Companies use M&A to bring in products and services that have languished elsewhere, but that will thrive with them. They also divest businesses that don't benefit from their own capabilities. Over time, all of this gravitational pull can realign an industry around its most coherent companies, those whose capabilities align most closely with their strategy. Many industries thus evolve toward a new equilibrium in which a few supercompetitors, each with a singular value proposition and a bespoke capabilities system to match, have carved up the market among them. These companies do different things well, and therefore, even though they're in the same industry or sector, they each attract a different part of the market to their "capabilities cluster" (see figure 6-1).

FIGURE 6-1

How industries evolve to a new equilibrium

Each of the three capabilities clusters in this industry has a dominant supercompetitor. Other companies (the smaller circles) try unsuccessfully to compete across the cluster boundaries. These smaller companies may ultimately become acquisition targets and be swallowed up by the supercompetitors.

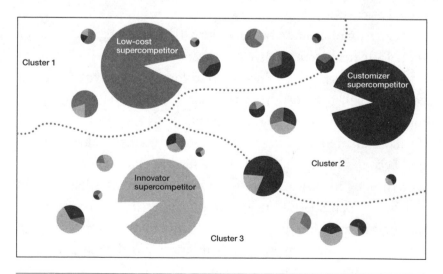

At this point, a virtuous cycle comes into play. The most highly skilled prospective employees are drawn to the supercompetitor because they know that more focused enterprises make better use of their talents and interests. The most proficient suppliers and distributors also find themselves more attuned to supercompetitors, which often invite them to play a strategic role in an environment where their work is valued highly. This adds to the success of these companies, which adds to their investment capital, which adds to the attraction. They become iconic names, at least within their industry: Apple, Frito-Lay, Haier, IKEA, Qualcomm, and Starbucks are among them.

Being a supercompetitor does not mean staying within one industry. Many coherent companies, including Amazon.com, Apple, Haier, IKEA, and Qualcomm, apply the same focus to several product or service categories. The single most important thing that enables a company to become a supercompetitor is its orientation to a few capabilities that work together. Supercompetitors have specialized around capabilities, not functions or products. They take advantage of the economics inherent to capabilities, which give them more leverage than mere economies of scale. The IT and human capital costs alone to support some of the great capabilities described in this book can run into millions or tens of millions of dollars. Therefore, the benefits accrued by coherent players are significant, and the industry evolves along with that.

One powerful example of this kind of industry evolution has occurred in consumer packaged goods (CPG). In the early 1990s, the CPG industry was dominated by large, diversified enterprises selling food, beverages, and personal-care products. Unilever, Procter & Gamble, Kraft, Colgate, Nestlé, and Sara Lee each owned a tremendous range of brands and business lines. Kraft, for example, made dairy-case products (including its own branded cheese and Philadelphia cream cheese), frozen foods (DiGiorno pizza), chocolate (Cadbury), chewing gum (Trident and Chiclets), and sweet and salty snacks (Oreo cookies and Ritz crackers among them).[12] Such different types of foods required a wide range of capabilities to produce and market. Unilever, Procter & Gamble, and Sara Lee were even more diverse. They thrived, nonetheless, because the benefits of scale gave them lower costs in back-office functions, broader access to distribution channels, and the deep pockets needed for expensive network television advertising.

But these advantages did not last. Starting in the 1990s, thanks to factors like more diverse consumer tastes and more accessible information technology, the barriers to entry dropped for smaller, more focused CPG competitors. Companies like Cabot Creamery, Amy's Kitchen, Godiva Chocolates, Green Mountain Coffee, and many others in North America and Europe found it easier to develop a following. These companies promoted their brands through the internet, avoiding the costs of television advertising altogether. The largest chain retailers, including Walmart, began to cultivate them. In this new world, the old, diversified incumbents found that their complex collections of loosely related brands and products were too unwieldy to sustain, and the old benefits of scale and size became liabilities.

So the large CPG companies began reworking their strategies. They each picked a group of categories where they could compete best and doubled down on these areas. The firms acquired other businesses that matched their strategies and shed businesses that didn't fit. Since the late 1990s, largely through mergers, acquisitions, and divestiture, the average number of segments per company has dropped by more than 25 percent, going from 4.3 segments on average in 1997 to 3.1 segments in 2015—as shown in one study that looked at fifteen such cases. The average company size in this industry has also decreased. Just about every CPG manufacturer has been affected.[13]

A map of the industry, now reorganized around capabilities systems, is barely recognizable from one of a decade ago. For example, in late 2014 and early 2015, Procter & Gamble spun off a number of well-known but isolated businesses: Iams pet food to Mars, Duracell batteries to Berkshire Hathaway, and Clairol, Wella and Covergirl cosmetics to a new business that would combine with Coty.[14] A new global snack company called Mondelez, spun off from Kraft, also contains former parts of Cadbury, Nabisco, and Danone. Mondelez's formerly disparate cookie and cracker product lines can now all take advantage of the same capabilities system, which relies on fast flavor innovation and a front-of-the-store distribution capability similar to that of Frito-Lay. Much of the rest of the old Kraft has combined with Heinz (under a deal brokered by Berkshire Hathaway) to become a source of processed and prepared foods: for example, packaged macaroni and cheese, condiments, and salad dressings. These products are sold primarily in the center of the supermarket, using different capabilities in distribution, brand marketing, and ongoing cost management (especially given the low growth of these categories). Nestlé, meanwhile, is morphing into a nutritional food, beverage, and cereal company, with former parts of Pfizer, Gerber, Novartis, Jenny Craig, and Ralston Purina under its umbrella. The old packaged-meat business from Sara Lee was temporarily renamed Hillshire Brands before being absorbed into the giant chicken producer Tyson Foods. (For an online diagram of the dynamics of CPG industry realignment, see our book's website: www.strategythatworks.com.)

Something similar has happened in a variety of other industries, including aerospace and defense, automobile rentals, and health care. Johnson Controls announced in mid-2015 that it was splitting into two separate companies with very different capabilities systems—one for auto interiors and car seats, and the other for batteries and climate-control equipment.[15] In the oil and gas industry, ExxonMobil and BP announced in 2014 that they would separate unconventional shale operations from their traditional operations. ConocoPhillips, Marathon, Murphy Oil and Total divested their downstream (refining and retail) operations so they could concentrate on oil and gas exploration; and oil and gas and chemical companies have generally reoriented themselves around more focused lines of business where they have the requisite capabilities to succeed.[16] In each case, the better fit between products and capabilities gave the spun-off entity more of a competitive edge. In all of these cases, the industry is realigning around supercompetitors, each one carving out an area where their value proposition and custom-made capabilities system allow them to dominate. This industry evolution unleashes imagination, innovation, and new forms of consumer insight that would have been far less likely under more-diverse enterprises.

One new competitor emerging in consumer packaged goods is Jacobs Douwe Egberts (JDE), a coffee business that consolidated parts of two former market leaders. Douwe Egberts was spun off from Sara Lee; Jacobs from Kraft. Under their old corporate parents, these businesses had never fully realized their potential. They fell within a broader umbrella structure, adding their needs to those of other members of the diverse portfolio, with only a small part of the overarching capabilities system relevant to them. Now, Douwe Egberts and Jacobs are part of the world's largest pure-play coffee and tea company. One of their main competitors will be Starbucks, which traditionally would have been seen as belonging to a different sector. JDE's biggest challenge is to build and refine the capabilities needed to maintain and grow its new position.

When thinking about strategy, executives often focus on the constraints of the industry around them—including well-established competitive positions and traditional sectors. In that context, the emergence of supercompetitors may seem like yet another threat to your existing business. But by looking ahead to the changing landscape of your industry, you can rethink your portfolio in a more transformative way. You can consider in advance how you could win if your industry changed in the same way that the CPG industry did, and you can put your attention squarely on the things your company does best, as a better platform for growth. Though focusing on a small group of capabilities may seem to narrow your scope, it gives you a much more clearly defined, stronger position in the sectors you choose and far more influence on the markets you care about. It gives you control over your destiny.

(The tool "Supercompetitor Workshop" outlines specific ways you can spur the leaders in your company to think in this distinctive, long-term direction.)

TOOL

Supercompetitor Workshop

A supercompetitor workshop is a powerful way to get the leadership team of an already successful company to think about taking control of the evolution of its industry. It can be conducted as a two-day session with an executive team: C-suite leaders, heads of main business units, the head of strategy, corporate development leaders, and heads of major functions (sales, marketing, HR, IT). The objectives are as follows:

As with the exercises in chapter 2, this session gives you a clearer sense of the value proposition and capabilities system that will serve you best. It goes further, however, because it helps you establish a supercompetitor value proposition: where you choose an area of your industry in which you can align other players to your leadership.

In an environment relatively unconstrained by day-to-day challenges, these four steps will spur your management team to think creatively about how to shape the future of your company and how to become a supercompetitor.

1. *Self-evaluation:* Examine your company's key strengths as they stand today, and compare them with your competitors' present strengths. Assess whether your unique capabilities are aligned with your strategy or whether there is a gap between your strategy and the execution of those capabilities.

2. *Supercompetitors and their capabilities:* Look at your company and competitors through a coherence lens. Brainstorm how value will be created in your market in five or ten years and how various value propositions might interact.

(continued)

3. *Comparison and gap analysis:* Consider your own company's potential in the world you imagined in step 2. Talk about where your company can have a right to win, in light of the capabilities you already have or can build.

4. *High-level roadmap:* Develop a consensus around the best approach for your company, and talk through a blueprint-like prospectus for how you might get there, including potential M&A opportunities.

FIGURE 6-2

Taking control of industry evolution: a supercompetitor workshop

SELF-EVALUATION	• How coherent are you today? • What are your key strengths? • What are your competitors doing?
SUPERCOMPETITORS AND THEIR CAPABILITIES	• How will the industry evolve around its potential supercompetitor models? Which are likely to prevail? • Which businesses will be traded to facilitate this new structure? • Which value-creation opportunities will be available in the future? • How attractive will they be (high level)? • What capabilities would a potential supercompetitor need to have in order to thrive?
COMPARISON AND GAP ANALYSIS	• Which supercompetitive model could fit your company best? • How big is the capabilities gap you would need to bridge . . . and could it be bridged? • Where will some of your competitors likely end up?
HIGH-LEVEL ROADMAP	• What's the way ahead? How can you best position your company in this new structure? • What capabilities need to be strengthened, and should they be linked into a system? • Who are your true competitors? • What changes to your portfolio (and the portfolios of other companies) might facilitate your desired future? • What sequence of moves (including M&A deals) could help make this happen?

Bold and Unafraid

"The greater danger for most of us lies not in setting our aim too high and falling short, but in setting our aim too low and achieving our mark," said Michelangelo.[1] The companies we celebrate in this book, and others like them, have managed to escape that fate.

They did it through leadership. Indeed, we would argue that the most critical quality in business leadership today is the ability to consistently close the gap between strategy and execution—or, better yet, to operate as if there is no gap. We are reminded of Warren Bennis' famous comment: "Managers are people who do things right and leaders are people who do the right thing."[2] This is often taken to mean, "leaders do strategy while managers execute." But in our view, the best leaders do both together (and we think Bennis would agree).

Some executives, focused on "doing the right thing," think they can delegate "doing things right." But this isolates them from the source of their company's strengths. Without that grounding, they may try many different approaches to strategy—growth strategies, M&A strategies, cost strategies, portfolio strategies, and innovation strategies—and never land one that truly fits their company. These are the executives who say, as we saw in chapter 1, that they have little confidence in their strategy, that their strategy is not understood across the organization, and that they lack the ability to execute it.

In our experience, great strategy and execution can't take place in isolation from each other. The two are closely linked. Great execution leads to better consideration of strategic issues because top executives understand what their company does well, and where it can gain in prowess. Similarly, great strategy leads to better execution because everyone in the organization understands where it is going and has the focused support and collaborative guidance to develop the highly sophisticated capabilities they need to get there.

The most important single catalyst is leadership. In our experience, great business leaders embrace the idea of strategies that work—strategies that connect the right destinations with the organization's current and future capabilities. They ask the tough but necessary questions about value creation:

Who do we want to be?

What is our chosen value proposition?

What can we do amazingly well that no one else can?

What other capabilities do we need to develop?

What path do we choose to get there?

By asking tough questions like these, top executives draw out an understanding of their company's identity—and lead the translation of that identity into everyday practice. They foster it in the enterprise's culture. They marshal resources in support of this identity. And they prepare the ground for taking their company to the next level. All this they do boldly, with the confidence that comes from having the right to win in the markets they have chosen and the modesty that comes from openness to the world at large.

This is an easier and more natural path than many people realize. It requires being bold and unafraid in the face of opposition. But that is a better way to live than always being chastened by conventional wisdom or the endless barrage of separate challenges from customers, investors, and employees.

Apparently, there are very few top executives who have mastered this type of leadership. In a survey of nearly seven hundred executives across a variety of industries, conducted by our firm in 2013, we asked respondents to rate the effectiveness of the top leaders of their companies. How many excelled at strategy? How many excelled at execution? The results are shown in figure 7-1. These

FIGURE 7-1

Top leaders' effectiveness at strategy development and execution

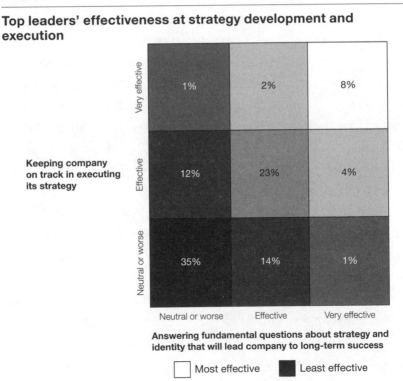

Keeping company on track in executing its strategy

	Very effective	1%	2%	8%
Effective	12%	23%	4%
Neutral or worse	35%	14%	1%
	Neutral or worse	Effective	Very effective

Answering fundamental questions about strategy and identity that will lead company to long-term success

☐ Most effective   ■ Least effective

responses are sobering: only 16 percent of top leaders are very effective at either strategy or execution (the combined top row and right-hand column). Only 8 percent were very effective at both (the white square), while 63 percent were rated neutral or worse on at least one dimension (the five darkest squares).[3]

But there is heartening news in one finding. More than half of the most effective people, that group of 16 percent at the top right, are skilled in both strategy and execution. This suggests that among the rest of us, those who become better strategists will probably gain skill at execution as well—and vice versa. Perhaps experience with distinctive capabilities expose businesspeople to both types of proficiency.

This correlation reflects the increasing recognition that great leaders must and can excel at both strategy and execution. And it suggests a way to develop that kind of leadership for your company. First, define the executive skills your leaders will require to win in your industry sector, given your company's particular value proposition and capabilities system. Second, set up opportunities for people to learn to master those skills, individually and collectively. Third, put your leadership on the line, and master and model those skills yourself, for the sake of the winning position that your enterprise deserves.

The five acts of coherent leadership described in this book (commiting to an identity, translating the strategic into the everyday, putting your culture to work, cutting costs to go stronger, and shaping your future) provide an opportunity to accomplish this. Think of them as a chance to create an engine of growth both for yourself personally and for the company.

For each of the acts of coherent leadership, there is a personal analogue that applies to the individual leader. For example:

Commit to an identity. The company differentiates itself and grows by being clear-minded about what it does best and sticking to its choices. This identity comprises the value proposition, distinctive capabilities, and portfolio of products and services all fitting together.

As a leader, you become a symbolic figure, a model of that commitment. You have something powerful to sell: a message about identity and a fundamental conviction that you need to stay with this identity over time. You demonstrate the courage of those convictions, recognizing that many will see this strategy as a leap of faith and that they will require your leadership to stay the course and see the benefits along the way.

Translate the strategic into the everyday. People blueprint, build, and bring to scale the capabilities that will deliver the company's value proposition. They do this in an original and effective way that transcends functional boundaries.

As a leader, you translate the strategic into the personal. You allow yourself to "get your hands in the mud," as Starbucks CEO Howard Schultz puts it.[4] You become the architect of the blueprint and the chief of builders. In these roles, you operate at a fine-grained-enough level of detail that you can see, sense, and touch the details of your capabilities system. But you also raise your view high enough that you clearly see how all your global capabilities fit together. Two kinds of perspectives, farsighted and nearsighted, are needed from you personally, and you can only develop them—and teach others to follow your example—if you are directly involved, at least to some major extent, with building and deploying your company's most important capabilities.

Put your culture to work. The company continually celebrates and leverages its cultural strengths. The people of your enterprise find it easy to think and act strategically because doing so fits with the "way we do things around here."

As a leader, you are infused with your company's culture. You are a primary champion of emotional commitment. You practice mutual accountability; everyone's success is important to you. Through teaching and learning, you devote yourself to the cultivation of collective mastery. You do all this in a way that matches the unique cultural attributes of your company, the attributes that set it apart, which are grounded in its capabilities system. You don't act like you come from a remote corner office; you act like you are one with the company's culture.

Cut costs to grow stronger. Your company prunes what doesn't matter to invest more in what does. It consistently allocates its resources with an eye toward strategic priorities.

As a leader, you do the same with your personal resources, particularly your time and attention. Are you devoting enough to the strategy and its requisite capabilities system? Or are you squandering too much time and attention on immediate demands, responding to everybody else's idea of what is important?

Shape the future. Having reached maturity, the company regularly reimagines its capabilities, creates demand, and realigns its industry on its own terms. Rather than being defined by external change, it has become a supercompetitor, in a position that attracts others to a world that it controls.

As a leader, you are one of the first to experience the constant challenge of external change. You can muster the fortitude (and humility) to recognize when change in yourself is required. You build an extremely capable team, knowing that ultimately the future will depend on developing the next generation of leaders.

In all of this leadership development work, your primary constraint is your own skill, and that of your colleagues. The next tool provides questions and behaviors that can help you and others in your company further develop these skills.

You will, of course, find many barriers, making it difficult to get answers to these questions or pursue these behaviors. You might be held back by ingrained incoherence: well-established capabilities that don't fit together, with champions who weren't involved in developing the strategy and compete with each other for investment. Another impediment may be an operating model where

TOOL

Questions and Behaviors for Leaders

The five acts	Leader questions	Leader behaviors
Commit to an identity	• Are we clear about the fundamentals of our strategy: who we are, who we're going to be, and how we choose to create value in the marketplace? • Are we investing in the capabilities that really matter? • Do most of the products and services we sell fit with our capabilities system? • Do we have the right to win in our chosen markets?	• Pursue healthy growth and stop chasing market opportunities where you have no right to win. • Be a role model for commitment to your chosen identity. • Make disciplined strategy and implementation choices. • Pay visible attention to efforts to build and deploy distinctive capabilities. • Take every opportunity to clearly communicate the identity and to share your conviction that the chosen path will lead to success. • Reward those who commit and confront those who don't.
Translate the strategic into the everyday	• How does each capability help us create and capture value? • How do the capabilities mutually reinforce one another? • What are the measures of our success? • What are the immediate gaps we need to fill, and how will we advance our capabilities over time?	• Focus on what your company does better than anyone else rather than on what it has (its brand and assets). • Think and talk capabilities rather than functions, encouraging all to transcend those boundaries. • Be close enough to the execution to understand your capabilities system in detail while always referring to the intended long-term blueprint. • Be the final arbiter, adjudicating on any implementation trade-offs that compromise your strategy.

(continued)

Put your culture to work	• Who are the critical informal leaders who can help most in committing to and living our chosen identity? • What are the critical few emotionally resonant traits of our culture that tie most closely to our chosen identity? • What critical few behaviors should we spread throughout the organization?	• Consistently and actively describe and live the critical few behaviors, and champion the traits of the company culture that reinforce your strategy. • Champion emotional commitment. • Foster mutual accountability among functions and business units. • Learn and teach to champion collective mastery and advance your own personal growth.
Cut costs to grow stronger	• How much of our expense budget is invested in our distinctive capabilities? • What current initiatives and projects are aligned to our strategy? Which are not? • How do our budgeting and continuous improvement processes align with our strategy?	• Be clear about what cost areas are critical to your capabilities system and invest in them visibly. • Be equally clear about the role of all other expenses. • Reduce investment in non-critical areas by setting aggressive cost targets. • Practice coherence by ensuring your own time and attention are devoted to what is most critical.
Shape your future	• How can we recharge and extend our capabilities system to confront change? • How can we leverage our customer relationships to better meet their known and unknown needs? • How can we step out in front of our industry to realign it around our strengths?	• Champion the aspiration to become a supercompetitor, and challenge your colleagues to define a viable path • Stop constantly reacting to market volatility but rather use change to further your identity • Invest in developing leaders and successors who share the same ambition

functions provide similar support or technologies for a wide range of businesses, which all demand different capabilities. Some members of the executive team or board may think that focusing on a single capabilities system or identity is too risky or difficult. Your company's established rewards and incentives may not yet align with your value proposition, or with the need to close the strategy-to-execution gap. And most of the time, there are probably too many things to do. In the melee of activity and requests, you can easily lose sight of the most important goal: to commit to an identity that can sustain your company and enable it to win, time after time.

But all of these barriers can be overcome—in fact, the five acts of unconventional leadership naturally lead an organization to overcome them. It may not be easy to start on this path, but it's a very rewarding path, and we know of no other path as reliable as this one.

Ultimately, the question of leadership is personal. Nearly every CEO that we've met has great aspirations to change the game, move beyond the constraints that his or her organization faces, and build the legacy that leaves years and years of growth.

Living with these five acts of leadership will no doubt turn people into well-rounded leaders—people who are comfortable with strategy and execution. They encourage a certain amount of curiosity about the world and are willing to think about strengths and weaknesses: their own and those of their enterprise. The practice of these five acts is an act of leadership development in itself.

We recognize that this approach represents a leap of faith. You have to be bold and unafraid to make it. It requires the courage of your convictions. But it is not a leap into the unknown; there is a great deal of precedent, and you have a lot of company.

This chapter is a call to action—an invitation to become a better leader through the alignment of strategy and execution. Coherence makes every aspect of leadership easier in the long run. It continually focuses your attention on the most important things your company does. It enables you to define a world that your company can help to create.

That is a worthwhile legacy for any leader in any enterprise.

A History of Strategy

The natural state of management has been incoherence. Strategy was not tied to execution in the past, at least not consistently.

The old questions in strategy were, Where are we going to go, and where are we going to grow? But the big current questions are, Who are we going to be, and how are we going to add value? If the latter set of questions represents strategy, then execution is extending that value proposition to market.

The yin and yang of strategic fad and fashion—the treadmill-like movement of business leadership from one trend to another over the past fifty years—has often led companies to make incoherent and ineffective moves. As writer Walter Kiechel notes, this pattern began in the 1960s, when business academics formalized the concept of strategy.[1] Since then, there have been four basic schools of strategic thought, whose proponents have argued back and forth through the years. Each school represents a different theory about the best way to gain a consistent right to win in the market.

Position

The position school proposes that the best way to win is by occupying an impregnable place in an industry or a market. This theory started with strategic planning in the 1960s—the origin of the strengths, weaknesses, opportunities, and threats (SWOT) analyses still prevalent today. A breakthrough in the school occurred with Bruce Henderson's growth-share matrix, which was more specific: the greatest advantage went to companies that held the leading position in market share for sectors with growth prospects.[2] This meant emphasizing the value of some divisions over others and basing those judgments primarily on the fit with external markets. Then, from the late 1970s to the early 1990s, Harvard Business School professor Michael Porter—probably the most influential thinker on corporate strategy in the institution's history—brought a higher level of economic sophistication and renewed vitality to the position school. He recast the turbulence of a company's business environment into a "value chain" and "five forces" (competitors, customers, suppliers, aspiring entrants, and substitute offerings): two frameworks that could be used to analyze the value potential and competitive intensity of any business. No matter what the specific answer, the underlying message was the same: business leaders could win by finding the right niche to dominate with first-mover advantage. This observation has been proven true, at least enough of the time, to be compellingly persuasive.[3]

But business leaders have also come to recognize the limits of the position school. Conventional strategic planning was resource-intensive and bureaucratic, and didn't necessarily correlate with profitability. Defending their position has also led many companies to get caught up in ruthless price wars and commoditization. To many corporate leaders in tough businesses or in highly regulated industries like electric power generation, staking out a position made them complacent; they saw no advantage in developing distinctive capabilities. Some companies tried to escape by seeking positions in new businesses: "blue oceans" where they often didn't know how to swim. These efforts generally failed. And too many companies with seemingly impregnable market positions, such as Nokia and Kodak, have seen their advantages fade when new competitors, such as Apple and Google, emerged.

Execution

The execution school, which began to be prominent in the West in the 1980s, started at the Harvard Business School's operations management department. In a seminal 1980 *Harvard Business Review* article titled "Managing Our Way to Economic Decline," William Abernathy and Robert Hayes proposed that competitive advantage came not from financial practices but from execution and operational excellence: the development and deployment of better processes, technologies, and products. The execution message was bolstered by manufacturers such as General Electric and Motorola, both of which provided influential examples of operations-oriented strategies with their focus on executive training and such practices as Six Sigma. Execution was also a basic tenet of the quality movement—the continuous-improvement practices that had been developed at Toyota and a few other Japanese companies during the previous few decades and were just then, in 1980, being brought back to the United States by W. Edwards Deming and several other well-known quality experts. The movement ultimately became known as lean management. The execution school gained further influence with the reengineering movement of the 1990s. This movement argued for redesigning processes from scratch and continues to be influential wherever changes in technology, particularly IT, lead to changes in organizational practices. It turned out that effective operational behavior can lead to far greater value.[4]

But execution-oriented ideas like reengineering, benchmarking, outsourcing, and change management also have limits—perhaps best articulated by Porter in his 1990 article "What Is Strategy?"[5] The ideas all led to better operations, but ignored the question of which businesses to operate in the first place. Execution-based practices are also vulnerable to competition. Nearly every aspect of operational excellence can be copied, and it often becomes industry standard. By the late 1990s, just about the entire global automobile industry had adopted some form of the Toyota Production System. The choice of capabilities, tied to any kind of value proposition, does not fit with the bottom-up continuous-improvement focus of the execution school.

Adaptation

The adaptation school of strategy started in the 1990s. It is most prominently represented by Henry Mintzberg, professor of management studies at McGill University. In his history *The Rise and Fall of Strategic Planning*, Mintzberg dismissed the position school as formulaic and execution as insufficient for strategic success. He sought a more creative, experimental approach to executive decision making. Executives could gain competitive advantage by experimenting with new ideas and directions, discarding those that don't work and adjusting their efforts on the fly to meet new challenges. In Mintzberg's words, they "let a thousand strategic flowers bloom . . . [using] an insightful style, to detect the patterns of success in these gardens of strategic flowers, rather than a cerebral style that favors analytical techniques to develop strategies in a hothouse."[6] Adaptation has helped many companies grow quickly and respond to external threats creatively. It has also been the most central guiding theme of Tom Peters's work, starting with his seminal business bestseller, *In Search of Excellence*.[7]

But the adaptation school is also seriously limited, because its freewheeling nature tends to lead to incoherence. A multitude of products and services that all have different capability requirements cannot possibly be brought into sync. The more diverse a company's efforts become, the more it costs to develop and apply the advantaged capabilities the company needs. Letting a thousand flowers bloom can lead to a field full of weeds—and to businesses that can't match the expertise and resources of more focused, coherent competitors.

Concentration

Hence the appeal of the fourth group of strategy thinkers—the concentration school. Its most prominent members were Gary Hamel and C. K. Prahalad, authors of *Competing for the Future* (1994).[8] They argued that the most effective companies owed their success to a select set of "core competencies": these were the bedrock skills and technological capabilities (e.g., new forms of hardware, software, systems, biotechnology, and financial engineering) that allowed companies to compete in distinctive ways. Their approach to capabilities was a foundational influence on the ideas in this book. In recent years, private equity firms have championed the idea of focusing on your core business. They acquire overextended companies and bring them back to their own core businesses as a way to promote growth and value.[9]

However, in practice, the concentration strategy often becomes a way of holding on to old approaches, even when they become outdated. Many companies (including private-equity firms) translate this strategy into slash-and-burn retrenchment. They cut costs and minimize investments in R&D and marketing to create a pared-down company that produces more profits at first, but that can't sustain the growth required for a healthy bottom line. When they seek to grow, it's through "adjacencies": products or services that seem related to their existing core businesses. But many adjacencies are less profitable than they were expected to be, partly because they may require very different capabilities—and partly because the truly successful game-changing leaps, like Apple's jump into consumer media or Amazon's foray into cloud computing, can't be managed from a concentration strategy alone.

Balancing the Schools of Thought

Not surprisingly, each of the four basic schools of thought (position, execution, adaptation, and concentration) has something significant to offer business strategists, as long as the ideas are adopted in an appropriately balanced way. But if you keep switching between them, as some companies do, you will simply end up using each one to compensate for the failings of the previous fashion. You'll never make time to go in your own chosen direction.

What we need is a theory of strategy that incorporates the best of all four points of view in practice. This type of theory can help you make strategic thinking a way of life. We believe that our approach to strategy and capabilities provides that theory. It suggests that the path to sustainable success, as the companies in this book have found, is through developing an identity all your own, grounded in your own way of capturing and delivering value and in your most distinctive capabilities. This identity is expressed as who you are and what you are great at doing, rather than where you are going and what you sell. Every day—instead of chasing unprofitable market opportunities, or getting mired in execution, or adapting incoherently, or being constrained by your core—you place a bet on your own company's identity. Every day, your company becomes closer to who you are. And in this way, you gain a consistent competitive advantage—a true right to win—in your chosen markets.

The Capable Company Research Project

This book is an effort to document how companies have narrowed the gap between strategy and execution in the face of competitive pressure and their own internal complacency. We began with a question: If a winning capabilities system is critical to capturing value, how do companies develop it, make use of it, and keep it alive?

There was little published research to work with. While writers like C. K. Prahalad, Gary Hamel, David Teece, Ikujiro Nonaka, Hirotaka Takeuchi, and Alfred D. Chandler had all marshaled evidence to show that distinctive capabilities were critically important, they had less to say about how companies went about developing them.[1]

We started with three simple hypotheses: First, we hypothesized that the best ways to build long-term capabilities are different from the best ways to boost short-term financial performance. Second, we theorized that if we could compare the stories of capabilities at different companies—the decisions that led the companies to learn to do extraordinary things—we would find some common actions and attributes among all the companies. Third, we believed that we could identify capable companies by reputation: that by polling a broad enough group of experts and senior managers, we could establish a credible list of companies to study.

We thus queried industry experts in our firm and some selected outsiders about which companies had distinguished themselves through what they could do consistently well. We also set up an online survey in which we asked executives to name the sources of success for the largest companies in their industry. We considered about fifty companies in light of these recommendations and then winnowed down the list with the following criteria:

- The companies we studied had to be clearly oriented toward the strategic approach in this book. Their capabilities system had to support an overall enterprise strategy and apply to most or all of their products and services. We excluded several diverse enterprises (Berkshire Hathaway, UTC, Unilever, Tata Group) because they embodied several strategies enabled by different capabilities systems at once.

- The companies had to be good performers compared with their industries—with either solid, steady shareholder returns and profitability figures or a credible explanation for why they had struggled. CEMEX, for example, qualified despite its near-bankruptcy during the 2008 financial crisis, because of the way the crisis had affected the building industries and because of the company's documented recovery.

- They had to be large, well-known, global companies that had reached a relative level of maturity in their operations.

- We looked for a broad range of industries and regional back- grounds. We hoped that people from any part of the world or any industry would want to learn from these examples.

- One criterion was important because we did *not* include it. We did not limit ourselves to clients of our management consulting practice. Our clients, which include many coherent and capable companies, have one thing in common: they have self-selected in asking for strategic or operational guidance. We did not exclude our clients, but we wanted to be sure that our sample was not limited to them.

- Finally, information about these companies and their capabilities had to be accessible to us—either through articles we commissioned for our magazine *strategy+business* (Haier, Lego, Starbucks); through informal conversations with people who knew the companies well (Frito-Lay, Qualcomm); through our direct in-depth experience (JCI-ASG, Pfizer's consumer division); through a body of memoirs and well-researched published material (Amazon, Apple, Inditex); through general observation of all these companies; and through our own intensive research, interviewing senior executives about the company's past and present.

Fourteen companies passed these criteria and became part of our research project. We conducted in-depth interviews at five of those companies: CEMEX, Danaher, Haier, IKEA, and Natura. In each of those five, we interviewed between six and eleven senior executives, people who had seen their capabilities develop firsthand.

We edited the transcripts of our interviews into roundtable-style discussions and had those approved by the interviewees and the companies as a whole, as a check on accuracy. We coded the roundtables, most of our other interviews, and our collections of published material, applying a method known as "grounded theory" to identify themes emerging from the material. We then sorted the themes to identify common patterns. In doing this, we tried to identify both elements that appeared consistently and elements that did not: for example, we looked for (but did not find) a common approach to organizational restructuring.

During a series of meetings among ourselves and with some advisers inside and outside the firm, we considered the factors that were present in all of these companies. Some of the most universal elements also resonated with our experience in helping other companies build distinctive capabilities of their own. Together, these factors added up to a common pattern, a developmental path, that in one way or another was present for all of the companies we had studied. In other words, we did not seek a compilation of best practices of successful companies, but attributes shared by companies that followed a common logic of value creation. The research consistently reinforced the view that this logic was prevalent among a particular type of successful company, that it was linked to success, and that it appeared in the context of the five unconventional acts.

As a final check, we compiled the identity profiles throughout this book and checked them with leaders at the companies or people who knew the companies well.

Puretone Ways to Play

Since 2008, we have conducted an ongoing research effort to identify the value propositions of companies around the world. This often involves deconstructing the "ways to play" of particular companies: breaking down the value they provide to customers into common strategic archetypes. We have identified fifteen of these "puretone" archetypes, as we call them. They are prevalent in companies around the world. Most companies combine two or more of them into a more distinctive strategy. You can use the puretones to identify another company's value proposition, or to design your own.

To illustrate and clarify each puretone "way to play," we have long used the examples listed here. They are meant to demonstrate each concept with real-life, generally understood examples. Some companies are listed under more than one puretone; their value proposition is bespoke to them, unlike any other, all distinctive variations on the archetypal puretone themes. Nonetheless, in looking at the list of examples, the essence of each value proposition may be easier to grasp.

TABLE C-1

Puretone ways to play

Puretone way to play (value proposition)	Definition	Examples of companies that incorporate these puretones	Comments
Aggregator	Provides the convenience and simplicity of a one-stop solution	Amazon Apple (through its App Store and iTunes) W.W. Grainger Inc Any peer-to-peer e-commerce business, where people exchange rooms, rides, goods, or services	These companies pull together multiple suppliers or sources under one common experience.
Category leader	Maintains top market share in a category and uses that position to shape and influence downstream channels and upstream supply markets, gaining leverage and customer loyalty	Most of the "supercompetitors" described in chapter 6 Coca-Cola Danaher's member companies Frito-Lay Intel L'Oréal GE Pfizer's consumer healthcare business in 2001–2006 (as described in this book) Starbucks Walmart	These companies often develop mass marketing capabilities that provide broad market appeal, combined with a high level of influence on both the value chain and the retail channels of the entire category.
Consolidator	Dominates an industry through acquisitions ("rolling up an industry") to provide either a value benefit to consumers or access to a platform with products and services that otherwise would not be possible	Danaher GE Many tech companies that use acquisition to build and maintain a platform, including Apple, Cisco Systems, Google, Microsoft, and Oracle.	Consolidators acquire rivals and offer customers access, technology, or prices that no smaller or less comprehensive company can provide.

Puretone way to play (value proposition)	Definition	Examples of companies that incorporate these puretones	Comments
Customizer	Leverages insight and market intelligence to offer tailored products or services	Burger King (with its "have it your way" campaign) Companies that build electronics and computer systems to order Frito-Lay (assortments tailored to the retail stores) Most B2B software development companies Haier Inditex	The internet, with its interoperability, automation of customer insight, global reach, and lowered transaction costs, has made it easier to succeed as a customizer.
Disintermediator	Helps customers bypass unreachable or more expensive distribution channels and parts of the value chain, thereby providing access to otherwise inaccessible services and products	NAPA Auto Parts (Genuine Parts Company) Priceline 3PLs (third-party logistics firms)	To deliver its way to play, a disintermediator must provide enhanced value for its customers, usually by cutting costs or aggregating volume. For example, the 3PLs provide "on-demand transportation"—in consumer packaged goods, these firms can take over an entire distribution chain, with capabilities they deploy on behalf of all their clients.
Experience provider	Builds enjoyment, engagement, and emotional attachment through strong brands or experiences	Apple Hotel chains with a design-based or specialty value proposition IKEA Lego McDonald's Sports car makers Natura Starbucks Virgin Airlines and other Virgin companies (Virgin Group)	Unlike premium players, these businesses can be viable at all price segments. In many US communities, for the price of a Happy Meal, McDonald's provides the most accessible and engaging indoor playground available. Experience providers can also include those manufacturers who make the use or purchase of their product feel like a noteworthy event.

(Continued)

TABLE C-1 *(Continued)*

Puretone ways to play

Puretone way to play (value proposition)	Definition	Examples of companies that incorporate these puretones	Comments
Fast follower	Leverages foundations laid by innovators to quickly introduce competing offerings, often at greater value or to a broader base of consumers	Generic pharmaceutical manufacturers Google (with Android) Hyundai Chinese *shan zhai* (innovative "knock-off" manufacturers)	Many successful innovations (e.g., the steamboat, electric power, television, personal computer) were spread through fast followers that successfully marketed someone else's innovation.
Innovator	Introduces new and creative products or services to the market	Apple Haier Inditex Leading-edge biotech companies Procter & Gamble Philips (Koninklijke Philips N.V.) Salesforce.com Under Armour	These are not just introducers of new products or services, but companies whose ongoing innovative capability enables them to consistently win and hold customers. There are many types of innovators, and the most successful ways to play clearly define the type of innovation and why it distinguishes a particular company.
Platform provider	Operates and oversees a shared resource or infrastructure	Electric power utilities Lego Microsoft (with Windows) New York Stock Exchange FedEx Conrail (CSX and Norfolk Southern Railway) Back-office transaction processors Natural resource providers (oil, natural gas, forest products, and mining companies)	These companies create a platform or resource that others can share by doing business with them. Whether they are heavily regulated or not, they have an implicit role as stewards of the resource they manage.

Puretone way to play (value proposition)	Definition	Examples of companies that incorporate these puretones	Comments
Premium player	Offers high-end products or services	Herman Miller Luxury automakers such as BMW Nordstrom Premium hotel chains such as Ritz-Carlton	Customers pay for both status and perceived value: customer service (Nordstrom), artistry (Herman Miller), performance (BMW).
Regulation navigator	Offers access to otherwise unreachable products and services by managing within government rules and oversight, and by influencing them	Pfizer's consumer healthcare business in 2001–2006 (as described in this book) Health insurance companies China National Off-Shore Oil Corporation (government owned) Industrial and Commercial Bank of China (government owned) Some trading companies (Mitsui)	These companies are viable in nations and sectors where governments control or regulate a large percentage of business activity. The CEO of a Turkish company once remarked that in a pre-deregulation environment, it was important to operate in many product lines, to have allies in multiple ministries, because pleasing the government was more important than pleasing customers. These companies can be vulnerable if regulation frameworks change.
Reputation player	As a trustworthy provider, charges a premium or gains privileged access to customers	CostCo Financial services companies with reputations for probity (which many have struggled to retain or rebuild since the mid-2000s) Natura Pfizer's consumer healthcare business in 2001–2006 (as described in this book) Tata Seventh Generation Volvo (Geely Automotive)	The reputational attribute is not necessarily altruistic, but it is tied to a value other than saving money. Volvo's reputation for safety was arguably a compelling factor in its 2010 purchase by the Chinese company Geely Motors. This way to play can backfire if a company lacks the capabilities or attention to follow through and its reputation erodes (BP, Enron, Honda and Toyota all experienced this), and it often depends on close connection with a dedicated, affiliated group of customers.

(*Continued*)

TABLE C-1 *(Continued)*

Puretone ways to play

Puretone way to play (value proposition)	Definition	Examples of companies that incorporate these puretones	Comments
Risk absorber	Mitigates or pools market risk for its customers	Commodity hedge funds New hybrid health care providers-payers, following the Kaiser Permanente model Many insurance companies	Risk absorbers enable others to extend entrepreneurially or help them navigate uncertainty.
Solutions provider	Provides bundled products and services that fully address customer needs	Ahlstrom (Oyj) CEMEX Haier Lockheed Martin	This group is also known as integrators, because the way to play depends on the capability to fit together disparate technologies and practices, including those from customers.
Value player	Offers lowest prices or tremendous value for comparable products and services	IKEA JetBlue McDonald's Ryanair Southwest Airlines Tata Motors (with the Nano) Walmart	Also known as low-cost producers, successful value players have the capabilities to sustain their position without falling into a commoditization spiral of price-based competition.

Examples of Table-Stakes Capabilities

For every industry, as we noted in chapter 5, there are table-stakes capabilities. Also called competitive necessities, these are the capabilities that every company has to develop, simply to remain current in its industry. They vary from one industry to the next, but they are found in every company within a sector.

Other capabilities are distinctive: difficult for others to copy, and providing competitive advantage. These become the elements of a differentiating capabilities system: the group of three to six mutually reinforcing capabilities that support a company's value proposition in a way that is difficult for other companies to copy or match.

In this appendix, for three industries, we show the table-stakes capabilities common to each and some ways (*in italics*) in which they could be adapted into distinctive capabilities. We hope these examples will be useful in helping you describe the table-stakes capabilities in your own industry and imagine ways in which you can develop some of them to a distinctive level.

Biopharmaceutical Companies

Drug discovery: Every pharma enterprise that engages in drug research must be able to identify biological pathways and drug-discovery platforms; evaluate and prioritize candidate drugs; manage academic and research partnerships; identify and develop the necessary life sciences talent to do this work; and manage the discovery program end to end. *This could become a distinctive capability for a company in a highly specialized field or with a unique group of patents.*

Clinical capabilities: All life sciences companies conduct clinical trials: identifying nuances in the regulatory and market landscape; designing trials for the appropriate geographic footprint (increasingly, a global footprint); managing contract research organizations; gathering competitive intelligence; and recruiting patients for testing. *A breakthrough innovation in clinical testing methods, if it could withstand regulatory scrutiny, might develop into a distinctive capability.*

Specialized production: Pharmaceutical companies have operational capabilities that include designing commercially scalable and compliant processes; optimizing costs and managing assets for global supply; and managing the supply chain and distribution channels, including track-and-trace processes and risks. *Highly efficient, cost-conscious production can, in some companies, become a distinctive capability if it leads to significant value or solutions-providing competitiveness.*

Market introduction and launch of new products: Biopharma companies depend on their ability to maintain a stream of new drugs. This capability includes the design of value- and risk-based pricing and accounting; managing commercial partnerships, including relationships with health-care providers and systems, such as integrated delivery networks (IDNs); engaging with physicians; outreaching to patients (to ensure they are taking the medications); and using new channels and digital platforms for these connections. *Working with particular categories of customers—for instance, being able to profitably deliver drugs for relatively rare diseases—could be a distinctive capability.*

Customer development: All pharma companies must have a basic capability in taking their products to market. This includes managing accounts; providing value-added services for patients (in part, to engage them); adapting the value proposition for different providers; and designing and performing outcome studies that will be used in the marketing campaigns. *For a company that combines this capability with drug development and market launch capabilities, targeting a particular group of patients or health-care providers, this capability could lead to distinction.*

Regulatory and medical affairs: Most biopharma companies must demonstrate this capability in proving their legitimacy. It might include managing research on health economics and outcomes; maintaining academic and research partnerships; contributing medical information to the industry; and demonstrating value to payers and providers to improve patient access. *In an opaque regulatory environment, some companies' insights or access could give them a distinctive capability.*

Retail Companies

Market insight: Retailers depend on their ability to connect with customers to understand their needs and tastes; predict future demand trends; select the most popular products that customers will want; and understand nuances at a local or store level. Increasingly, this capability involves consumer data and sophisticated analytics. *Some retailers go further, gaining privileged access to customers as discussed in chapter 6.*

Assortment management: Product development and merchandising combine in a capability common to all retailers, which involves designing the right set of products that match customer preferences (often working closely with manufacturers to do so); selecting them in an appropriate assortment for each venue; keeping the assortment on trend through new product introductions and/or seasonal changes; assembling the optimal mix of sizes, units, colors, flavors, fabrics, fits, and other factors; and developing innovative features at the retail level to augment what manufacturers have given them. *A retailer like Apple, IKEA, Inditex, or Starbucks that manufactures some of its offerings will often seek to develop a distinctive capability in this area.*

Supply chain logistics: Every retailer must manage a vendor base to ensure quality of product and competitive cost; develop an agile supply chain that can react to demand and avoid understocking or overstocking; design a pipeline that can deliver a localized assortment, with different product mixes to different stores; manage optimal inventory levels across supply nodes, providing end-to-end visibility down to the stock-keeping unit (SKU) level; deliver an omnichannel experience (matching online and brick-and-mortar venues); and replenish shelves on a just-in-time basis to optimize sales. *A few companies, like Inditex—and on the consumer products manufacturing side, Frito-Lay and Natura—have taken this capability to the level of operational excellence where it becomes distinctive.*

Retail environment: Large multinational retailers must be proficient in several related activities. These include identifying and securing real estate to balance sales, cost, and brand image; developing and managing a store footprint that optimally serves each geographic market; optimizing backroom (noncustomer-facing) operations for the minimum cost and desired in-stock levels; and managing in-store (customer-facing) operations to deliver the desired store experience at competitive costs; and integrating brick-and-mortar, online, and smartphone-based customer experiences. *Innovations (such as IKEA's warehouse design and Apple's Genius Bar) and continuous improvement (as at Amazon, Inditex, and Starbucks) can give some retailers a distinctive edge with this capability, especially when it is integrated with insights into customer experience.*

Communication: Every retailer must have a threshold level of competence in creating a brand that attracts customers, both face-to-face and online. This includes managing brand coherence across channels; driving customer awareness and traffic to a sales channel; cross-selling or up-selling products to existing customers; incenting new trials for new or lapsed customers; conducting ongoing analytics to continuously improve marketing efforts; and devising effective pricing and promotional strategies that create long-term value. *Skilled retailing marketers can create targeted relationships with segments of consumers focused on distinctive experience or a customized value proposition.*

Omnichannel sales and service: Retailers must provide an integrated digital offering that allows customers to buy products when, where, and how they want. These retailers must manage an end-to-end customer experience from home to store and back to the home, to improve the customer relationship. They must also develop customer retention and loyalty programs that create long-term value. *A few retailers, such as Burberry and Restoration Hardware, have turned this capability into a distinctive art form.*

Software Technology

Product development: Software companies are known first and foremost for their offerings. They must capture market and consumer insights, often monitoring customer usage closely to do so; they must identify and translate customer requirements into a compelling product architecture, increasingly a "software-as-a-service" (SaaS) architecture; they must rapidly prototype, test, and beta manage these products in an agile fashion; they must develop clear, predictable product strategies and road maps; they must manage the innovation portfolio and pipeline; and they must do all of this in a timely fashion, maintaining quality in their product releases. *The industry has improved its table-stakes capabilities in this regard over the years, so a company can no longer distinguish itself by simply meeting this standard, but a company that has developed new channels or integrated, network-based solutions can still gain a distinctive edge.*

Customer segmenting and targeting: Technology companies have learned, over time, how to build a table-stakes branding and customer-awareness capability. This includes developing highly personalized campaigns and offers; optimizing customer segmentation to generate high customer demand and a sense of lifetime value; delivering personalized messaging across channels; creating long-standing, profitable marketing partnerships and alliances; and developing a disciplined ability in pricing, discounting, and promotion. *Some software companies—Apple and Google are noted for this—have parlayed this capability to establish distinctive branding capabilities that attract loyal customers to the company's identity.*

Customer management: This table-stakes capability is often unseen outside the industry, but it drives much of its growth. It includes the building of sales teams for specific buyers and account acquisition; developing compensation models based on customer lifetime value, deal size, and margin; managing the lead-generation and sales pipeline, for both direct and indirect customers; managing and executing a robust web presence with sophisticated e-commerce abilities; and having the ability to monitor and model customer engagement. *Qualcomm's licensing prowess is one example of how a company can adapt a sales capability into its own distinctive form.*

Quote-to-cash and operations: In the evolving world of cloud-based software, conventional operations and cash-flow capabilities have rapidly moved in new directions for all software companies. These now include automating and streamlining quote-to-cash (QtC) processes for SaaS ordering, billing, and customer management; developing dynamic configurability for personalization and solution selling (also known as "low-touch offers"); and managing operational activities that are often outsourced or offshored, including transaction processing, compliance monitoring, and the production of necessary reports. *Amazon's development of a distinctive operational capability shows what is possible in this domain.*

Customer support and service: While this is a table-stakes capability for the entire industry, many companies' services are still lagging behind customer demand. The capability includes developing compensation models that provide variable, performance-driven incentives for front-line support staff; maintaining and continuously improving service effectiveness (utilizations, cycle times, etc.); developing self-service offerings and capabilities (including user communities) with a viable user interface that is compelling, not frustrating; and executing user education and after-sales consulting. *Those focused on service quality or value can turn this into an advantage.*

Selected Bibliography

Of the many works that we drew on during the writing of this book, the following were particularly focused on closing the gap between strategy and execution:

Barnett, William P. *The Red Queen Among Organizations: How Competitiveness Evolves.* Princeton, NJ: Princeton University Press, 2008. How companies that follow the logic of their industry inevitably develop similar capabilities; the only way out is to seek another path.

Chandler, Alfred D., Jr. *Shaping the Industrial Century: The Remarkable Story of the Evolution of the Modern Chemical and Pharmaceutical Industries.* Cambridge, MA: Harvard University Press, 2005. The eminent business historian's last book before his death describes how a mature industry reshaped itself, time and again, by using its capabilities as a platform for growth.

Dahlvig, Anders. *The IKEA Edge: Building Global Growth and Social Good at the World's Most Iconic Home Store.* New York: McGraw-Hill, 2011. The author is one of IKEA's former CEOs.

Fischer, Bill, Umberto Lago, and Fang Liu. *Reinventing Giants: How Chinese Global Competitor Haier Has Changed the Way Big Companies*

Transform. San Francisco: Jossey-Bass, 2013. This complete version of the remarkable story of Haier's capabilities system provides CEO Zhang Ruimin's approach to identity.

Gill, Michael Gates. *How Starbucks Saved My Life: A Son of Privilege Learns to Live Like Everyone Else*. New York: Penguin, 2007. The author provides a front-line view of a company with little gap between strategy and execution.

Isaacson, Walter. *Steve Jobs*. New York: Simon & Schuster, 2011. Apple's extraordinary capabilities reflected and transcended those of its founder, exile, and strategic leader.

Kiechel, Walter, III. *The Lords of Strategy: The Secret Intellectual History of the New Corporate World*. Boston: Harvard Business Review Press, 2010. How ideas of what companies should be and do have evolved, typically in an ad hoc way, and why the most powerful ideas are frequently ignored.

Koenigsaecker, George. *Leading the Lean Enterprise Transformation*. Boca Raton, FL: CRC Press/Productivity Press, 2009. One of many guides to lean management, this also provides an insider's look at the evolution of the Danaher Business System.

Lafley, A.G., and Roger L. Martin. *Playing to Win: How Strategy Really Works*. Boston: Harvard Business Review Press, 2013. We don't feature Procter & Gamble in *Strategy That Works* because the story of its capabilities system is told here so completely.

Lashinsky, Adam. *Inside Apple: How America's Most Admired—and Secretive—Company Really Works*. London: Hachette, 2012. This guide explains how this iconic company develops and maintains its iconic capabilities.

Leinwand, Paul, and Cesare Mainardi. *The Essential Advantage: How to Win With a Capabilities-Driven Strategy*. Boston: Harvard Business Review Press, 2011. Our original definition of coherence lays the groundwork for the five unconventional acts of *Strategy That Works*.

Mock, Dave. *The Qualcomm Equation: How a Fledgling Telecom Company Forged a New Path to Big Profits and Market Dominance*.

New York: AMACOM, 2005. Qualcomm developed an effective capabilities system while carving out a distinctive high-tech identity.

Montgomery, Cynthia. *The Strategist: Be the Leader Your Business Needs*. New York: HarperCollins, 2012. Strategy as identity, with extraordinarily high stakes; the opening contrasts Masco, which lost millions trying to dominate the furniture business, with IKEA.

Nonaka, Ikujiro, and Hirotaka Takeuchi. *The Knowledge-Creating Company: How Japanese Companies Create the Dynamics of Innovation*. New York: Oxford University Press, 1995. This book is the original source on the interplay between tacit and explicit knowledge.

Rossman, John. *The Amazon Way: 14 Leadership Principles Behind the World's Most Disruptive Company*. North Charleston, SC: CreateSpace, 2014. Published by Amazon's own imprint, this guide reveals its compelling capabilities and compulsive culture.

Rumelt, Richard. *Good Strategy, Bad Strategy: The Difference and Why It Matters*. New York: Crown Business, 2011. Every distinctive capability should have, underlying it, the kind of strategic logic that Rumelt describes here.

Senge, Peter. *The Fifth Discipline: The Art and Practice of the Learning Organization*. 2nd ed. New York: Random House, 2006. A collection of attitudes and habitual practices, on an individual level, helps people develop distinctive capabilities and a culture of collective mastery.

Sviokla, John, and Mitch Cohen. *The Self-Made Billionaire Effect: How Extreme Producers Create Massive Value*. New York: Portfolio/ Penguin, 2014. Could it be that every distinctive capability needs a few people with distinctive personalities?

NOTES

Chapter 1

1. References to Strategy& or "our firm" in *Strategy That Works* refer to a strategy consulting enterprise that navigated a series of changes in structure during the time the authors and their colleagues were developing the ideas in this book. Before April 2008, this enterprise was the global commercial strategy business in the management consulting firm Booz Allen Hamilton. Starting April 2008 it was an independent global consulting firm, Booz & Company. As of July 2015, it is Strategy&, a global team of practical strategists integrated within the PwC network of firms. For more about PwC's Strategy&, see www.strategyand.pwc.com. For further details about how the PwC network is structured, see www.pwc.com/structure.

2. This study was conducted through an interactive survey and self-analysis tool called the Coherence Profiler. These figures reflect results gathered between 2010 and 2015. The profiler and more detail on results are available at "Our Leading Research on Strategy," Strategy&, 2015, http://www.strategyand.pwc.com/global/home/what-we-think/cds_home/the_concept/our_leading_research_on_strategy.

3. "Companies Spend Money and Time at Odds With Their Own Strategy," the Strategy& group of PwC, based on data from the *Fit-for-Growth* index profiler: http://www.strategyand.pwc.com/global/home/what-we-think/reports-white-papers/article-display/fitforgrowth-info-graphic-indexprofiler-results. *Fit for Growth* is a registered service mark of PwC in the United States.

4. "Companies Spend Money and Time at Odds With Their Own Strategy," ibid.

5. Paul Leinwand and Cesare Mainardi, "What Drives a Company's Success?" Strategy&, October 28, 2013, www.strategyand.pwc.com/global/home/what-we-think/reports-white-papers/article-display/what-drives-a-companys-success. Originally conducted and published by Booz & Company.

6. IKEA Systems B.V., "Who We Are," accessed July 3, 2015, http://franchisor.ikea.com/who-we-are-2-2/.

7. Natura Cosméticos S.A., "Individual and Consolidated Financial Statements," December 31, 2014, http://natu.infoinvest.com.br/enu/5179/1DemonstraesFinanceirasIngles1.pdf.

8. Bob Tita, "Danaher to Split Up Businesses, Buy Pall for $13.6 Billion," *Wall Street Journal*, May 13, 2015, www.wsj.com/articles/danaher-to-buy-pall-for-13-6-billion-split-up-businesses-1431518043. See also "Danaher Reports Record Fourth Quarter and Full Year 2014 Results," Danaher press release, January 27, 2015, http://phx.corporate-ir.net/phoenix.zhtml?c=82105&p=irol-newsArticle&ID=2010728.

9. Paul Leinwand and Cesare Mainardi, "The Coherence Premium," *Harvard Business Review* 88, no. 6 (June 2010): 86–92.

10. Leinwand and Mainardi, "What Drives a Company's Success?" op. cit.

11. J. Neely, John Jullens, and Joerg Krings, "Deals That Win," *strategy+business*, July 14, 2015, http://www.strategy-business.com/article/00346.

12. Gerald Adolph, Cesare Mainardi, and J. Neely, "The Capabilities Premium in M&A," *strategy+business*, February 22, 2012, http://www.strategy-business.com/article/12105.

13. "Management by walking around": Thomas J. Peters and Robert H. Waterman, Jr., *In Search of Excellence: Lessons from America's Best Run Companies* (New York: HarperBusiness, 1982, 2004), 289; "level five leadership": Jim Collins, *Good to Great: Why Some Companies Make the Leap . . . And Others Don't* (New York: HarperCollins, 2001), 17ff.

14. The quotes from individuals at CEMEX, Danaher, IKEA, and Natura come from interviews that were edited into roundtable-style articles, published or to be published by *strategy+business*. These are: Thomas A. Stewart, interviewer, "CEMEX's Strategic Mix" (published April 13, 2015; http://www.strategy-business.com/article/00325); George Roth and Art Kleiner, interviewers, "The Danaher Zone" (in progress); Per-Ola Karlsson, Marco Kesteloo, and Nadia Kubis, interviewers, "The Idea of IKEA," (in progress); and Thomas A. Stewart, interviewer, "Beauty, Business, Brazil" (about Natura, in progress). Other quotes were taken from interviews with the authors.

15. Jon Katzenbach, Rutger von Post, and James Thomas, "The Critical Few: Components of a Truly Effective Culture," *strategy+business*, February 11, 2014, http://strategy-business.com/article/00237; also a forthcoming book on the subject by the authors.

16. Deniz Caglar, Jaya Pandrangi, and John Plansky, "Is Your Company Fit for Growth?" *strategy+business*, May 29, 2012, http://www.strategy-business.com/article/12205; and the *Fit for Growth* index, http://www.strategyand.pwc.com/global/home/what-we-think/fitforgrowth.

17. Clive G. Jones, John H. Lawton and Moshe Shachak, "Organisms as ecosystem engineers," *Oikos* 69, no. 3 (April 1994): 373–386.

18. Quotes about IKEA come from "The Idea of IKEA," and from Ingvar Kamprad, *The Testament of a Furniture Dealer: A Little IKEA Dictionary* (IKEA, 1976). We also drew on Michael I. Norton, Daniel Mochon and Dan Ariely, The "IKEA Effect: When Labor Leads to Love," Harvard Business School Working Paper 11-091, 2011; "The Secret of IKEA's Success," *The Economist*, Feb 24, 2011; Linda Matchan, "Cheap Thrills: Its prices are just one way IKEA is altering how America decorates," *Boston Globe*, Nov 3, 2005; Kerstin Gustafsson, Gunilla Jönson, David Smith, and Leigh Sparks, "Packaging logistics and retailers' profitability: an IKEA case study," Lund University, 2004; J. Klevås, "Design for packaging logistics," International Design Conference— Design 2006, Dubrovnik, Croatia; and Deniz Caglar, Marco Kesteloo, and Art Kleiner, "How Ikea Reassembled Its Growth Strategy," *strategy+business*, May 7, 2012. http://www.strategy-business.com/article/00111.

19. References to job titles for IKEA executives draw upon the company's description of its organizational structure: "About the IKEA Group: Welcome Inside Our Company," accessed July 26, 2015; http://www.ikea .com/ms/en_GB/about-the-ikea-group/company-information/#organisation.

Chapter 2

1. Walter Isaacson, *Steve Jobs* (New York: Simon & Schuster, 2011).

2. Ibid., 326; Chloe Albanesius, "Steve Jobs vs. Everyone: His Best Fights," *PC Magazine Online*, October 5, 2011, http://www.pcmag.com/ article2/0,2817,2391784,00.asp.

3. "Steve Jobs Keynote Macworld 2001 SF," video uploaded by Evgeny Z, November 8, 2011, *YouTube*, http://www.youtube.com/ watch?v=pICctkS12fY.

4. Ken Favaro and Art Kleiner, "The Thought Leader Interview: Cynthia Montgomery," *strategy+business*, February 26, 2013, http://www .strategy-business.com/article/00163?pg=all.

5. Barry Jaruzelski, John Loehr, and Richard Holman, "The Global Innovation 1000: Navigating the Digital Future," *strategy+business*, October 22, 2013, http://www.strategy-business.com/article/00221.

6. Sources on Apple include Isaacson, Albanesius, and Favaro and Kleiner, op. cit., along with: Adam Lashinsky, *Inside Apple: How America's Most Admired—and Secretive—Company Really Works* (New York: Business Plus, 2012), 126; David B. Yoffie and Michael Slind, "Apple Computer 2006," Harvard Business School Case Study 9-706-496; David B. Yoffie and Penelope Rossano, "Apple Inc. in 2012," Harvard Business School Case Study 9-712-490; John Boddie, "Has Apple Hit the Right Disruptive Notes?" *Strategy&Innovation*, Harvard Business School Publishing, 2005; Ken Mark, "Apple Inc.: iPod and iTunes," Ivey Case Study 905M46, 2007; and Luc Wathieu, "Apple Stores," Harvard Business School Case Study 9-502-063, 2010.

7. Joseph A. Michelli, *Leading the Starbucks Way: 5 Principles for Connecting with Your Customers, Your Products and Your People* (New York: McGraw-Hill Education, 2014), 4.

8. Bill Fischer, Umberto Lago, and Fang Liu, *Reinventing Giants: How Chinese Global Competitor Haier Has Changed the Way Big Companies Transform* (San Francisco: Jossey-Bass, 2013).

9. Art Kleiner, "China's Philosopher-CEO Zhang Ruimin," *strategy+business*, November 10, 2014, http://www.strategy-business.com/article/00296; Fischer, Lago, and Liu, *Reinventing Giants*, op. cit.

10. Jeannie Jinsheng Yi and Shawn Xian Ye, *The Haier Way: The Making of a Chinese Business Leader and a Global Brand* (Paramus, NJ: Homa & Seka Books, 2003), 27.

11. Sources on Haier include Fischer et al., Jinsheng and Shawn, and Kleiner, op.cit.; and Bill Fischer, Umberto Lago, and Fang Liu, "The Haier Road to Growth," *strategy+business*, April 27, 2015, http://www.strategy-business.com/article/00323.

12. Correspondence with CEMEX public affairs.

13. Clayton M. Christensen, *The Innovator's Dilemma: When New Technologies Cause Great Firms to Fail* (Boston: Harvard Business School Press, 1997), 31ff.

14. Gary Hamel and C. K. Prahalad, *Competing for the Future* (Boston: Harvard Business School Press, 1994), 247.

15. Sam Frizell, "Meet the Robots Shipping Your Amazon Orders," *Time*, Dec 1, 2014; David Cardinal, "Amazon Deploys 10,000 Robot Workers, a Year after Obama's Famous Amazon Jobs Speech," *ExtremeTech*, May 30, 2014, http://www.extremetech.com/extreme/183254-amazon-deploys-10000-robot-workers-a-year-after-obamas-famous-amazon-jobs-speech.

16. Kaj Grichnik and Conrad Winkler, with Jeffrey Rothfeder, *Make or Break: How Manufacturers Can Leap from Decline to Revitalization* (New York: McGraw-Hill, 2008), 1ff.

17. U.S. Securities and Exchange Commission, "Division of Corporation Finance: Standard Industrial Classification (SIC) Code List," last modified January 3, 2011, www.sec.gov/info/edgar/siccodes.htm.

18. "History of Smith Corona," Smith Corona web page, accessed July 9, 2015, www.smithcorona.com/history; Erwin Danneels, "Trying to Become a Different Type of Company: Dynamic Capability at Smith Corona," *Strategic Management Journal* 32, no. 1 (January 2011): 1–31.

19. "2012 re:Invent Day 2: Fireside Chat with Jeff Bezos & Werner Vogels" Amazon Web Services, youtube video, November 29, 2012: https://www.youtube.com/watch?v=O4MtQGRIIuA. Quote starts about 4:30.

20. J. P. Mangalindan, "Why Amazon's Fire Phone Failed," *Fortune*, Sept. 29, 2014; http://fortune.com/2014/09/29/why-amazons-fire-phone-failed/.

21. Tony F, "Tesla Batteries as Backup to Power Homes?" *Tesla Forums*, blog, August 16, 2011, http://my.teslamotors.com/fr_CH/forum/forums/tesla-batteries-backup-power-homes.

22. Gerald Adolph and Kim David Greenwood, "Grow From Your Strengths," *strategy+business*, August 18, 2015, http://www.strategy-business.com/article/00354?gko=478fb.

23. This trigger was inspired by "I Can Do That" by Marvin Hamlisch and Edward Kleban in *A Chorus Line*, 1975.

24. "The Danaher Zone," op cit.; Richard McCormack, "A Manager's Guide to Implementing Lean," (interview with George Koenigsaecker), *Manufacturing and Technology News*, May 16, 2001, http://www.manufacturingnews.com/news/01/georgek.html; George Koenigsaecker, *Leading the Lean Enterprise Transformation* (Boca Raton, FL: CRC Press 2009).

25. Natura Cosméticos S.A., *Natura Brasil Annual Report 2012*, https://www.naturabrasil.fr/en/about-us/our-annual-reports.

26. Howard Schultz and Dori Jones Yang, *Pour Your Heart into It: How Starbucks Built a Company One Cup at a Time* (New York: Hyperion, 1997), 6.

27. Michael Gates Gill, *How Starbucks Saved My Life: A Son of Privilege Learns to Live Like Everyone Else* (New York: Gotham Books, 2007); Tom Ehrenfeld, "Starbucks and the Power of Story," *strategy+business*, June 10, 2008, http://www.strategy-business.com/article/08211.

28. Keith Oliver, Edouard Samakh, and Peter Heckmann, "Rebuilding Lego, Brick by Brick," *strategy+business*, August 29, 2007, www.strategy-business.com/article/07306.

Chapter 3

1. PepsiCo, Annual Report, 2013, www.pepsico.com/Assets/Download/PEP_Annual_Report_2013.pdf.

2. Brian Cornell and Tom Greco, presentation at Thomson Reuters Streetevents, PEP—PepsiCo at CAGNY Conference, February 20, 2014, edited transcript, www.pepsico.com/docs/album/Investor/pep-transcript-2014-02-20t18_45.pdf?sfvrsn=2.

3. Candace Choi, "Cappuccino Potato Chips? America Says No Way," Associated Press, October 20, 2014.

4. Trefis Team, "Frito-Lay Dominates U.S. Salty Snacks, But Rising Cracker Sales Could Stall Growth," *Forbes*, June 27, 2014, www.forbes.com/sites/greatspeculations/2014/06/27/frito-lay-dominates-u-s-salty-snacks-but-rising-cracker-sales-could-stall-growth; Trefis Team, "PepsiCo Rides on Growth in Frito-Lay and Developing Markets in the First Quarter," *Forbes*, April 21, 2014, http://www.forbes.com/sites/greatspeculations/2014/04/21/pepsico-rides-on-growth-in-frito-lay-and-developing-markets-in-the-first-quarter/; Anthony A. Verstraete, "Frito-Lay: Case Study in Using MIS for Competitive Advantage," Smeal College of Business, Penn State University, 1994.

5. Mike Cooke and Edward H. Baker, "Helping the CIO Lead" [interview with Charles ("Charlie") Feld], *strategy+business*, December 13, 2010; http://www.strategy-business.com/article/00055.

6. James L. McKenney, Duncan Copeland, and Richard O. Mason, *Waves of Change: Business Evolution Through Information Technology* (Boston: Harvard Business School Press, 1995), 190.

7. Indra Nooyi, Q4 2013 PepsiCo Earnings Conference Call transcript, Thomson Reuters StreetEvents, February 13, 2014, https://www.pepsico .com/docs/album/Investor/q4_2013_pep_transcript.pdf?sfvrsn=2; Brian Cornell, "Winning in North America," Strategy Presentation at 2014 Consumer Analyst Group of NY conference, February 20, 2014: http://www .slideshare.net/Foodsfluidsandbeyond/pep-cagny-2014; Katy Askew, "PepsiCo confident on US snacks despite slowing sales," *Just-Food*, September 4, 2014: http://www.just-food.com/analysis/pepsico-confident-on-us-snacks -despite-slowing-sales_id127785.aspx; Sharon Bailey, "Why PepsiCo's operating margins are still under pressure," *Market Realist*, Feb 25, 2015, http:// marketrealist.com/2015/02/pepsicos-operating-margins-still-pressure/.

8. Lashinsky, *Inside Apple*, op. cit.

9. Oliver, Samakh, and Heckmann, "Rebuilding Lego, Brick by Brick," op. cit.

10. "The Danaher Zone," op. cit.

11. Bob Tita, "Johnson Controls to Spin Off Automotive Business," July 25, 2015. *Wall Street Journal,* http://www.wsj.com/articles/ johnson-controls-to-spin-off-automotive-business-1437742476.

12. For more on the strategic context of this story, see Paul Leinwand and Cesare Mainardi, *The Essential Advantage: How to Win with a Capabilities-Driven Strategy* (Boston: Harvard Business Review Press, 2011), 50–54.

13. Johnson Controls, Inc., *Annual Report Pursuant to Section 13 or 15(d) of the Securities Exchange Act of 1934 for the Fiscal Year Ended September 30, 2014* (Washington, DC: US Securities and Exchange Commission, 2014), www.johnsoncontrols.com/content/dam/WWW/jci/corporate/ investors/2014/JCI%202014%2010-K.pdf, 26.

14. Consumer Product Information Database, "Listerine Antiseptic Mouthwash, Original" May 22, 2008, http://whatsinproducts.com/types/ type_detail/1/9569/standard/Listerine%20Antiseptic%20Mouthwash,%20 Original-05/22/2008/10-001-115.

15. David Gelles, "Coke and McDonald's, Growing Together Since 1955," *New York Times*, May 15, 2014, www.nytimes.com/2014/05/16/ business/coke-and-mcdonalds-working-hand-in-hand-since-1955.html. The story comes from an interview with a former consultant to McDonald's.

16. Sarah Germano, "Under Armour Turns Ambitions to Electronic Apparel, Monitoring Apps," *Wall Street Journal*, February 27, 2015; Adam Auriemma, "With Digital Fitness Trackers, CEOs Band Together."

Wall Street Journal, March 12, 2014; John Phung, "The History of Under Armour—A Mastermind for Performance Apparel," *SearchWarp*, January 12, 2006, http://searchwarp.com/swa33442.htm; Drake Baer, "Here's How Under Armour Grew into a $15 Billion Athletic-Apparel Empire," *Business Insider*, February 19, 2015, http://www.businessinsider.com/history-of-under-armour-2015-2?op=1; Daniel Roberts, "Under Armour Gets Serious," *Fortune*, October 26, 2011; http://fortune.com/2011/10/26/under-armour-gets-serious/.

17. Deborah Arthurs, "Now We Know Who to Blame! Flat-Pack Revolution Sparked When an IKEA Designer Sawed the Legs Off a Table to Fit It in His Car," *Daily Mail*, July 19, 2013, www.dailymail.co.uk/femail/article-2370113/Ikea-designer-Gillis-Lundgren-sparked-flat-pack-revolution-sawing-table-legs-fit-car.html; "Ikea Relaunches First Flat-Pack Table," *DeZeen*, July 22, 2013, www.dezeen.com/2013/07/22/ikea-revives-three-legged-diy-side-table; IKEA, "The IKEA Product Range," IKEA web page, http://franchisor.ikea.com/product-for-a-better-everyday-life, accessed July 3, 2015.

18. "The Idea of IKEA," op. cit.

19. Amit Bagaria, "Uniqlo vs Zara vs H&M vs the World of Fashion Retailing," ReTales, *ETRetail.com* blog, February 10, 2014, http://retail.economictimes.indiatimes.com/re-tales/Uniqlo-vs-Zara-vs-H-M-vs-the-world-of-fashion-retailing/91.

20. Joe Avella, producer, "The One Reason Zara Is Dominating the Fashion Industry Right Now," video, *Business Insider*, July 14, 2015; http://www.businessinsider.com/zara-dominating-beating-competition-fashion-industry-2015-7.

21. At the end of fiscal year 2014, Inditex operated 6,683 stores in eighty-eight markets. Inditex, "FY2014 Results: 1 February 2014 to 31 January 2015," accessed July 3, 2015, www.inditex.com/documents/10279/145048/Full+year+2014+Results.pdf/244e2a9f-12bd-4509-ad06-470e7f10800b.

22. Paloma Díaz Soloaga and Mercedes Monjo, "Caso Zara: la empresa donde todo comunica (Zara Case Study: The Company Where Everything Communicates)," *Harvard Deusto Marketing y Ventas* 101 (November–December 2010): 60–68; Zeynep Ton, Elena Corsi, and Vincent Dessain, "Zara: Managing Stores for Fast Fashion," case 9-610-042 (Boston: Harvard Business School, revised January 19, 2010).

23. Ton, Corsi, and Dessain, "Zara: Managing Stores for Fast Fashion," op. cit.

24. Rodrigo Orihuela, "Inditex Sales Growth Hits Two-Year High as More Stores Open," BloombergBusiness, March 18, 2015; http://www.bloomberg.com/news/articles/2015-03-18/inditex-full-year-profit-meets-estimates-on-zara-chain-expansion.

25. Dave Mock, *The Qualcomm Equation: How a Fledgling Telecom Company Forged a New Path to Big Profits and Market Dominance* (New York: AMACOM American Management Association, 2005), 168; Paul McLellan, "A Brief History of Qualcomm," *SemiWiki*, January 29, 2014, www.semiwiki .com/forum/content/3123-brief-history-qualcomm.html.

26. Chris Chiaccia, "Qualcomm Has a Huge Target on It from Jana Partners—Here's the Investor Letter in Its Entirety," *The Street*, April 13, 2015, www.thestreet.com/story/13110333/1/qualcomm-has-a-huge-target-on-it-from-jana-partners--heres-the-investor-letter-in-its-entirety.html.

27. Mock, *The Qualcomm Equation,* op. cit., 153–154.

28. Qualcomm, "Qualcomm Announces Fourth Quarter and Fiscal 2014 Results, Fiscal 2014 Revenues $26.5 billion, GAAP EPS $4.65, Non-GAAP EPS $5.27," press release, Qualcomm, San Diego, CA, November 5, 2014, http://files.shareholder.com/downloads/QCOM/0x0x791877/4610a277-ca86-4da7-8b11-8618efec1d2a/FY%202014%20 4th%20Quarter%20Earnings%20Release.pdf.

29. PwC Digital Services, "Upping the Ante" (video), 2015: http:// digital.pwc.com/upping-the-ante.

30. These two companies were Southdown, purchased in 2000, and RMC, a large multinational with presence in the U.S. and Europe, purchased in 2005. See Donald R. Lessard and Cate Reavis, "CEMEX: Globalization 'The CEMEX Way,'" MIT Case study 09-039, March 5, 2009, https://mitsloan.mit.edu/LearningEdge/CaseDocs/09%20039%20 CEMEX%20%20Lessard.pdf.

31. Scott Kirsner, "Acquisition Puts Amazon Rivals in Awkward Spot," *Boston Globe*, December 1, 2013, www.bostonglobe.com/ business/2013/12/01/will-amazon-owned-robot-maker-sell-tailer-rivals/ FON7bVNKvfzS2sHnBHzfLM/story.html; Dave Smith, "Chart of the Day: Amazon's Biggest Acquisitions," *Business Insider*, August 26, 2014, www.businessinsider.com/chart-of-the-day-amazons-biggest-acquisitions-2014-8.

32. Neely, Jullens, and Krings, "Deals That Win," op. cit.; Adolph, Mainardi, and Neely, "The Capabilities Premium in M&A," op. cit.

33. "The Danaher Zone," op. cit.

34. "The Deal: Qualcomm Divests Omnitracs for $800MM," August 23, 2013, http://www.thestreet.com/story/12017187/1/the-deal-qualcomm -divests-omnitracs-for-800m.html.

35. Ashok Divakaran, Gary L. Neilson, and Jaya Pandrangi, "How to Design a Winning Company," *strategy+business*, August 27, 2013, http:// www.strategy-business.com/article/00194; Gary L. Neilson, Karla L. Martin, and Elizabeth Powers, "Secrets to Successful Strategy Execution," *Harvard Business Review* 86, no. 6 (June 2008), 60–70; PWC, *10 Minutes*

on Organizational DNA, 2014, http://www.pwc.com/en_US/us/10minutes/assets/pwc-10minutes-organizational-dna.pdf.

36. Edgar H. Schein, *The Corporate Culture Survival Guide* (San Francisco: Jossey-Bass, 2009); Art Kleiner, "The Cult of Three Cultures," *strategy+business,* July 1, 2001, http://www.strategy-business.com/article/19868.

37. Leinwand and Mainardi, *The Essential Advantage,* op. cit., 185–186.

38. Ikujiro Nonaka and Hirotaka Takeuchi, *The Knowledge-Creating Company: How Japanese Companies Create the Dynamics of Innovation* (New York: Oxford University Press, 1995).

39. Robert Putnam, "Recipes," in Peter M. Senge et al., *Fifth Discipline Fieldbook: Strategies and Tools for Building a Learning Organization* (New York: Currency, 1994); Richard R. Nelson and Sidney G. Winter, *An Evolutionary Theory of Economic Change* (Cambridge, MA: Belknap Press of Harvard University Press, 1982); Markus C. Becker, "The Concept of Routines Twenty Years After Nelson and Winter (1982): A Review of the Literature," working paper 03-06, Research Unit for Industrial Dynamics, University of Southern Denmark, Department of Marketing, Odense, 2002, www3.druid.dk/wp/20030006.pdf.

40. Nicholas Ind, Oriol Iglesias, and Majken Schultz, "How Adidas found its Second Wind," *strategy+business,* August 18, 2015, http://strategy-business.com/article/00352.

41. "The Idea of IKEA," op. cit.

Chapter 4

1. Thomas A. Stewart, "CEMEX's Strategic Mix," *strategy+business,* April 13, 2015, http://www.strategy-business.com/article/00325.

2. Kleiner, "China's Philosopher-CEO Zhang Ruimin," op. cit.

3. Edgar H. Schein, *Organizational Culture and Leadership* (San Francisco: Jossey-Bass, 2010), 7.

4. "Natura Annual Report, 2012," op. cit., 3.

5. Stewart, "Beauty, Business, Brazil," op. cit.

6. Joseph Mitchell, *Leading the Starbucks Way: 5 Principles for Connecting with Your Customers, Your Products and Your People* (New York: McGraw-Hill Education, 2014), 12.

7. Natura's ad copy comes from the company's English-language website, https://www.naturabrasil.fr/en, accessed August 12, 2015; all other quotes in the section are from Stewart, "Beauty, Business, Brazil," op. cit.

8. John Elkington, *Cannibals with Forks: The Triple Bottom Line of 21st Century Business* (Mankato, MN: Capstone, 1997).

9. Jon R. Katzenbach and Douglas K. Smith, *The Wisdom of Teams: Creating the High-Performance Organization* (Boston: Harvard Business School Press, 1993).

10. Lashinsky, *Inside Apple*, op. cit., 46.

11. IKEA, "Our Business in Brief," http://inter.ikea.com/en/about-us/business-in-brief/; and "The Secret of IKEA's Success," *The Economist*, Feb 24 2011, http://www.economist.com/node/18229400.

12. "The Idea of IKEA," op. cit.

13. McCormack, "A Manager's Guide to Implementing Lean," op. cit.

14. "The Danaher Zone," op. cit.

15. Lashinsky, *Inside Apple*, op. cit., 76.

16. For more on the critical few theory and practice, see the Katzenbach Center site: http://www.strategyand.pwc.com/global/home/what-we-think/katzenbach-center.

17. Stewart, "CEMEX's Strategic Mix," op. cit.

18. Art Kleiner, "The Thought Leader Interview: Douglas Conant," *strategy+business*, August 28, 2012, http://www.strategy-business.com/article/00128.

19. Kleiner, "China's Philosopher-CEO Zhang Ruimin," op. cit.

Chapter 5

1. Peter Fabris, "CIO Hall of Fame: Charles Feld," *CIO Magazine*, September 15, 1997, www.cio.com/article/101855/CIO_Hall_of_Fame_Charles_Feld; Mike Cooke and Edward Baker, "Helping the CIO Lead," *strategy+business*, December 13, 2010, www.strategy-business.com/article/00055?pg=all.

2. Leinwand and Mainardi, *The Essential Advantage*, op. cit.; interview with Shaun Holliday.

3. James L. McKenney, Duncan Copeland, and Richard O. Mason, *Waves of Change: Business Evolution Through Information Technology* (Boston: Harvard Business School Press, 1995), 194.

4. George Lazarus, "Eagle's Plants Have Landed in the Lap of Frito-Lay," *Chicago Tribune*, February 8, 1996, http://articles.chicagotribune.com/1996-02-08/business/9602080224_1_frito-frito-lay-salty-snacks.

5. These four categories are part of the Fit for Growth approach pioneered at Strategy& to help companies rethink their expense profiles in light of their strategies. Deniz Caglar, Pandrangi, and Plansky, "Is Your Company Fit for Growth?", op. cit.

6. Erin Ailworth, "Who Will Hire a Petroleum Engineer Now? The Oil Slump Casts a Cloud over the Ranks of Students Who Flooded into the Industry," *Wall Street Journal*, May 8, 2015, http://www.wsj.com/articles/who-will-hire-a-petroleum-engineer-now-1431130173.

7. Dave Mock, *The Qualcomm Equation: How a Fledgling Telecom Company Forged a New Path to Big Profits and Market Dominance* (New York: AMACOM American Management Association, 2005), 113.

8. Ibid., 138.

9. Shumeet Banerji, Paul Leinwand, and Cesare Mainardi, *Cut Costs, Grow Stronger: A Strategic Approach to What to Cut and What to Keep* (Boston: Harvard Business Press, 2009).

10. David Tweed, "Brick by Brick: Inside Lego," *Bloomberg*, April 17, 2013, www.bloomberg.com/video/brick-by-brick-inside-lego-4-17-Slb-mZEQnSfyC~y1eSm9Fag.html.

11. Oliver, Samakh, and Heckmann, "Rebuilding Lego, Brick by Brick," op. cit.

12. Ibid.

13. Jørgen Vig Knudstorp, quoted in ibid.

14. Ibid.

Chapter 6

1. Kleiner, "China's Philosopher-CEO Zhang Ruimin," op. cit.

2. Ibid.

3. IKEA, "Providing Patterns for Success," IKEA web page, http://franchisor.ikea.com/providing-a-pattern-for-success, accessed July 3, 2015.

4. Hadley Malcolm, "Ikea Wants to Get a Little More Personal," *USA Today*, June 14, 2015, www.usatoday.com/story/money/2015/06/12/ikea-30th-anniversary-us-expansion/71066656.

5. "The Idea of IKEA," op. cit.

6. Beth Howitt, "How Ikea Took Over the World," *Fortune*, March 15, 2015, http://fortune.com/ikea-world-domination.

7. World Business Council for Sustainable Development, Cement Sustainability Initiative, "Sustainability Benefits of Concrete," www.wbcsdcement.org/index.php/about-cement/benefits-of-concrete, accessed July 3, 2015.

8. Stewart, "CEMEX's Strategic Mix," op. cit.

9. Attributed to Kay on http://www.smalltalk.org/alankay.html, a web page maintained by the Active Information Corporation, accessed August 13, 2015.

10. Roberts, "Under Armour Gets Serious," op. cit.

11. Thomas N. Hubbard, Paul Leinwand, and Cesare Mainardi, "The New Supercompetitors," *strategy+business*, August 8, 2014, http://www.strategy-business.com/article/00272.

12. Trident and Chiclets had been part of Pfizer in the early 2000s. Pfizer sold them to Cadbury in 2002, and Kraft acquired them when it acquired Cadbury in 2010.

13. Phil Wahba, "Procter & Gamble Selling Beauty Brands Like Clairol, Covergirl to Coty for $12.5 Billion" *Fortune*, July 9, 2015, http://fortune.com/2015/07/09/procter-gamble-coty/.

14. Hubbard, Leinwand, and Mainardi, "The New Supercompetitors," op. cit.

15. Bob Tita, "Johnson Controls to spin off automotive business," *Marketwatch*, July 25, 2015, http://www.marketwatch.com/story/johnson-controls-to-spin-off-automotive-business-2015-07-25.

16. Viren Doshi and Georges Chehade, "The New Volatile World of Oil and Gas," *strategy+business*, February 19, 2015. http://www.strategy-business.com/blog/The-New-Volatile-World-of-Oil-and-Gas.

Chapter 7

1. E. C. McKenzie, *Mac's Giant Book of Quips and Quotes* (Baker Book House, 1980); the attribution of this quote is disputed according to Wikiquotes, http://en.wikiquote.org/wiki/Michelangelo.

2. Warren Bennis and Burt Nanus, *Leaders: Strategies for Taking Charge* (New York, Harper & Row, 1985), 20.

3. Leinwand and Mainardi," What Drives a Company's Success," op. cit.

4. Howard Schultz, *Onward: How Starbucks Fought for Its Life Without Losing Its Soul* (New York: Rodale, 2011), 97.

Appendix A

1. This appendix was adapted from Cesare Mainardi, with Art Kleiner, "The Right to Win," *strategy+business*, November 23, 2010, http://www.strategy-business.com/article/10407. It was based in part on Walter Kiechel, *The Lords of Strategy: The Secret Intellectual History of the New Corporate World* (Boston: Harvard Business Review Press, 2010); Walter Kiechel, "Seven Chapters of Strategic Wisdom," *strategy+business*, February 23, 2010, http://www.strategy-business.com/article/10109; and Art Kleiner, *The Age of Heretics: A History of the Radical Thinkers Who Reinvented Corporate Management*, 2nd ed. (San Francisco: Jossey-Bass, 2008).

2. Bruce Henderson, "The Development of Business Strategy," in Carl W. Stern and Michael S. Deimler, eds., *The Boston Consulting Group on Strategy: Classic Concepts and New Perspectives* (New York: Wiley, 2006).

3. Michael E. Porter, *Competitive Strategy: Techniques for Analyzing Industries and Competitors* (Florence, MA and Washington, DC: Free Press, 1980, rev. ed. 1998).

4. Robert H. Hayes and William J. Abernathy, "Managing Our Way to Economic Decline," *Harvard Business Review* 58, no. 4 (July/August 1980).

5. Michael E. Porter, "What Is Strategy?" *Harvard Business Review*, 74, no. 6 (November/December 1996); and Michael E. Porter, "The Five Competitive Forces That Shape Strategy," *Harvard Business Review* 57, no. 2 (March/April 1979).

6. Henry Mintzberg, *The Rise and Fall of Strategic Planning: Reconceiving Roles for Planning, Plans, Planners* (Florence, MA and Washington, DC: Free Press, 1994).

7. Thomas J. Peters and Robert H. Waterman Jr., *In Search of Excellence: Lessons from America's Best-Run Companies* (New York: Harper & Row, 1982).

8. Gary Hamel and C. K. Prahalad, *Competing for the Future* (Boston: Harvard Business School Press, 1994).

9. Chris Zook with James Allen, *Profit from the Core: Growth Strategy in an Era of Turbulence* (Boston: Harvard Business School Press, 2001); and Chris Zook with James Allen, *Profit from the Core: A Return to Growth in Turbulent Times* rev. ed. (Boston: Harvard Business Review Press, 2010).

Appendix B

1. Gary Hamel and C. K. Prahalad, *Competing for the Future*, op. cit.; David Teece, *Dynamic Capabilities and Strategic Management* (New York: Oxford University Press, 2009); Ikujiro Nonaka and Hirotaka Takeuchi, *The Knowledge-Creating Company*, op. cit.; Art Kleiner, "Professor Chandler's Revolution," *strategy+business*, April 9, 2002, http://www.strategy-business.com/article/18594?gko=103b7; and Alfred D. Chandler Jr., *Inventing the Electronic Century: The Epic Story of the Consumer Electronics and Computer Industries* (New York: Simon & Schuster, Free Press, 2001).

INDEX

Index

ACKNOWLEDGMENTS

We could not have produced this book, like everything we have written on capabilities and strategy, without the significant efforts of many of our colleagues at Strategy&, the global team of practical strategists integrated within the PwC network of firms. Much of our motivation in writing *Strategy That Works* has been driven by the wish to collect the tremendous collegial insight, intelligence, and creativity of this group—at Strategy& and before that at Booz & Company—and bring it together for a larger business audience.

We thank our clients, who gave us the opportunity to develop these insights with them and often illuminated (through their strategies and execution) the meaning and value of the five unconventional acts. And we thank the companies that cooperated with the research for this book, allowing us to interview and learn from their executives at length: CEMEX, Danaher, Haier, IKEA, and Natura.

As for specific individuals, we should start with the team that led the research and editing and that generated the book's tremendous insights. Campaign director Nadia Kubis oversaw most of this activity and participated directly and instrumentally in generating ideas. Hers was a steady, strong voice of deep commitment, logical consistency, and advocacy for the reader's interests throughout many iterations. She conducted much of the research and played a major role in developing the innovative applications, tools, and approaches around capabilities so that companies and organizations of all kinds can benefit from our perspective.

Acknowledgments

The book's research manager until spring 2015, Josselyn Simpson, shepherded our fact-gathering efforts, organized much of the fact-checking and iteration, and added a great deal of insight. Her commitment to quality and integrity has left an impression on every page. Thomas A. Stewart, former chief marketing and knowledge officer of Booz & Company, championed the book, participated in its gestation, and conducted interviews. If this book has a sense of compelling yet light-hearted gravitas, it owes much of that to Tom. George Roth, researcher at MIT Sloan School and visiting professor at the University of New Hampshire, Durham, helped us design the research methods, commented consistently on our findings, and conducted interviews. Drawing on his years of experience with organizational learning and capabilities building gave us a much richer perspective.

Acting campaign manager Jennifer Zelinsky joined us at a critical time and brought the book to completion. Writers Rob Hertzberg and Joe Cahill contributed to early drafts. Information graphics specialist Linda Eckstein created some of the exhibits. Researchers Ariel Lelchook (Gettysburg College), Gaelle Pierre (NYU), and Yukika Awazu (Bentley University) coded materials on the companies we studied. Paul Michelman commented on the manuscript at a critical time. Kate Pinkerton oversaw the project at its inception; other former team members included Jennifer Ding and Marc Johnson.

We had an outstanding team of Booz & Company/Strategy& leaders providing guidance and thought leadership during the entire project. They are experts in their fields, and we were fortunate to have them involved in this effort. The book started with a gathering in New Orleans in May 2011. The participants included Ken Favaro, Alan Gemes, Paul Hyde, Les Moeller, Stephanie O'Connor, Kasturi Rangan, Joachim Rotering, and Jack Topdjian. A second pivotal conversation took place in September of that year in New York, with Gerald Adolph, Jono Anderson, Marty Bollinger, Mike Connolly, Roman Friedrich, David Hovenden, Minoo Javanmardian, J. Neely, Randy Starr, and Yan Yao.

Also attending that meeting were Jon R. Katzenbach and Gary L. Neilson, both eminent authors in their own right; they continued to help us, refining our material on culture and organization, respectively. We borrowed many of Katzenbach's insights for chapter 4 ("Put Your Culture to Work,"), and he and fellow partner Rutger von Post read our drafts on culture and helped us clarify our thinking. Gerald Adolph, Peter Mensing and Richard Rawlinson, made similarly important contributions to the book, which incorporates many of their critiques and insights. We also benefited from the guidance of Shaun Holliday (whose background at Frito-Lay and McDonald's gave us critical insight into those companies, and who also provided a keen innovator's perspective), and Marc Robinson (former leader of Pfizer Consumer Healthcare, who keenly understood how readers might perceive this book).

Some of our colleagues also played a critical role in helping us research and reflect on the companies we studied. Fernando Fernandes, Per-Ola Karlsson, and Marco Kesteloo were directly involved in our research efforts; Jose Baquero, Coen de Vuijst, Evan Hirsh, Edward Tse, and Michelle Wang made valuable contributions to them. People from outside our firm who did the same included Lubna Dajani, Brian Hackett, and Grace Leung.

Many of our colleagues, past and present, have been working on these ideas for years, applying the capability lens as a central driver of differentiation with clients. Some whose insights or actions made a difference to *Strategy That Works* included DeAnne Aguirre, Gary Ahlquist, Shumeet Banerji, Matthias Bäumler, Deniz Caglar, Niko Canner, Vinay Couto, Adrienne Crowther, Jay Davis, Rick Edmunds, Matt Egol, Nick Hodson, John Jullens, Alex Kandybin, Per-Ola Karlsson, Rich Kauffeld, Dirk Klemm, Steffen Lauster, Jens Nackmayr, Rich Parkin, Thomas Ripsam, Karim Sabbagh, Andrew Schmahl, Bert Shelton, Behdad Shahsavari, KB Shriram, Hannu Suonio, Chris Vollmer, and Tom Williams. In particular, we want to thank two partners from our Booz Allen Hamilton days who opened the door to this way of thinking: Jack McGrath and Keith Oliver. We add a special note of appreciation for Mike Connolly, Ivan de Souza, and Les Moeller, who have supported the capabilities-driven strategy platform for years.

Our colleagues at PwC were instrumental in supporting this project and seeing its potential. We particularly want to thank Dean Arnold, Randy Browning, Dan DiFilippo, Miles Everson, Rob Gittings, Casey Kirkpatrick, David Lancefield, John Maxwell, Bob Moritz, Dennis Nally, Phil O'Prey, Tony Poulter, Juan Pujadas, John Sviokla, Robert Swaak, and Ashley Unwin. We also want to thank some of our PwC colleagues for their insights about companies and capabilities. These include Michael Brandmeyer, Antonia Cusumano, Ron Chopoorian, John Tripp Davis, Kim David Greenwood, David Marston, Arnout van der Rest, David Warren, and Kevin Zhang.

As we write this, an emerging community of PwC principals, partners, directors, and staff is continuing to work on the concept and practice of capabilities-driven strategy, helping to carry forward the ideas in this book. Champions from the PwC network worldwide include Cristina Ampil, Jim Ashby, Dom Baumeister, Mike Beck, Peter Behner, Igor Belokrinitsky, Erich Butters, Marie Carr, Ben Chelovich, Joyjit Saha Choudhury, John Corrigan, Annabel Dennison, Peter Gassmann, Vlad Gil, Marcus Gloger, Jay Godla, Dan Hays, Julia Heskel, Hunter Hohlt, Michael Horvath, Toshiya Imai, Todd Jirovec, Kaleb Johannes, Ganesh Kalpundi, Thomas Kavanaugh, Jason Kim, Hans-Jörg Kutschera, J. P. Leisure, Ed Lesnau, Patrick Maher, Michael Mariani, Sergio Meneses, Marcus Morawietz, Nils Naujok, Barry Neal, Hector Nelson, Rich Parkin, Arjun Patel, Anand Rao, Greg Rotz, Vijay Sarathy, Andy Schmahl, Sean Sell, Samrat Sharma, John Siciliano, Milind Singh, Jai Sinha, Suzanne Snowden, Michael Spellacy, Hugo Trepant, Shashank Tripathi, Caitlyn Truong, Aaron Tweadey, Richard Viereckl, Roger Wery, Huchu Xu, Nir Zepkowitz, and a growing number of others.

Strategy That Works also reflects the influence of our colleagues at Northwestern University's Kellogg School of Management. We wish to acknowledge the intellectual contribution of Thomas N. Hubbard, whose research and thinking were critical in developing the "supercompetitors" concept, and Dean Sally Blount, who provided context and conversation in which the ideas of this book came to life. We are also grateful to Harvard Business School professor Robert Eccles, IESE/NYU professor Pankaj Ghemawat, IMD professor Phil Rosenzweig, and MIT Sloan School professor Donald Sull for their commentary and perspective.

We also have had support from a great marketing team to ensure these ideas reach the market. These include Joanne Alam, Mark Bowerman, Kevin Considine, Charity Delich, Deirdre Flynn, Siobhan Ford, Peter Hahn, Meike Hegge, Howard Kravitz, Jeannette Leong, Ann Nash, Ilona Steffen, Tria Tedford, Rebecca Weaver, and Dexter Webb. We also thank Frank Sommerfield of Sommerfield Communications. Margaret (Maggie) Kashmir, Tara Owen, and Jonathan Trippett made tireless efforts and devoted incessant creativity to helping this book and its authors develop the presence that our message deserves. Maggie has played a key role in realizing the potential of the messages and communicating them to a diverse audience, Tara has helped improve the language we've been using since our very first article, and Jonathan has always been a wonderful thought partnter, able to connect great aspiration with making it happen.

At Harvard Business Review Press, once again we were fortunate to work closely with editor Melinda Merino. This book also benefited from the quality of attention of Sally Ashworth, Courtney Cashman, Julie Devoll, Dave Lievens, and Keith Pfeffer.

Nothing much would get done without the individuals that support us at the office, who have helped in so many ways: Natasha Andre, Pascale Lattouf, Jane McCauley, and Debbie Page. The *strategy+business* team stepped in at times to fill gaps left by Art's

Acknowledgments

work on this book, particularly, Laura Geller, Dan Gross, Gretchen Hall, Elizabeth Johnson, and Melanie Rodier.

Our respective families were incredibly supportive, pushing us and making it possible for us to spend nights, weekends, and long hours to complete this book. They saw the value in bringing these ideas to life and the energy in our commitment, and reminded us of that during the various challenges along the way. Thank you: Te, Cia, and G.G.; Wendy, Cesare Evan, Avery and Amelia; and Faith, Frances, Elizabeth, Constance, and Harrison.

—Paul Leinwand, Cesare Mainardi, Art Kleiner

ABOUT THE AUTHORS

Paul Leinwand is Global Managing Director, Capabilities-Driven Strategy and Growth, with Strategy&, PwC's strategy consulting business, and a principal with PwC U.S. He advises companies in many industries and regions on enterprise strategy and has coauthored a number of works on capabilities-driven strategy, including the books *Cut Costs and Grow Stronger* (with Shumeet Banerji and Cesare Mainardi, Harvard Business Review Press, 2009) and *The Essential Advantage* (with Cesare Mainardi, Harvard Business Review Press, 2011), as well as articles in *Harvard Business Review* and *strategy+business*. Leinwand is an adjunct professor of strategy at the Kellogg School of Management. He holds a master's degree in management with distinction from the Kellogg Graduate School of Management at Northwestern University and a bachelor of arts in Political Science from Washington University in St. Louis.

Cesare Mainardi is a leading thinker on business strategy. He is one of the principal architects of the capabilities-driven strategy approach and has used it to help transform the fortunes of some of the world's leading companies. This is the third book he has coauthored on the subject, all for Harvard Business Review Press. During his thirty years as a management consultant, Mainardi held many senior leadership positions with Booz Allen Hamilton and Booz & Company (now Strategy&, the strategy consulting group at PwC). He was elected global CEO of that enterprise in April 2012 and served in that role until July 2015. He is an adjunct professor of strategy at the Kellogg School of Management at Northwestern University and a member of the school's Global Advisory Board. Mainardi attended Northwestern, where he earned a bachelor of science degree in industrial engineering, a master's degree in manufacturing engineering, and an MBA from the Kellogg School.

Art Kleiner is a management writer and the editor-in-chief of *strategy+business,* the award-winning management magazine published by PwC. His books include *The Age of Heretics: A History of the Radical Thinkers Who Reinvented Corporate Management* and *Who Really Matters: The Core Group Theory of Power, Privilege, and Success.* He is the editorial director of the bestselling *Fifth Discipline Fieldbook* series with Peter Senge, and a faculty member at New York University's Interactive Telecommunications Program. Kleiner has a master's degree in journalism from the University of California at Berkeley.

Note: Certain individuals have roles across PwC or Strategy& and their titles reflect this. PwC refers to the PwC network and/or one or more of its member firms, each of which is a separate legal entity. Please see www.pwc.com/structure for further details. Mentions of Strategy& refer to PwC's strategy consulting business. For more about Strategy& see www.strategyand.pwc.com.